THE Traumatized & At-Risk Youth Toolbox

Over 160 Attachment-Informed Interventions for Working with Kids and Families in Foster Care and Beyond

Jeanette Yoffe, MA, MFT

THE TRAUMATIZED AND AT-RISK YOUTH TOOLBOX

Published by
PESI Publishing, Inc.
3839 White Ave
Eau Claire, WI 54703

Cover and interior design by Emily Dyer
Editing by Gretchen Panzer

ISBN 9781683738329 (print)
ISBN 9781683738336 (ePUB)
ISBN 9781683738343 (ePDF)

PESI Publishing
pesipublishing.com

Dedicated to my birth family, my foster family,
and my adoptive family for instilling in me the
strength to heal, the compassion to help others,
and the resilience to inspire change.

Table of Contents

Chapter 5: Managing Anger, Frustration, and Aggression 91

Chapter 6: Managing Sadness, Grief, Despair, and Heartbreak 113

Chapter 7: Managing Shame, Humiliation, and Guilt 133

Phase 3 | What Happened to You? 149

Chapter 8: Trauma Psychoeducation 151

Chapter 9: My First Family, My Identity 167

Preface

As a person who entered the foster care system at 18 months old and who was attempted to be placed in a permanent home many times before finally being adopted at age 7, I have firsthand knowledge of the complex emotional journey and challenges children are faced with and forced to overcome.

One of my more positive memories of the placement attempts that happened predominantly between the ages of 4 and 7 was my social worker at the time. She was a woman named Barbara who was assigned to my case but who very much valued me as a human being and guided me with great compassion throughout the process. When I look back on that very traumatic time, I understand her own honest empathy was a huge factor in building my resilience and sense of self-worth through what was a terribly dehumanizing and stressful process.

Thankfully, my adopted family treated me as their own and with love, but they had other adopted children in the home—some born drug addicted, others sexually abused—so I grew up with firsthand experiential knowledge of my own siblings dealing with abandonment, abuse, neglect, loss, and all the various forms of trauma associated with foster care and adoption.

In college, I studied acting, which I loved (and still do), and looking back at that time with the insight I have gained over the years, I realize that it wasn't just the love of performing and the sound of applause that attracted me to that field. It was the search for identity and the exploration of character that fascinated me and further increased my ability to empathize with others—to "walk a mile in their shoes."

This compassion and empathy eventually led me to the decision to become a professional psychotherapist. I wanted to have a real impact on people's lives, especially those in foster care, and give them the insights born of my experience. The education I gained at Antioch University and by working at foster care agencies while getting my required hours to become licensed only added to my breadth of knowledge. I combined my own experience with the opinions, ideas, and theories of experts in the field and in academia. I began my own practice in Los Angeles—Yoffe Therapy—and have since helped hundreds of children and families become stronger, more resilient, and happier in their day-to-day lives. Nearly every day, I serve foster parents, birth parents, children, teens, and adults who are dealing with the complex set of emotions and issues involved with foster care.

All of my personal and professional experience informs and amplifies the interventions found in this book. The therapeutic techniques were honed in the field and specifically tailored to working with traumatized children, teenagers, and families within the foster care system. Most of these interventions can also be used to support clients who have not been in foster care but have experienced other forms of separation, loss, and trauma. I not only draw from my personal history and education but also synthesize the latest research of other experts and my associates in the field. As you work your way through this book, I hope you find it useful, cathartic, emotional, effective, practical, and—most of all—respectful of the foster care experience.

I wish you all the best,

Jeanette Yoffe

Introduction

When I first set out to work with foster care youth, I was confident that my personal and professional experiences had prepared me for the role. I told myself, "Oh, I can do that! I know foster care from the inside out." But then the experience shook me from the *outside in*. I sat with infants who were detoxing from crack. I sat with a 7-year-old telling me how their mom abused them. I sat with a 17-year-old who shared about his sister's murder for the first time. I sat with a 9-year-old boy who had been in 11 foster homes and couldn't stop hitting his head against the wall from all the pain of rejection and abandonment. They all believed it was their fault.

As I sat with each one of them, my heart hurt. I would drive home crying, angry, and wanting to act, to fix a broken system, to advocate for each one of them—and most importantly, to find relief and provide healing. I kept asking myself, "What can I do? What can I do to change the system? What is best practice for these children?"

So I dug deep. I asked myself what I had needed growing up in foster care, because no one had known what to do for me either. I began to try out different interventions with kids—interventions that could contain their immense feelings of rage, pain, grief, and loss. Interventions that could provide a symbol of acknowledgment of the "foster care experience." Interventions that could counteract the feeling of being "not good enough." I wanted these children to know that they were worthy of my time, my dedication, and my repair as their therapist.

That is what led me to write this manual. In *The Traumatized and At-Risk Youth Toolbox*, you'll find over 160 therapeutic interventions you can use with children, teens, and families navigating the foster care system and beyond. It is designed for any trusted adult working with children and adolescents in this capacity, including marriage and family therapists, social workers, psychologists, psychiatrists, counselors, educational therapists, client welfare case managers, school social workers, and school counselors.

The interventions in this manual promote healing from a trauma- and attachment-informed lens by integrating the child's fragmented experiences into a coherent narrative while promoting a sense of safety, trust, and resilience. They are designed to help children heal through creative interaction by tapping into their natural instincts of playfulness and curiosity. These interventions and approaches were developed out of a lifetime of experience, both lived and learned.

The interventions are inspired by the following principles:

1. **Play therapy:** For younger children and those who struggle to verbalize their feelings due to early trauma, play therapy can be highly effective. Through play, children can express their emotions, experiences, and perceptions indirectly.

2. **Art and creative expression:** Art therapy allows children to express and project their experiences through drawing, painting, sculpting, and other creative activities. This can provide insights into their feelings and experiences related to trauma.

3. **Psychoeducation:** Using visual explanations can help children make sense of their traumatic experience in a way that they can understand. This can help them see that trauma can be caused by various events and may affect how they think, feel, and behave.

4. **Metaphors:** Children may use metaphors or symbolic language to describe their emotions or experiences. Paying attention to these metaphors can allow caregivers and therapists to better understand the child's perspective.

5. **Storytelling:** Encouraging children to tell stories or write narratives can help them process and communicate their thoughts and feelings about the trauma in a structured and meaningful way.

6. **Validation and empathy:** Validating children's feelings and showing empathy can encourage them to be open about their experience. It's essential to listen actively, without judgment, and acknowledge their experiences.

7. **Time and patience:** It's important to remember that processing trauma takes time. Children may not be ready to talk about their experiences immediately, and patience is needed as they navigate their emotions and find the words to express themselves.

The techniques, approaches, and strategies in this book cover the variety of situations that foster youth face, while also covering the various stages of the foster care journey, from placement to reunification or adoption. As you read through the manual, you'll notice that the interventions are categorized into five different phases:

1. Creating Safety
2. Building Coping Skills
3. "What Happened to You?"
4. Regaining Control, Self-Esteem, and Acceptance
5. Building Family Trust, Bonding, and Attachment

It is important to familiarize yourself with the interventions in each phase so you can determine which interventions are effective for each individual client. I also recommend moving through the phases in order, particularly the first two phases, as children must have a sense of safety in their bodies and have adaptive coping skills in place before moving into trauma psychoeducation and processing.

In addition, use your best judgment when choosing interventions, as children who have experienced trauma have at least a two-year emotional and psychological delay. A client's chronological age may be 13 years old, but they may have the maturity level of a 5-year-old. Therefore, as you choose interventions, keep in mind the child's emotional and psychological age. The way you do this is by observing—watching and listening to their verbal and nonverbal communication throughout each session. One size does not fit all. Treating trauma is an experiment of using different modalities and interventions.

As you introduce the interventions, keep in mind that foster children either want to please or expect to be rejected. Therefore, it is crucial to help them feel *needed* (e.g., "I need your help with this"), *connected* (e.g., "I believe in you"), and *important* (e.g., "I know you can help me"). I also recommend structuring each session using a 10-30-10 format: offering 10 minutes for connecting, 30 minutes for utilizing an intervention, and 10 minutes for allowing the child some "you are the boss" time (e.g., relaxing, drawing, playing a game). This helps create a safe and nonjudgmental space where children can share openly and work through their feelings at their own pace.

Finally, I want to emphasize that although this book is primarily geared for foster care youth, it can be used for any at-risk or traumatized children who struggle with anxiety, fear, worry, stress, anger, aggression, frustration, poor impulse control, grief, loss, or depression. It is especially beneficial for kids who exhibit any combination of the following diagnoses:

- Posttraumatic stress disorder
- Attention-deficit/hyperactivity disorder
- Reactive attachment disorder
- Sensory integration disorder
- Disinhibited social engagement disorder
- Oppositional defiant disorder
- Major depressive disorder

Children who enter foster care are unique. Not only have they experienced multiple traumas that led to their foster care placement in the first place, but they have experienced trauma to their primary attachment bonds. This is not to mention that upon entering the system, they continue to experience serial trauma in the form of going to court, losing control of their lives, having a system determine their fate, and being handed over to total strangers who are responsible for meeting their needs for safety, security, and sustenance.

This manual has techniques to process all these experiences and more. By creating a safe and supportive environment, implementing the various therapeutic tips and techniques inside, and providing empathetic support, you can help your clients gradually find the words to communicate and move through their trauma to begin their healing journey. Let's get started.

PHASE 1

Creating Safety

Teaching traumatized clients skills to feel safe in their bodies, be able to express their feelings, and have a sense of emotional containment is crucial for several reasons.

First, it plays a significant role in restoring trust. Trauma can profoundly impact a client's sense of safety and trust in themselves and the world around them. By equipping them with tools to help them feel emotionally safe, we begin to rebuild that trust and provide a foundation for regaining a sense of confidence and security.

Second, creating safety is essential for emotional regulation. When clients feel safe, they are better equipped to manage and express their emotions in healthy ways. This reduces the risk of emotional dysregulation and helps them navigate their emotional experiences more effectively.

In his book *In an Unspoken Voice: How the Body Releases Trauma and Restores Goodness*, Peter A. Levine (2010) emphasizes the importance of self-regulation in trauma recovery. He explains that trauma is an injury caused by fright, helplessness, and loss, which can be healed by engaging the body's innate capacity to self-regulate high states of arousal and intense emotions. Levine integrates insights from biology, neuroscience, and body-oriented psychotherapy, showcasing how the body can restore balance and healing through somatic experiencing and other therapeutic practices.

Additionally, a sense of safety contributes to overall physical well-being. It can begin to alleviate stress-related symptoms such as muscle tension, headaches, and digestive issues, leading to improved physical and mental health.

The following chapters offer a variety of interventions to help clients calm their body and mind, explore their feelings and sensations, and manage their most difficult and painful emotions. These interventions were inspired by the teachings of Levine (2010), Laurel Parnell (2008), Susan Kaiser Greenland (2016), Colleen West (2021), Michael Balint (1968), and Marshall Bertram Rosenberg (2015).

CHAPTER 1

Feeling Safe in My Body

Distress Hill

Age Range
4–17

Goals:

- Give clients a sense of control by identifying and measuring the intensity of their distress or discomfort related to any therapy interventions, questions, thoughts, or emotions.

Materials:

- *Distress Hill* handout*

Directions:

1. Explain to the client that they are going to learn how to communicate in session when they are feeling stressed so they can create a sense of control in the room. You can use the following script:

   Imagine stress is like a stone that shows up in your pocket when you have too many things to do or when something worries you or makes you feel uncomfortable. The more stress you feel, the heavier and larger the stone. The weight of the stone can make your body feel weak, cause your heart to beat faster, or make your shoulders hurt or your stomach feel queasy.

   But guess what? You can lessen the burden on your body! Just like superheroes have powers to handle tough situations, you have powers too. Our tendency is to try to hide the stress stone, even if it's so huge that everyone can see it and we can barely move it. So how do you keep your stress stone from getting bigger? You "name it to tame it!"

   Sharing the feelings and talking about them will shrink a boulder back down to a tiny pebble that fits easily in your pocket. Everyone has a few pebbles they carry around. Acknowledging the feelings will help us make progress together. Please feel free to communicate with me, your therapist, your "level of distress" anytime during our sessions together. And I will ask you from time to time too.

   We are going to practice this de-stress technique right here, right now. How does this sound?

2. Use the *Distress Hill* handout to explain the 1–10 rating scale for subjective units of distress. You can say: "Take a look at each stone, starting from 0 and going up to 10, and let me know which one best describes the size of your stress. Is it a tiny pebble in your pocket, a huge boulder you can't even budge, or somewhere in between?"

3. React appropriately to their response and encourage them to share their distress level with you anytime: "Great job! Just by telling me, you've shrunk it a few sizes. So anytime you feel it getting heavier, you just let me know and we'll shrink it back down again."

---

* You can make the scale more interactive by cutting out the figures with their stones and inviting the client to take the one that represents their level of distress and place it on the hill.

Distress Hill

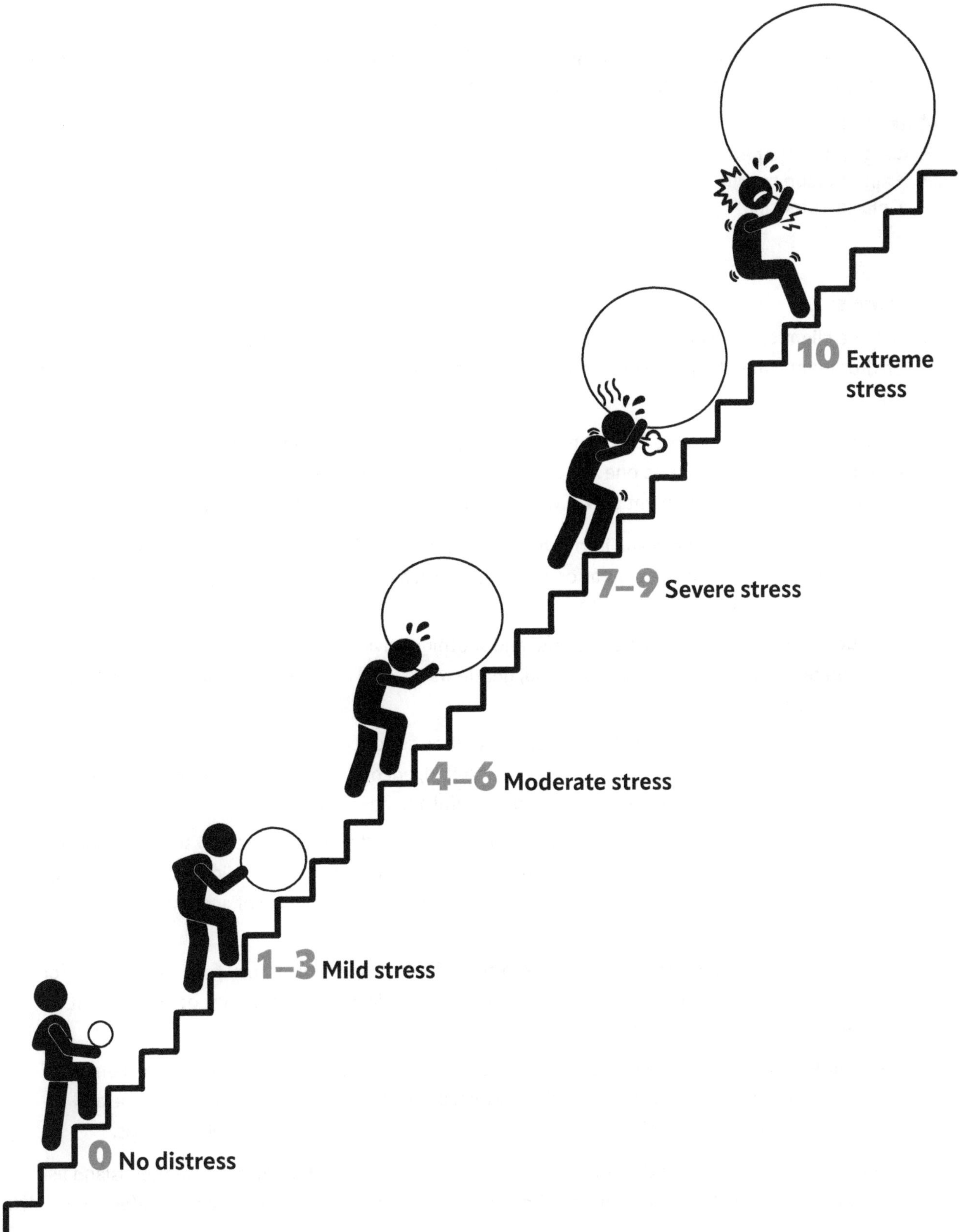

My Island of Safety

Age Range
4–17

Goals:

- Help clients visualize a safe and comforting place where they can feel protected, secure, and free from the debilitating effects of trauma and stress.

Materials:

- Large poster paper
- Paper person cutout
- Coloring utensils
- Glue

Directions:

1. Ask the client to imagine an "island of safety": a special place that provides a calm and nurturing environment where there are no conflicts, stress, or pain and where they can feel a sense of relief and safety.
2. Instruct them to draw a large island on the poster board. Then ask them to put a protective barrier around the entire island so no one and nothing can enter without their permission, including unwanted feelings. (They might draw a wall, security cameras, big rocks, laser beams, etc.).
3. Instruct them to divide the island into five parts. Describe the five following areas and ask the client to draw and label each of these areas on their island. Each one serves a unique purpose in the therapeutic process:
    - **Beach of calmness:** This is a peaceful and soothing environment where the client can rest and feel calm. It may include soft sand, gentle waves, and comfortable seating areas for quiet relaxation.
    - **Forest of exploration:** The forest area symbolizes curiosity and discovery. It could have winding paths, trees to climb, and hidden treasures to find, encouraging the client to explore their thoughts, emotions, and experiences in a playful and adventurous way.
    - **Mountain of strength:** The mountain represents inner strength, resilience, and empowerment. Climbing the mountain could symbolize overcoming challenges and building confidence. At the top, there could be a lookout point where the client can gain a sense of accomplishment and perspective.
    - **Lake of reflection:** The lake area offers a space for introspection. It may have calm waters for peaceful contemplation and reflection, with elements like stepping-stones or bridges that represent progress and growth.
    - **Garden of positivity:** This area is dedicated to nurturing positive emotions, self-esteem, and connection. It could have colorful flowers, butterflies, and other symbols of hope and encouragement, reminding the client of their strengths and supportive relationships.
4. After the client has drawn and named these areas, ask them to place themselves on their island using their paper person cutout. Invite them to imagine themselves living on their island of safety. Ask which

area they would like to spend time in and join them in their experience, following their lead as they explore the areas. Guide the client with processing questions to explore their sense of safety, such as:

- How does it feel to be here in [*name the area*]?
- What physical sensations are you experiencing right now?
- What do you like to do in this area?

5. Ask them what more they will need to feel safe, and follow their lead.
6. Invite them to name their island of safety. Reassure them that this is now their special place where they can always go to feel a sense of relief.

Safety Superhero Powers

Age Range
4–17

Goals:

- Provide clients with tools and techniques for expressing and embodying feelings of strength and safety.
- Help clients learn to feel safe within their body, begin engaging again, and rebuild a sense of stability and security within themselves.

Materials:

- Paper and coloring utensils
- Calm, magical, or heroic music
- Superhero dress-up clothes and props (optional)

Directions:

1. Explain to the client, "We are going to activate your safety superhero powers by creating your safety superhero character." Start the music to ignite inspiration.
2. For younger clients, offer the dress-up clothes and props to help them embody their superhero. This can make the experience more tangible and fun.
3. Provide the coloring materials and read the following descriptions of special safety superhero powers that the client can choose from. They can draw, write, or simply imagine their superhero embodying these qualities. Discuss which items the client would like to put on their hero and why:
    - **Calmness cape:** The superhero can wrap themselves and others in an invisible cloak that instantly makes them feel calm and relaxed by taking five to eight deep breaths to activate it.
    - **Shield of serenity:** This shield can be activated to protect the superhero from any negative feelings or stress, creating a safe emotional barrier. What color is it? What is the texture? The temperature?
    - **Grounding boots:** These special boots help the superhero stay firmly grounded and centered, no matter what's happening around them. What color are they? How heavy are they? What are they made of?
    - **Heart-light beam:** The superhero can emit a warm, comforting light from their heart, which soothes and reassures both themselves and others. Let out a very long breath to activate it.
    - **Comforting whisper:** This is a soft whisper that can instantly comfort and reassure anyone who hears it. What are the words being whispered?
    - **Protection bubble:** The superhero can create a protective bubble around themselves and others that shields them from fear and harm. What color is it? What is the texture? The temperature?
    - **Bravery belt:** Wearing this belt gives the superhero the courage to face any fear or challenge with confidence. What are the words engraved on the belt?
    - **Peaceful pulse:** The superhero's heartbeat emits a rhythmic pulse that promotes a sense of peace and tranquility. You can drum, tap, sing, or play an instrument that represents that pulse.

- **Healing self-hug:** A self-hug from the superhero can heal emotional wounds and provide a deep sense of safety and love. Have the client cross their arms, place their hands on their shoulders, and hug themselves for a count of 10.
- **Focus field:** This field helps the superhero focus and remain calm in stressful situations, blocking out distractions. Designate where the field is in the universe and how it is activated.
- **Echo of encouragement:** The superhero can create a mantra of encouraging words (for ideas, see the *Affirmation "Me Cards"* intervention on page 282). Have the client recite three affirmations out loud while you echo each affirmation for them.
- **Relaxation rays:** These rays can be emitted to help anyone feel instantly relaxed and free from tension. Teach the client a muscle relaxation technique to activate it: squeeze your hands into fists, hold for 10 seconds, and release the rays of relaxation. What colors are the rays? What is the texture? The temperature?
- **Wisdom wave:** The superhero can send out a wave of wisdom that reassures others they are safe, kind and gentle. Practice the wave.
- **Resilience ring:** This ring provides the superhero with resilience, helping them to bounce back from difficult situations. What is the ring made of? What color is it?
- **Safety signal:** The superhero can send out a signal that alerts their allies to provide help and support. Designate and practice a safety signal the client can use with you and other trusted adults when they need safety and support.

4. Invite the client to name their superhero.
5. Teach the client to use a simple anchoring technique (like pressing their hand to their heart, taking a deep breath, or another grounding technique they create on their own) as a way to activate their inner superhero's powers when they feel unsafe or anxious.

My Sensory Smoke Detector

Age Range **4–17**

Goals:

- Help clients recognize and respond to their sensory triggers using effective coping strategies.
- Enhance clients' sense of safety and control in their body.

Materials:

- *Action Coping Zones*, *Arrow Coping Cards*, and *Sensory Detector Cards* templates
- "The Safety Dance" song by Men Without Hats (optional)

Directions:

1. Before the session, make copies of the three templates; cut out the individual zones and cards. Some premade cards are included, but you should also make copies of the blank templates and personalize the cards to ensure they address the most relevant sensory triggers for each client and offer suitable coping strategies. Consider the following categories: sight, sound, touch, smell, taste, movement, and sensations.
2. In session, explain to the client that they are going to be a detective and learn how a smoke detector works, alerting us to danger so we can act. Relate this to how their body has "smoke detectors" for sensory alerts and emotional experiences that can signal potential danger or discomfort. Discuss how recognizing these alerts can help them "smoke detect" and recognize when they may need to use their coping strategies or seek help.
3. Place the three action coping zones in front of the client and explain what they represent:
   - **Grounding zone:** This zone involves using grounding techniques to calm themselves.
   - **Safety zone:** This represents physical, predesignated safe spaces where the client can go.
   - **Communication zone:** This reminds the client that they can communicate their feelings and seek help from a trusted adult.
4. Show them the arrow coping cards one at a time. Have the client place each card in the appropriate action coping zone. (For example, an arrow card that says "practice deep breathing" would go in the grounding zone.)
5. Next show them the sensory detector cards one at a time. Have the client identify what they can do when they encounter each sensory experience, using the action zones they have created as a guide. (For instance, if the detector card says "loud noise," the client may choose the grounding zone, where they have put cards like "practice deep breathing" and "use noise-canceling headphones.")
6. At the end of the activity, you can invite the client to listen, sing, and dance to "The Safety Dance."

Action Coping Zones

Grounding Zone

Safety Zone

Communication Zone

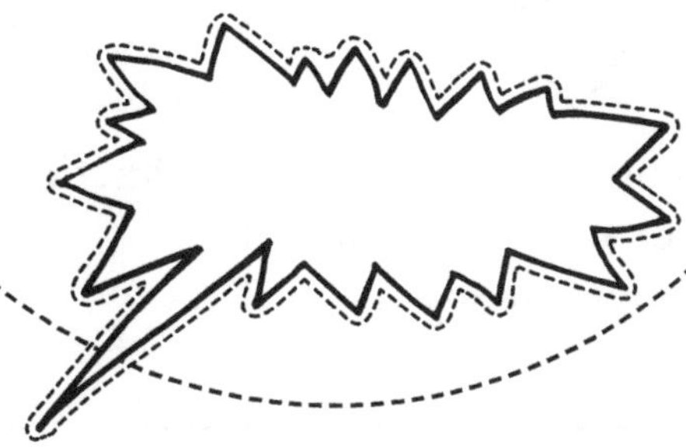

Arrow Coping Cards

Wear sunglasses or a visor

Use noise-canceling headphones or earplugs

Keep a small flashlight or nightlight nearby

Identify the sound and remind yourself it is not a threat

Play soft, soothing music or white noise

Drink a soothing beverage like milk or juice

Gently massage the area or apply a cold pack to relieve pain

Move away from the smell and tell an adult if necessary

Drink cool water or use a cool cloth on your forehead or neck

Hold on to a stable object or sit down until you feel steady

Practice deep breathing

Replace the uncomfortable texture with something soothing, like a soft blanket

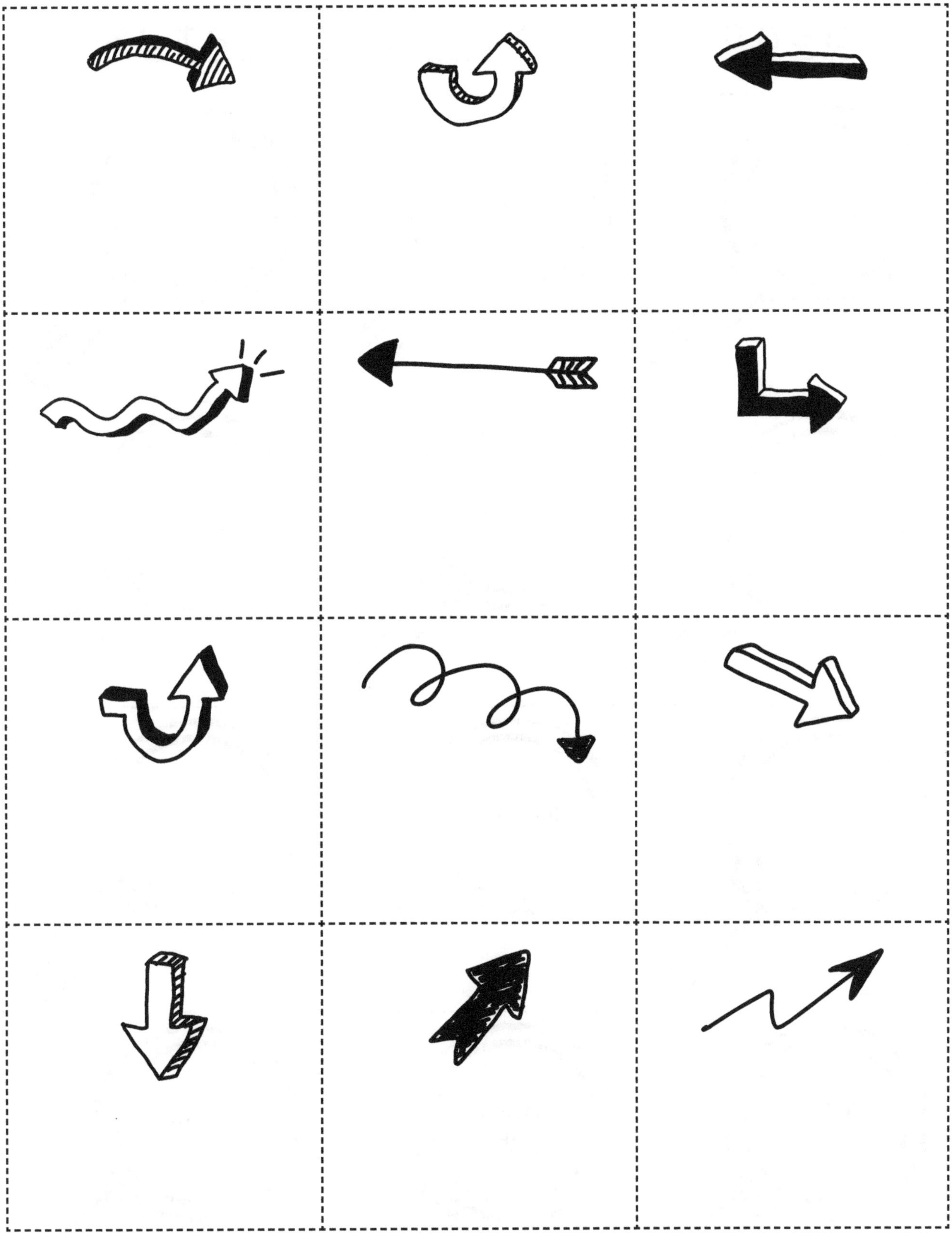

Sensory Detector Cards

Bright light	Darkness	Loud noise
Annoying noise	Silence	Sharp or rough
Pressure or pain	Bad odor	Yucky taste
Jolt or shake	Racing heartbeat	Sweating

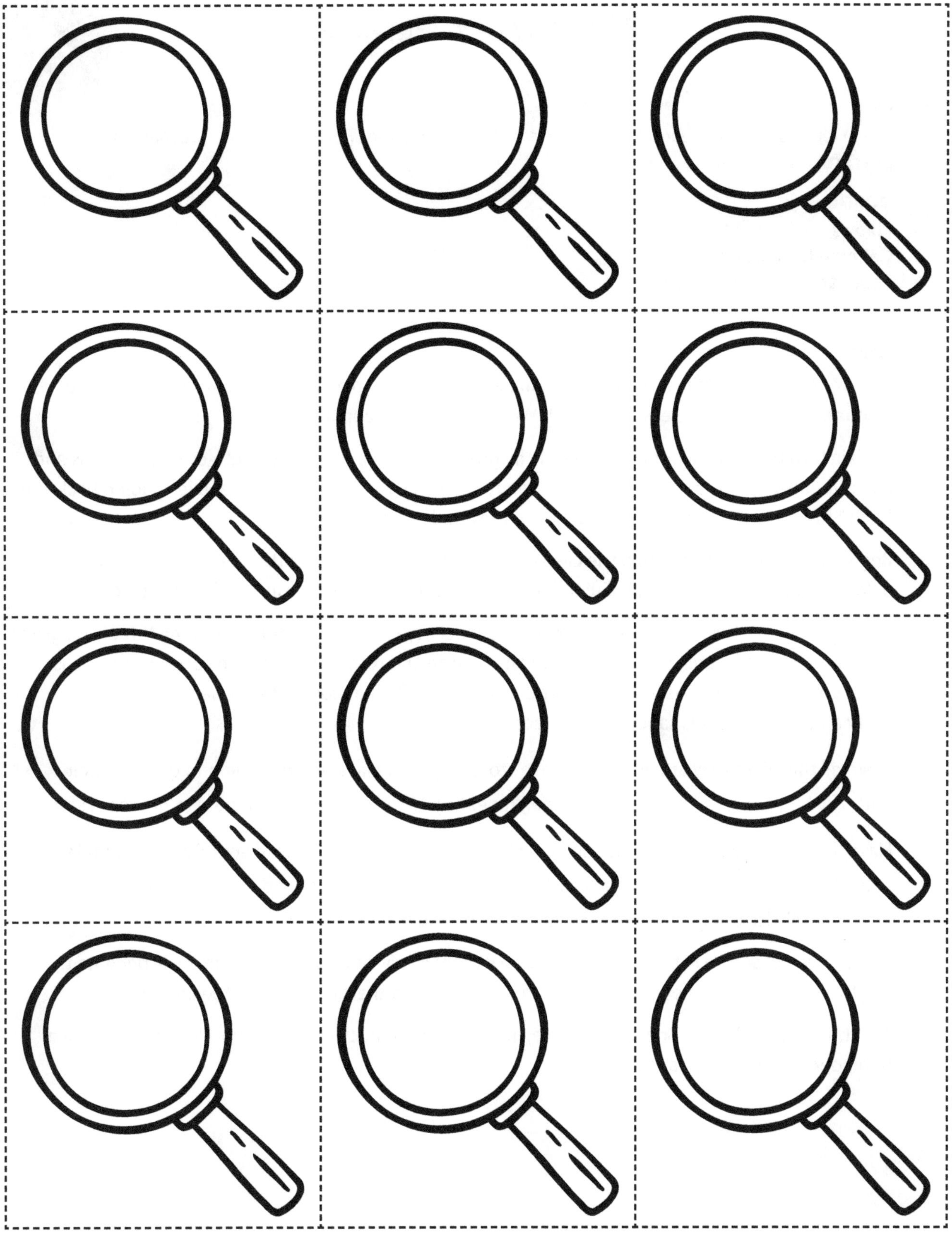

My Inner Peace

Age Range **4–17**

Goals:

- Teach clients bilateral resource tapping, a self-regulation tool, to develop an internal resource of a peaceful place within.

Materials:

- Pillows and blankets
- Calming background music
- Paper and coloring utensils

Directions:

1. Explain to the client: "We are going to create a safe, peaceful place inside you where you can go anytime you're feeling stressed or upset. We will do this by tapping in."
2. Explain how to tap in bilaterally: "You start by giving yourself a 'butterfly hug'—cross your arms and place your hands on your shoulders. Then gently tap on each shoulder, right and left, going back and forth." Model and practice with the client so they understand.
3. Begin the music and encourage the client to get comfortable, either sitting or lying down, using pillows and blankets as needed. Guide them in taking a few deep, relaxing breaths in and out.
4. Tell them: "Imagine a calm place that makes you feel at peace." Ask them to describe this place, giving them time between each prompt so they can visualize and respond: "Describe your surroundings. What do you hear? See? Is it hot or cool? Breezy or calm? What colors do you see? What objects? Relax and settle into this sanctuary of peace."
5. Now tell the client they are going to "tap in" to this special place. Instruct them to get into their butterfly hug and gently tap each shoulder, repeating 16 times. Count with them to get them started.
6. Have the client take a deep breath and check in: "Are you in your special place? Do you feel safe and relaxed?" If not, ask them if any part of their body feels more relaxed and continue the tapping process while focusing on where they feel relaxed, allowing the feeling to spread.
7. Once they feel secure in their special place, ask them to give it a name. This name will become their cue to return anytime they feel the need to tap in and find the calm they are feeling now.
8. Ask the client to draw their peaceful place, in as little or as much detail as they like, to have a visual reminder of feeling at peace within.

My Protective Figure

Age Range
4–17

Goals:

- Teach clients bilateral resource tapping, a self-regulation tool, to develop an internal resource of a protective figure.

Materials:

- Pillows and blankets
- Calming background music
- Paper and coloring utensils

Directions:

1. Explain to the client: "We are going to create and imagine a helpful resource and internal figure that is supportive and protective, special just for you. We will do this by tapping in."
2. Explain how to tap in bilaterally: "You start by giving yourself a 'butterfly hug'—cross your arms and place your hands on your shoulders. Then gently tap on each shoulder, right and left, going back and forth." Model and practice with the client so they understand.
3. Begin the music and encourage the client to get comfortable, either sitting or lying down, using pillows and blankets as needed. Guide them in taking a few deep, relaxing breaths in and out.
4. Tell them: "Imagine a figure that makes you feel protected. It can be someone you know or would like to meet, even an animal or a character from a book or movie. Let the image of your protective figure come to your mind now." Wait 10 seconds.
5. Ask them to describe this figure, giving them time between each prompt so they can visualize and respond: "Once you have this figure in your mind's eye, get more specific. Imagine their facial features. What colors are their skin, hair, and eyes? What are they are wearing? What do they sound like? Smell like?"
6. Now tell the client they are going to "tap in" to this protective figure. Instruct them to get into their butterfly hug and gently tap each shoulder, repeating 16 times. Count with them to get them started.
7. Check in with the client. If they haven't quite gotten a clear image of their protector, have them tap in again.
8. Once a clear image has been achieved, tell the client: "Now bring your protective figure close to you and give them a warm, caring embrace. Feel their protective energy surround you. You are fiercely protected and wrapped in a gentle bubble of protection. Know that you can call upon this figure whenever you need them, and they will care for you and keep you safe. By tapping in to them, you will feel this sense of safety and protection."
9. Ask the client to give their protective figure a name. This will become a cue word that can be used at any time to bring the figure quickly into their mind's eye and allow them to tap in to its protective effect.
10. Ask the client to draw their protective figure, in as much or as little detail as they like, to have a visual reminder of their internal resource of feeling protected within.

My Loving Figure

Age Range
4–17

Goals:

- Teach clients bilateral resource tapping, a self-regulation tool, to develop an internal resource of a loving figure.

Materials:

- Pillows and blankets
- Calming background music
- Paper and coloring utensils

Directions:

1. Explain to the client: "We are going to create and imagine a helpful resource and internal figure that is supportive and loving, special just for you. We will do this by tapping in."
2. Explain how to tap in bilaterally: "You start by giving yourself a 'butterfly hug'—cross your arms and place your hands on your shoulders. Then gently tap on each shoulder, right and left, going back and forth." Model and practice with the client so they understand.
3. Begin the music and encourage the client to get comfortable, either sitting or lying down, using pillows and blankets as needed. Guide them in taking a few deep, relaxing breaths in and out.
4. Tell them: "Imagine a loving figure that makes you feel loved, wanted, and unconditionally accepted. It can be someone you know or would like to meet, even an animal or a character from a book or movie. Let the image of your loving figure come to your mind now." Wait 10 seconds.
5. Ask them to describe this figure, giving them time between each prompt so they can visualize and respond: "Once you have this figure in your mind's eye, get more specific. Imagine their facial features. What colors are their skin, hair, and eyes? What are they are wearing? What do they sound like? Smell like? What are the colors of love that surround your figure?"
6. Now tell the client they are going to "tap in" to this loving figure. Instruct them to get into their butterfly hug and gently tap each shoulder, repeating 16 times. Count with them to get them started.
7. Check in with the client. If they haven't quite gotten a clear image of their loving figure, have them tap in again.
8. Once a clear image has been achieved, tell the client: "Now bring your loving figure close to you and give them a warm, caring embrace. Feel their loving energy surround you. You are fiercely loved and wrapped in a gentle bubble of warmth. You are surrounded by love and light and you are cared for. You can call upon this figure whenever you need to feel lovable again. By tapping in to them, you will feel this sense of love and support."
9. Ask the client to give their loving figure a name. This will become a cue word that can be used at any time to bring the figure quickly into their mind's eye and allow them to tap in to its loving effect.
10. Ask the client to draw their loving figure, in as much or as little detail as they like, to have a visual reminder of their internal resource of feeling loved within.

My Calm Box

Age Range
4–12

Goals:

- Help clients internalize a sense of safety in their world, initiate self-control, and provide a container for their anxiety, fears, or feelings of helplessness.

Materials:

- A large box in which the client can fit (e.g., a refrigerator box)
- Arts and crafts materials

Directions:

1. Inform the client that they are going to create a "calm box" where they can go to feel safe and secure when the outside world feels unmanageable or out of control. Describe how this special box will help them calm down and be peaceful with the help of special items the client chooses to place in there. Explain that the calm box is very private—no one else can open the box or know what the client does in it. They have control.
2. Make a list of things the client wants to put inside their box, which they can gather at home or you can provide as appropriate. Prompt them with examples of soothing items (e.g., pillows, blankets, a flashlight, a device to play music or watch videos, books, paper and coloring utensils, their favorite stuffed animals, a water bottle, snacks, a pacifier, a baby bottle).
3. Designate where this box will go in their home (usually in their room).
4. Encourage the client to decorate their box inside and out to create significance and importance.
5. Have them create an entry with a special code to enter the box.
6. Invite the client to give their calm box a name so they can claim it as their own, such as:
    - Calm Corner
    - Peaceful Portal
    - Inner Peaceful Place
    - Chill Zone
    - Safe Bubble
    - Mindful Me Space
    - Reset Room
    - Brave Base
    - Breathe Box
    - Zen Den
    - Cozy Cove
    - Heart Haven

Breathing Snow Globe

Age Range
4–17

Goals:

- Teach clients communication skills.
- Help clients understand how the brain works.
- Practice breathing and self-regulation.

Materials:

- *I Statements* handout
- Large clear bottle or jar with a secure lid
- Water
- Glitter in blue, red, yellow, purple, and green
- Glycerin
- Lavender oil (optional; assess for allergies before use)
- Video player

Directions:

1. Explain to the client that they are going to learn about how our brains work so they can understand what drives their feelings and what they can do to help themselves when they have big feelings.
2. Teach and practice "I statements" using the *I Statements* handout.
3. Watch the YouTube video "Just Breathe" by Julie Bayer Salzman and Josh Salzman (Wavecrest Films): https://www.youtube.com/watch?v=RVA2N6tX2cg
4. Explain to the client that they are going to make a "breathing snow globe" to help them learn how to slow down and calm their brain.
5. Lay out the glitter tubes and explain which feeling each color represents: blue is sad, red is mad, yellow is happy, purple is scared, and green is irritated.
6. Fill the bottle with water, leaving some room at the top.
7. Ask the client to express their feelings by adding the different colors into the bottle, one by one, encouraging them to share about each feeling as they do so.
8. Add two teaspoons of glycerin to the bottle (this will allow the glitter to move slowly). Secure the top of the bottle with the cap.
9. Instruct the client to shake their finished snow globe, then watch the glitter (their feelings) settle. Provide a few drops of lavender oil in the palms of their hands or have them imagine breathing in a relaxing or pleasant smell, such as a birthday cake. Encourage them to breathe deeply, settling their inner feelings just as the glitter settles in the bottle.
10. The client can bring their snow globe home and use it whenever they need help calming themselves.

I Statements

"I Feel . . ."

(Basic Feelings)

- Sad
- Mad
- Scared
- Glad
- Other:

"I Need . . ."

(The Five A's)

- Autonomy or alone time
- Affection
- Attention
- Appreciation
- Acknowledgment

Calming My Body

Age Range
4–13

Goals:

- Teach clients tools for calming the mind and body.

Materials:

- *CALM* handout

Directions:

1. Explain to the client that they are going to learn to calm their body in creative ways with the acronym CALM:
    - **<u>C</u>ount slowly—from 1 to 10.** This can help distract the mind and slow down the body's stress response. Encourage the client to use this technique whenever they start to feel anxious or upset.
    - **<u>A</u>ffirmations—say three out loud.** Affirmations can help shift the client's focus from negative thoughts to positive ones. Teach them to repeat their favorite affirmations whenever they need reassurance (for ideas, see the *Affirmation "Me Cards"* intervention on page 282).
    - **<u>L</u>isten to your breath—in and out.** Focusing on deep, slow breaths can calm the nervous system. Teach the client to take deep breaths in through the nose and out through the mouth. Practice this regularly and encourage them to use it whenever they need to relax.
    - **<u>M</u>uscle relaxation—squeeze and release.** Progressive muscle relaxation involves tensing and then relaxing different muscle groups to release physical tension. Guide the client through a simple routine, starting from their toes and working up to their head, to help them feel more relaxed.

CALM

Count slowly—from 1 to 10.

Affirmations—say three out loud.

Listen to your breath—in and out.

Muscle relaxation—squeeze and release.

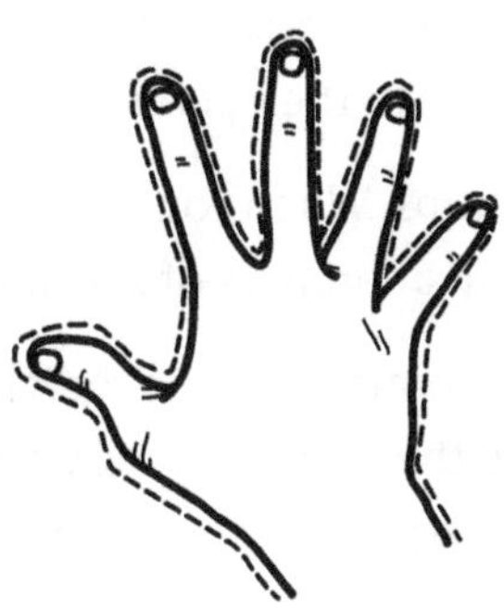

"Captain, May I?" with Hula Hoops

Age Range
5–13

Goals:

- Help clients understand personal boundaries, foster open and clear communication, and learn impulse control.

Note: This game is great for family sessions, and it is especially useful with clients who have major control issues and create intense power struggles with their parents. I have seen dramatic results with clients who have learned to stop and think before acting. Most clients really enjoy this game. The hula hoops give them a container in order to feel secure, and the rules give them a structure to adhere to, all the while earning points and being rewarded for their efforts.

Materials:

- Hula hoops® (as many as there are players)
- *"Captain, May I?" Rules* handout
- Reward point tokens (e.g., pennies, poker chips)
- Assortment of snacks and/or toys (e.g., stuffed animals, toy cars, dolls)

Directions:

1. Inform the players that the game is called "Captain, May I?" and they are going to earn points for stopping, relaxing, and thinking before they act. This includes listening, following instructions, sharing, engaging, and respecting others.
2. Place the hula hoops on the ground, close enough together that the players will be able to pass or toss items to each other while each sitting inside a hoop. Lay out the toys/snacks all around the hula hoops, but inform the players that they cannot touch them until the game begins.
3. Instruct each player to pick a hoop and sit inside it. Explain that just as each player is surrounded by a physical hula hoop, we all have "invisible hula hoops"—boundaries—in the world. No one can enter our hula hoop without our permission, and we cannot enter other people's hula hoops without their permission.
4. Explain that you will serve as the "captain" and hand out reward point tokens when the players follow the rules. Go over the *"Captain, May I?" Rules* handout and place it where the players can reference it throughout the game. The point values can be changed depending on the behavior you want to target. A good idea is to work with the parent to create an incentive for the client—for example, if they earn 30 points they will win a special time with their parent, such as going for a bike ride together.
5. Start the game, having the players take turns. When you award tokens to a player, ask them to identify what they earned points for; this instills an awareness of self and the actions taken.
6. During the game, encourage the client to notice how big their hula hoop is, how much space they have around them, and the space around the other players. Connect this back to the "invisible hula hoops" to help them understand the concept of personal space and boundaries—where they end and others begin.

"Captain, May I?" Rules

★ 1. Each player must say "Captain, may I?" when beginning each turn. (2 points)

★ 2. Ask for a toy and wait for the answer "yes" or "no." (1 point)

★ 3. Accept a "no" answer with no talking back. (5 points)

★ 4. Give a toy/snack to another player. (2 points)

★ 5. Give kind words to another player. (5 points)

★ 6. Use eye contact when speaking. (10 points)

★ 7. Say "please" and "thank you." (5 points)

★ 8. Stay inside your own hula hoop. (10 points)

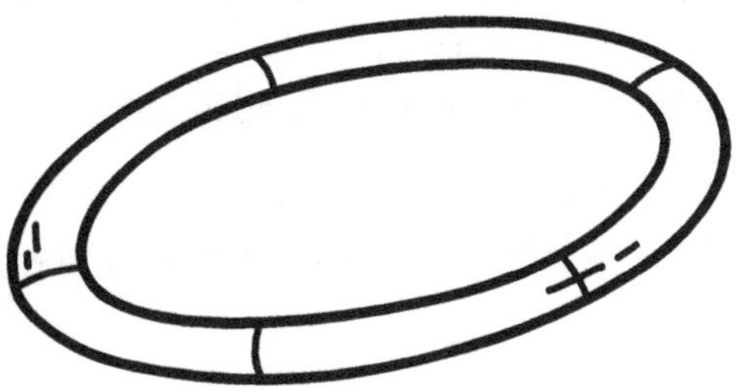

My Inner Strength Cord

Age Range **4–17**

Goals:

- Help clients recognize and harness their inner strength by connecting and grounding with the earth.

Materials:

- Two hula hoops

Directions:

1. Explain that the client is going to learn how to ground their body when they feel insecure or unstable. Place the hula hoops on the ground. Have the client stand outside of their hula hoop and stand a few feet away, facing them.
2. Tell the client that together you will be exploring how loose and unsettled we can feel in our bodies. Ask them to give you a little, gentle push on your shoulders and explain that you will not resist the motion but will let your body be like a ragdoll.
3. Then ask the client permission to give them a gentle little push on their shoulders so they can feel loose and unsettled in their body, like a ragdoll.
4. Instruct the client to stand inside their hula hoop boundary. Stand in your hula hoop as well, so everyone feels a sense of safety and security in their space.
5. Read the following script to the client, going slowly and pausing between each prompt so they have time to visualize the images and follow the instructions:
    a. We are going to create our inner strength cord. Please stand in your hula hoop and know this is your safe space. Stand with your hands at your sides and your feet apart. You can close your eyes if that feels comfortable for you.
    b. Take a deep breath in through your nose . . . see if you can hold it for three seconds . . . and then release the air through your mouth like a flat tire by flapping your lips together like a horse or blowing lip bubbles.
    c. Let's breathe like this two more times. Take a deep breath in through your nose . . . hold it for three seconds . . . and release the air like a flat tire by flapping your lips together like a horse or blowing lip bubbles. One more time: breathe in . . . hold for three seconds . . . and release like a flat tire.
    d. Now I want you to imagine that from your belly button to the center of the earth you are connected by a cord. This cord is so strong, it is unbreakable. It can be made of anything you can imagine—a ray of light, a ray of love, a vacuum hose, titanium, or even a strong rope. You get to decide what your unbreakable cord is made of and imagine that now.
    e. It is important to make sure your cord feels like a gravitational pull from your belly button to the center of our planet. Once you feel that gravitational pull, you can open your eyes and ask me

to give you another gentle push on your shoulders . . . and you can give me a gentle push on my shoulders.

f. You know you are successful when you can feel the difference in your body. You now feel an inner strength like never before. You now feel more full inside, more powerful, and a greater sense of belonging to yourself and to our planet.

g. Congratulations—you have created your inner strength cord. You can imagine this anytime you need it. Say, for instance, before you go to school, before a big test, before you enter your classroom, before a visit with your family or siblings, or before any special important event that could cause you to feel insecure and unstable. The more you imagine it, the greater you will feel!

CHAPTER 2

Exploring Feelings

Feelings Conference Table

Age Range
7–17

Goals:

- Help clients understand, explore, identify, and organize their feelings to gain a sense of self-control.

Materials:

- *Conference Table* handout (laminated or in a sheet protector) and cards (cut out)
- Feelings chart (such as the one in the *Feelings in My Heart* intervention on page 35)
- Clay or play-dough in at least seven colors
- Small wooden peg doll
- Hors d'oeuvres flags (white/plain)
- Dry-erase or permanent markers
- Resealable bag or other container
- Bell

Directions:

Session 1

1. Introduce the activity to the client: "You are going to bring all of your feelings together at a conference table because they are all on your team. They tell you how to feel, what to say, and how to act. So, we are going to learn how to gain self-control by giving all of your feelings a chance to be heard and seen, one by one, because there are no 'bad' feelings—all feelings, whether we like it or not, have a seat at the conference table."
2. Instruct the client to choose up to seven feelings from the feelings chart and begin to customize them by choosing the color of the clay or play-dough for each feeling. Have them imagine and mold what figure, character, or animal that feeling will become. Then ask them to give each feeling a name; write it down on a flag and stick it to the feeling.
3. Give the client the wooden peg doll and tell them the doll represents them, the boss of all their feelings. Have them color and customize the doll however they wish.
4. Ask the client to seat the boss and each feeling in chairs at the conference table (on the handout) one by one. Do not instruct where to place them, as it is very informative to witness where they put each feeling, especially as it relates to the proximity of their doll, the boss of all their feelings.
5. Ask the client to give their "feelings team" a name. Give some examples, like "the Heart Racers," "the Dodgers," "the Wild Bunch," "the Confusions," or the client's first name (e.g., "the Jennifers"). Brainstorm with the client until they get excited and have found the right team name. Write this on the handout.
6. Explain to the client that they are now going to have a meeting to understand what each feeling represents and how they can best work together to achieve a sense of happiness and self-control. To do this, you will be conducting a "feelings interview," in which you will pose questions to a feeling and the client will answer in the voice of that feeling (e.g., saying in a gruff voice, "I am Anger and I am aggressive"). Make it fun!

7. During the interview, ask each feeling to state their name and describe themselves. Then ask them to share a story about how that feeling came to be in the client's life. This will help you identify underlying emotional or psychological vulnerabilities related to the feelings and choose appropriate interventions from this book to use with the client.
8. Preserve the feelings conference table for future sessions by placing the handout and figures into a large resealable plastic bag (or similar container) and labeling it with the client's name.

Session 2

1. Have the client set up their feelings conference table with the boss and feelings figures.
2. Explain that in this conference table meeting the client—the team's boss—will ask the questions and do some "feelings management" to help them further organize their feelings and achieve a greater sense of control.
3. Introduce the bell and the "rant" and "rave" cards. Explain that the client can allow any feeling, one at a time, to rant (speak or shout angrily about being that feeling) or rave (speak or shout excitedly about being that feeling). The client can play with the figure and be the feeling's voice (e.g., "I'm Sad and this is how I feel about it . . ."). The full process is as follows:
    a. The client picks a feeling.
    b. The client places the rant or rave card in the middle of the table and rants or raves as that feeling.
    c. You will ring the bell once the client has expressed what they needed to as that feeling.
    d. The client picks the next feeling to act out.

Session 3 and Beyond

1. Have the client set up their feelings conference table with the boss and feelings figures.
2. Explain that today they will do more feelings management to help the feelings learn to share, decide, problem-solve, or vent about people, places, or things in the client's life. Place the "share," "decide," "problem-solve," and "vent" cards on the table.
3. Explain that the client, as the boss of the feelings team, gets to choose feelings one by one to be in charge for a turn and use one of the three cards. The client can instruct you to role-play different feelings and help the feeling that is in charge that turn.
4. As the play unfolds, ask *who*, *what*, *when*, and *how* questions to process with the client. Start by asking, "Who is the feeling in charge right now?" After the client identifies the feeling, repeat it out loud (e.g., "Sad is in charge, everybody").
5. Then ask, "What does [*feeling name*] want to share, decide, or problem-solve about?" Let the client respond as that feeling. They can share, ask the other feelings questions, and so on. You can answer the questions by role-playing as the other feelings or ask the client what those feelings should say, if you don't know how to answer. Always follow the client's lead.

6. Ask processing questions to go more deeply into the thoughts and behaviors of the feeling—for example:
    - What is Anger fighting for?
    - What does Anger need?
    - What does Anger want to happen?
    - What does Anger think about their aggression?
    - What does Anger do with their aggression?
7. Have the client take turns with different feelings, repeating the same steps.
8. Invite the client to speak as themselves (the boss) on behalf of the whole team and ask processing questions to integrate the feelings—for example:
    - How does a team work together?
    - What is a problem in your life that they could be solving together?
    - Could they brainstorm ideas to work through this problem?
9. At the end, you can say (or encourage the client as the boss to say), "Meeting over! See you next time and anytime we need to figure our feelings out."

Conference Table

Conference Table Cards

RANT Speak or shout **angrily** about being that feeling.	**RAVE** Speak or shout **excitedly** about being that feeling.
SHARE Offer a story, an idea, or advice.	**DECIDE** Make a choice.
PROBLEM-SOLVE Find a solution.	**VENT** Let out stressful thoughts and feelings.

Feelings in My Heart

Age Range
4–17

Goals:

- Help clients explore, identify, express, and organize complex feelings to gain a sense of self-control.

Materials:

- *Feelings Chart* worksheet
- *Feelings Map Legend* handout
- Paper
- Coloring utensils

Directions:

1. Explain to the client that they are going to explore the feelings in their heart. On a piece of paper, draw a large heart outline to serve as the client's feelings map.
2. Invite them to color in the *Feelings Chart* worksheet. They can choose which colors represent each feeling to them.
3. Next show them the *Feelings Map Legend* handout. Explain how this legend shows the meaning of feelings through textures, rhythms, and shapes, which helps them understand the qualities within each emotion.
4. Ask the client to choose a feeling in their heart and draw that feeling on the heart map. You can help them by prompting:
    a. Where is this feeling located in the heart shape? (Top, bottom, middle, left, right, everywhere, nowhere, inside, outside?)
    b. What size is the feeling?
    c. What color is it?
    d. Draw the rhythm, weight, or texture of the feeling.
    e. What is the temperature of the feeling? (Hot, cold, warm, frozen, boiling, icy, toasty, chilling?)
5. Repeat the previous step for each feeling.
6. Process with the client using prompts such as:
    - Tell me a story about a feeling.
    - When does this feeling happen?
    - Which feeling is most intense for you at this moment?
    - Which feeling is least intense?
    - Which feelings are good?
    - Which feeling should we pay attention to?
    - If the feeling had words, what would they want us to know?
    - How can we help that feeling?
    - What does that feeling need?

Feelings Chart

I feel . . .

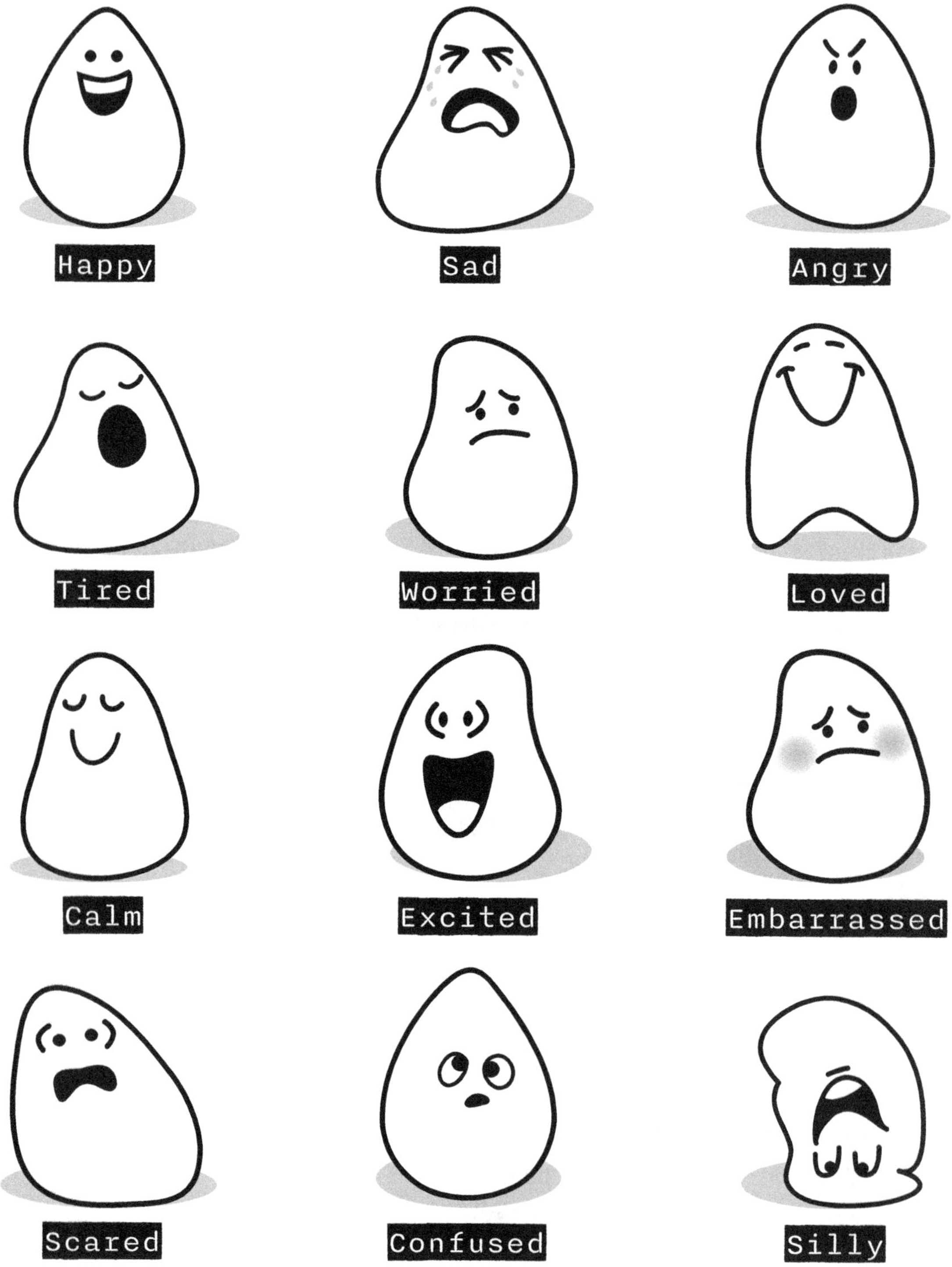

Feelings Map Legend

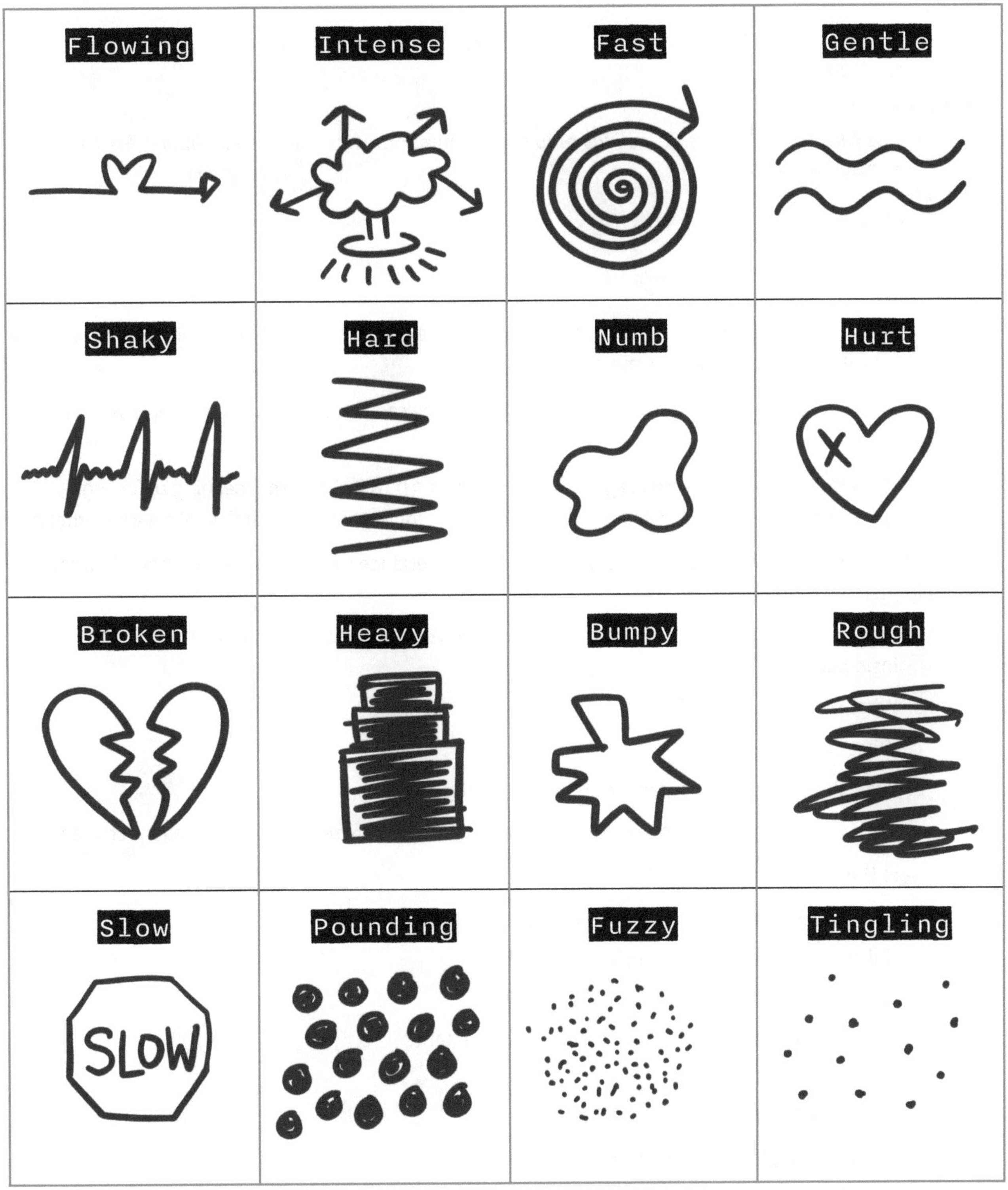

Feelings in My Body

Age Range
4–17

Goals:

- Help clients explore, identify, express, and organize complex feelings to gain a sense of self-control.

Materials:

- *Feelings Chart* worksheet and *Feelings Map Legend* handout (found in the *Feelings in My Heart* intervention on page 35)
- Paper
- Coloring utensils

Directions:

1. Explain to the client that they are going to explore the feelings in their body. On a piece of paper, draw a large body outline to represent the client.
2. Invite them to color in the *Feelings Chart* worksheet. They can choose which colors represent each feeling to them.
3. Next show them the *Feelings Map Legend* handout. Explain how it shows the meaning of feelings through textures, rhythms, and shapes, which helps them understand the qualities within each emotion.
4. Ask the client to choose a feeling and draw how they experience that feeling in their body. You can help them by prompting:
    a. Where in your body do you experience this feeling? (A specific body part, everywhere, nowhere, inside, outside?)
    b. What size is the feeling?
    c. What color is it?
    d. Draw the rhythm, weight, or texture of the feeling.
    e. What is the temperature of the feeling? (Hot, cold, warm, frozen, boiling, icy, toasty, chilling?)
5. Repeat the previous step for each feeling.
6. Process with the client using prompts such as:
    - Tell me a story about a feeling in your body.
    - When does this feeling happen?
    - Which feeling is most intense for you at this moment?
    - Which feeling is least intense?
    - Which feeling feels good to you?
    - Which feeling needs the most attention?
    - If the feeling had words, what would they want us to know?
    - How can we help that feeling?
    - What does that feeling need?

Feeling Spirals

Age Range
7–17

Goals:

- Teach clients how not talking about feelings can spiral over time and lead to losing self-control.

Materials:

- Play-dough in a variety of colors
- *Feeling Spirals* handout

Directions:

1. Introduce the topic using the metaphor of a tornado:

   Today we are going to learn how feelings can spiral and sometimes grow harmful, like wind that spirals into a tornado. Feelings can happen at any time, out of nowhere. Something happens that makes you feel happy, sad, scared, or mad. At first, the feeling is like a gentle breeze. It's important to acknowledge and manage the feeling. If you don't, it might start to spiral, growing into a strong wind—a mood—that pushes against anything in its path. And if you don't talk about the mood, then it can grow even bigger—into an attitude, which is like an out-of-control tornado. Together we're going to explore some feelings and learn how to manage them before they spiral out of control into a damaging storm.

2. Introduce the *Feeling Spirals* handout. Ask the client to choose one of the four main feelings shown—happy, sad, scared, or angry—and give this feeling a color (e.g., red for anger). Instruct them to take a small piece of that color play-dough to form the center of a feeling spiral. (It may be helpful to draw a spiral on a piece of paper as an outline for the client to follow.) Explain that this basic feeling happens all the time and is nothing but a gentle breeze that comes and goes.

3. Next have them look at the moods associated with that feeling. Have them select a different color of play-dough for each mood and mold those colors around the center color in a spiral. As they are doing this, you can encourage storytelling around each element by prompting, "Tell me a story about this mood."

4. Have the client read through the attitudes associated with the core feeling and add more play-dough, making the spiral grow even larger. Once again, they can talk about each attitude as they create their own vortex around that core feeling.

5. Once the tornado is complete, discuss further how feelings can spiral, sometimes out of control. You can use processing questions such as:
   - Will you tell me a story about when you have felt [*happy/sad/scared/angry*]?
   - How does this feeling turn into a mood?
   - What happens next that creates an attitude?

Feeling Spirals

Manage feeling spirals before they grow into a tornado!

Feeling	**Happy**	**Sad**	**Scared**	**Angry**
Mood	Joyful Grateful Peaceful Hopeful	Lonely Heartbroken Disappointed Hopeless	Anxious Dreading Fearful Despairing	Annoyed Frustrated Irritated Bitter
Attitude	Positive Gratitude Solitude Confident	Quiet Teary Discouraged Humorless	Horrified Shocked Doubtful On edge	Negative Furious Aggressive Argumentative

Feeling Poems

Age Range
7–17

Goals:

- Help clients bring meaning to their experience and put words to their feelings.

Materials:

- Paper and writing or coloring utensils

Directions:

1. Explain to the client that they are going to bring meaning to their feelings and experiences with the use of poetry. They can explore any feeling or experience they have encountered (e.g., happy, mad, homelessness, abandonment).
2. Have the client create an acrostic poem by first writing down the feeling or experience vertically in capital letters and then, building off each capital letter horizontally, writing a word, phrase, or sentence. For example:

   Foster love.

   Other family.

   Share their home.

   Teach about families.

   Ever after—not!!!

   Really hurts.

   Can't stay.

   Angry sometimes.

   Ritalin. Yuck!

   Exit to home.

3. Have them read the result from top to bottom to hear their poem.

Feeling Helper Cards

Age Range
7–14

Goals:

- Provide a tool for clients to use in session or at home to communicate their feelings and needs more clearly with their caregivers.

Materials:

- *Feeling Helper Cards* template
- Scissors
- Coloring utensils
- Small resealable bag

Directions:

1. Before the session, make several copies of the *Feeling Helper Cards* template and cut out the cards. You may wish to use thicker paper or index cards for sturdier cards.
2. In session, explain to the client that they are going to learn a new tool to communicate what they need by creating "feeling helper cards." The client can use these cards in session or at home with their caregivers to more clearly express their feelings and needs.
3. Identify the feelings and needs that the client would like to be able to share with their caregivers, and write each one down on a card. Here are some examples:
    - Help me remember.
    - Let me be mad.
    - Let me be scared.
    - Let me cry.
    - Just listen.
    - Don't talk me out of my feelings.
    - Don't try to fix me.
    - Don't give up on me.
    - Ask if I need help with anything.
    - Please tell me this was not my fault.
4. The client can also color and customize their cards, then put them in a resealable bag that they can carry with them.

Feeling Helper Cards

Feeling Helper Cards

Feeling Helper Cards

Feeling Helper Cards

Feeling Helper Cards

This Is My Boundary, This Is My Space

Age Range
7–17

Goals:

- Teach clients how to communicate their feelings and boundaries with their caregivers.

Note: This intervention is done with the caregiver and client together in session. The exercise consists of the client expressing their boundaries and the caregiver honoring them; it is *not* done in the reversal for the caregiver. It is about the caregiver meeting and understanding the client's needs.

Materials:

- Paper and writing utensils

Directions:

1. Explain that they will be exploring how much space or closeness the client needs from the caregiver when they are experiencing different feelings.
2. Instruct the client to stand in one corner of the room and instruct the caregiver to stand in the opposite corner of the room.
3. Tell the client they will say out loud, "This is my boundary, this is my space when I'm feeling [*choose a feeling*]." As soon as the client states the feeling, the caregiver starts stepping slowly toward the client, one foot at a time. The client will say "stop" when they feel the caregiver has come close enough, and the caregiver will stop accordingly.
4. Ask the caregiver to look around and acknowledge the space this feeling needs. Some feelings may result in an embrace; others may require the entire distance. You or the caregiver should write these distances down on a piece of paper so they will remember.
5. Continue this process for other feelings until the caregiver understands how they can best support the client in different scenarios.

Lights! Camera! Feelings!

Age Range
6–12

Goals:

- Give clients a creative opportunity to explore feelings and communication between family members while fostering bonding and attachment.

Materials:

- Blank index cards
- Coloring utensils
- Magazine clippings of feeling faces and glue
- Bowl, hat, or similar container
- Movie slate (optional)
- Assortment of costumes and props (optional)

Directions:

1. This game is designed for caregiver or family sessions. Explain to the clients that they will be playing a version of charades called "Lights! Camera! Feelings!" They will be like actors in a TV show or movie, and you will be the director.
2. Use the index cards to make feeling cards that will be the actors' prompts. The clients can write words, draw pictures, or glue magazine clippings of faces onto the cards to represent different feelings (e.g., smiley, angry, sad, bossy, friendly). Put the completed feeling cards in a bowl or hat.
3. Choose who will be the first "actor" and have them pick a feeling card. After they look at it and have a moment to consider it, you as the director will say, "Lights, camera, feeling, action!" and lower the clapboard movie slate, signaling it's time for the actor to portray that feeling as if on a stage or movie set.
4. The actor portrays the feeling using facial expressions, miming, and body movements but no words. The other players yell "Cut!" when they want to guess the feeling. If their guess is correct, they get to go onstage and be the next actor. If it is wrong, you will say, "Lights, camera, feeling, action!" to direct the original actor to continue.
5. If the client is having a hard time expressing a feeling, offer them notes as the director. You might encourage them to think of a time in their life when they have had that feeling before, help them act out the feeling by joining them in the scene, or offer costumes and props to inspire them to get into character.

Variation:

This game can also be used as a projection game where the client is the director and tells the actor what to feel and how to feel it. It can be very interesting to see what events the client wants you or their caregiver or family member to act out. The client is then given full liberty to yell "Cut!" and make changes as they see fit.

Feelings Expert

Age Range
7–17

Goals:

- Encourage clients to express their feelings and experiences.

Note: This fun and moving exercise works well in caregiver or family sessions. It serves as a great projection test as the client shares what they know about emotions. Many of these clients are experts. And what's shareable is more bearable, as Daniel Siegel says.

Materials:

- "Expert" props and costume pieces (e.g., clipboard, fake reading glasses)
- Deck of feeling faces (this can be purchased or created, as described in the *Lights! Camera! Feelings!* intervention on page 45)
- Timer (optional)

Directions:

1. Explain to the client they are going to have fun talking about their feelings by pretending to be an expert on the feeling that they will pull out of a deck of feeling faces. Encourage them to use the available props and costume pieces, such as a clipboard and fake reading glasses, to get into character.
2. Also let them know that after their presentation, there will be a Q&A where the audience (you and any family members present) can ask questions. Please follow the client's lead and cues as to what they need. They may want their presentation to be timed or to be allowed to speak for as long as they would like.
3. Have the client pull a feeling face out of the deck and examine it. Ask them to begin their presentation by stating, "Hello, my name is Dr. _____ and I am an expert in [*feeling*]." Let them talk freely about what the feeling means to them, what can cause the feeling, or anything else they have to say about it.
4. After the expert has finished their presentation, it's time for the Q&A. You and any other audience members can ask questions such as:
    - How many years have you been an expert in this feeling?
    - Is there a cure for this feeling?
    - How does one live with this feeling their whole life?
    - If I know someone with this feeling, how can I help them?
    - Is there one piece of advice you have about this feeling?

Let the Feelings Out

Age Range
7–17

Goals:

- Teach clients movement and body-up regulation skills to work through and release feelings.

Materials:

- *Let the Feelings Out* worksheet
- Index cards
- Writing or coloring utensils

Directions:

1. Explain to the client that they are going to learn ways to let their feelings out.
2. Using the *Let the Feelings Out* worksheet, take turns with the client reading each coping activity out loud. Explain, model, or practice activities with the client as needed. Have the client circle or highlight the ones that feel good to them. They can also come up with their own ideas to add to the list.
3. Have the client write down their chosen activities on separate index cards. Encourage the client to take these cards home and display them so they will serve as reminders to use the skills, such as on the client's desk or on their bedroom wall.

Let the Feelings Out

- Act it out
- Bike it out
- Breathe it out
- Build it out
- Cartwheel it out
- Carve it out
- Clap it out
- Clean it out
- Climb it out
- Collage it out
- Color it out
- Cook it out
- Cry it out
- Dance it out
- Draw it out
- Drum it out
- Hike it out
- Hug it out
- Hula hoop it out
- Hum it out
- Juggle it out
- Jump it out
- Jump rope it out
- Kick it out
- Laugh it out
- Play it out
- Punch it out
- Read it out
- Rest it out
- Rock it out
- Run it out
- Scream it out
- Sculpt it out
- Sew it out
- Shake it out
- Shout it out
- Sing it out
- Sit it out
- Sketch it out
- Sleep it out
- Snuggle it out
- Stick it out
- Stomp it out
- Story tell it out
- Stretch it out
- Sweat it out
- Swim it out
- Talk it out
- Tap it out
- Think it out
- Throw it out
- Walk it out
- Wash it out
- Whistle it out
- White it out
- Write it out
- Yell it out

CHAPTER 3

Emotion Containers

My Safe

Age Range
4–17

Goals:

- Provide clients with a safe space to store and externalize undesirable thoughts, feelings, and memories.
- Reduce feelings of anxiety, fear, and helplessness.
- Increase emotional regulation, self-control, and a sense of safety.

Materials:

- Lockbox (or any box with a lid and duct tape)
- Paper and coloring utensils
- Other arts and crafts supplies (e.g., play-dough, stickers, popsicle sticks)

Directions:

1. Show the client the lockbox and explain that it is a safe where they can store everything that is getting in the way of their peace and happiness. You can say:

   A safe is a locked area, large or small, that no one else can enter or look inside unless they are allowed. Usually, it's where valuable items are placed for safekeeping. But today, you are going to create a safe to store your thoughts, feelings, and memories that are dangerous, scary, or painful. These might be images or words that remind you of people, places, and things that are frightening or uncomfortable. You can also include any thoughts that keep popping up in your mind when you don't want them to. You are going to put all that stuff into this safe, so it gets out of your head and into a place that you can control.

2. Open the box and invite the client to give shape to their unwanted thoughts, feelings, and memories. This can include words, phrases, stories, pictures, sculptures, people's names, and so on. Explain that they do not have to tell you what they are putting in their safe but you are there to help them create the items if they want you to. Listen closely to what they say and encourage them to be as specific as possible without pressuring them.

3. Instruct the client to place all of these unwanted things into the box, close the lid, and lock it or tape it up so nothing can get out unless they want it to. Allow the client to choose how much tape they use and whether they throw away the key or keep it. Process with the client how it feels to have all the danger locked up in a box that they can hold in their hands.

4. Then ask them where they would like their safe to be stored: in the therapy room or at home with them. If it will be left in your office, make sure the client labels it with their name and have a predesignated place where you keep clients' safes, so they are assured it will be well cared for and accessible should they need to add something to it.

Complaint Department

Age Range
5–17

Goals:

- Allow clients to externalize, express, and let go of past grievances, frustration, hopelessness, and helplessness.
- Increase emotional stability, regulation, relief, and validation.

Materials:

- "Clerk" props and costume pieces (e.g., post or police officer cap, service bell)
- Clipboard with paper and a writing utensil
- Rubber stamp and ink pad

Directions:

1. Tell the client that in this session they are going to be visiting the "complaint department," where they get to complain about anything and everything they ever wanted to. Prompt them to begin thinking about experiences they have had in the past or present—all the worst and wrong stuff they and their family have had to deal with. This will be an opportunity to get it all off their chest. Provide examples of complaints to help with normalizing and brainstorming (e.g., foster care, housing, parents, waiting, bullies, bills, bugs).
2. The clerk at the complaint department—which can be you or a caregiver, if present—wears the cap and holds the clipboard and ink pad. Instruct the client to sit across the room. When the clerk is ready, they will say, "Next! This is the complaint department. What can I have you complain about today? We take complaints very seriously here. We are all ears."
3. As the client shares their complaints, the clerk writes down, as best as possible, every word so they can read back pieces of it. Some clients speak very fast, so it is all right to say, "Please slow down. I want to make sure I get this all written down. We take your complaints very seriously here." Or "Can you repeat that once again? That was important and a really good complaint."
4. The clerk can be very animated and encourage the client to continue by saying, "I get it! Give me more!" Once the client is done, the clerk will read back their complaints and say, "Thank you for your complaints! They will be filed immediately." Then the clerk stamps the paper and places it to the side.
5. This can be done at many sessions to encourage the client to share new or ongoing complaints.

My Shipping Container

Age Range
5–17

Goals:

- Provide clients with a safe space to store and externalize undesirable thoughts, feelings, and memories.
- Reduce dysregulation, anxiety, and feelings of helplessness.
- Increase emotional stability, hope, and a sense of self-control.

Materials:

- *Shipping Container* worksheet
- Coloring utensils

Directions:

1. Give the client the *Shipping Container* worksheet and explain the activity. You can use the following script:

   Today you will be creating your own imaginary shipping container. You can fill your container with any unwanted thoughts, feelings, and memories that keep coming up in your mind, as well as people, places, and things that keep bothering you. It helps to have a place to put all these thoughts and feelings so they are not all stuck in your head, mixing together and becoming confusing and frustrating.

2. Have the client draw pictures or write words (e.g., the names of people, places, or things) on the worksheet to represent placing all of these troublesome and irritating things inside their container.
3. Tell them that they are now going to seal the container shut and ship it out to sea so they don't have to carry these uncomfortable feelings inside anymore. They can leave the container at sea until they are ready to bring it back and unpack it, one thing at a time, making it easier to deal with these troubles.
4. Invite them to scrunch the worksheet into a ball or fold it and speak to the container out loud. You can encourage them with phrases like "I'm sending you out to sea. Leave me alone. I need some peace. When I want to deal with you I will; right now I'm not. You need to know who's the boss of me—me!"
5. Inform the client that you will make sure their container gets on the ship that's headed out to sea later that day and if they need to, they can have it come back to add more feelings or deal with them one by one when they are ready.

Shipping Container

Suitcase of Memories

Age Range
7–17

Goals:

- Support clients who have experienced multiple foster care placements or similar changes in homes (e.g., kinship care, housing instability) by providing emotional containment of negative experiences as well as a place to access positive experiences, promoting a sense of control, self-confidence, and hope.

Materials:

- Large piece of cardboard or poster board
- Coloring utensils
- Stickers and magazine clippings of people, places, things, and words
- Glue and scissors
- Variety of additional arts and crafts supplies

Directions:

1. In advance, draw, cut out, or print out and glue a large outline of a suitcase on the cardboard or poster board.
2. In session, show the client the suitcase and explain that they are going to create a collage about their experience of moving from home to home.
3. Encourage them to use the art supplies of their choice to represent different things they remember, both positive and negative, about their past homes. This can include people, pets, foods, smells, places, feelings, and so on. They might wish to create different compartments or sections within the suitcase to organize their memories and feelings.
4. If they could use further guidance, prompt them by asking questions such as:
    - What do you think you had in your suitcase when you first moved?
    - What do you remember always bringing from house to house?
    - Did you save any keepsakes or souvenirs from any homes?
    - Who are some of the people you remember and why?

Variation:

For older or tech-savvy clients, consider creating digital versions of the suitcase using apps or online tools to store photos, videos, and written reflections.

Scar Jars Inside Me

Age Range
8–17

Goals:

- Help clients identify the emotional scars they have hidden, denied, or deflected.
- Help clients face, cope, and heal from the psychological trauma they have endured.

Materials:

- *Invisible Scars* handout
- Three small clear jars with lids (eight-ounce plastic jars are recommended)
- Variety of arts and crafts supplies (e.g., play-dough, paints, puzzle pieces, slips of paper, coloring utensils, googly eyes, glue, rocks)

Directions:

1. Explain the activity to the client. You can use the following script:

   With the help of arts and crafts, you are going to identify the invisible scars that you hold inside. Scars are created by painful experiences and can only heal if treated carefully. We often hide our scars because we think that if we can't see them, we won't think about the pain that caused them. But if we don't think about our scars sometimes, they won't fully heal and will be stuck inside us.

   To help your scars heal and cause no more pain, you are going to bring them out of the body into the light. This will allow you to see them clearly and even befriend them. You will put your scars in a new, special container—a scar jar—where they can heal and fade away over time.

2. Show the client the list of invisible scars. They get to decide which three scars they want to bring to light.

3. Invite the client to manifest each scar through arts and crafts. You can prompt them by asking, "What does this scar feel like? What does it look like? Is it heavy? Scary?" and so on. The client can use the mediums available to represent different people, feelings, or objects and put each scar in its own jar. They can even decorate or label the jar itself.

4. While the client is preparing each jar, encourage dialogue about what caused this scar, what it felt like at the time, and what it feels like now to bring it out of hiding and put it somewhere it can be seen and heal.

5. When the client is finished, place the three jars on a shelf or table and let the client know that if there are any more scars they'd like to heal they can do this again at another time.

Invisible Scars

- Chaos inside me
- Longing inside me
- Sadness inside me
- Rage inside me
- Panic inside me
- Darkness inside me
- Anger inside me
- Confusion inside me
- Disappointment inside me
- Hate inside me
- Pain inside me
- Rejections inside me
- Abandonment inside me
- Hurt inside me
- Fear inside me
- Puzzles inside me
- Questions inside me
- Emptiness inside me
- Loss inside me
- Love inside me in spite of it all!

Privacy Me Box

Age Range
4–17

Goals:

- Create a safe space for clients to strengthen their sense of agency, self-control, identity, and potential after abuse, neglect, or emotional harm.
- Alleviate shame, humiliation, and fear.
- Empower clients to protect their personal space and information.

Materials:

- Box with a lid
- *Privacy Affirmations* handout
- Scissors
- Variety of arts and crafts supplies (e.g., paints, mirror pieces, craft gems, stickers, markers, glue)

Directions:

1. Explain to the client that no matter what they have experienced or been told, they have a right to their own privacy. They are not required to tell anyone how they feel or what happened to them. To help them understand this, they are going to make a "privacy me box" to remind them that they are in control of their feelings and experiences and it's okay to wait until they are ready to share and can trust in the people they choose to open up to.
2. Invite them to use the arts and crafts supplies to decorate the box. This is their box; encourage them to make it their own.
3. Provide them with the *Privacy Affirmations* handout and scissors. Instruct them to cut out the affirmations that resonate with them and place these in their box.
4. Inform them that these affirmations can be taken out and read aloud as part of daily routines, during therapy sessions, or as reminders when they face situations where their privacy might feel challenged. The affirmations will help reinforce the importance of their personal boundaries and empower them to maintain control over their own stories and experiences.

Privacy Affirmations

I have the right to keep my personal thoughts and feelings private.

It's okay to say no when I don't want to share something about myself.

I deserve to have my own space and boundaries respected.

My privacy is important, and I can protect it by speaking up.

I am in control of what I choose to share with others.

It's okay to set limits on what I talk about and with whom.

I can trust myself to know when to keep things private.

My personal information is mine to share only when I feel comfortable.

I am strong and capable of setting healthy boundaries.

My feelings and experiences are my own, and I choose who to share them with.

I have the right to feel safe and secure in my personal space.

I respect my own privacy, and others will respect it too.

It's okay to keep some things to myself; I don't owe anyone my story.

I can protect my privacy by being clear about my boundaries.

My privacy matters, and I deserve to feel comfortable and safe.

The Recycling Plant

Age Range
4–17

Goals:

- Lessen the pain of past trauma and reduce the sense of victimization and hopelessness.
- Increase clients' sense of control over their environment, teach about perspective, and encourage optimism.

Materials:

- Colored paper cut into strips
- Writing or coloring utensils
- Paper shredder
- Balloon
- Two bowls
- Mod Podge® paper-mache glue
- Piece of string
- Scissors
- Decorative materials (e.g., glitter, paints, stickers)

Directions:

Session 1

1. Explain to the client that they have the power to transform something wasteful or hurtful into something reusable, helpful, and even beautiful. They are going to explore and prove this concept by recycling some negative feelings into something cool and useful.
2. Have the client write about a negative person, place, or experience on the strips of paper.
3. Ask the client to carefully place the strips of paper into the shredder and collect the shreds into a pile.
4. Blow up the balloon, tie the end, and place it in one of the bowls. Pour some paper-mache glue into the other bowl.
5. Invite the client to dip the shreds in glue and place them on the balloon. Have them cover the balloon, apart from the tied-off end.
6. When all the shreds have been stuck to the balloon, tie a string to the end of the balloon and hang it up to dry. (Make sure you put something underneath to catch any drippings of glue). Inform the client that at the next session it will be dry, and they can complete the recycling transformation from something ugly into something cool.

Session 2

1. Pop the balloon and cut the dried paper-mache shape in half to make a bowl.
2. Invite the client to decorate their bowl using the materials you have available (paints, stickers, glitter, etc.), covering the shreds as they desire. One method that works well is to use a paintbrush to spread some glue on the inside of the bowl, let it dry for a few minutes, then spread more glue inside and swirl glitter around to coat the inside of the bowl.

3. Once the client is satisfied with their bowl, ask them how it feels to recycle their pain into something new and useful. Continue processing by asking questions such as:
    - How do you feel about your recycled bowl?
    - What will you use your bowl for?
    - What did you learn about yourself from this experience?
    - How can you use what you've learned from this experience to help yourself in the future?

Flush It Away

Age Range
4–14

Goals:

- Help clients verbalize, externalize, and release feelings, thoughts, and memories.
- Reduce anxiety and helplessness; increase self-empathy and confidence.

Materials:

- Toilet paper
- Thin black ball-point marker
- Toilet available

Directions:

1. Explain to the client that they are going to carefully write feelings, thoughts, and memories they are holding inside onto the toilet paper and flush all the toxic ones away.
2. Prompt them with experiences to write on the paper, such as:
   - A bully once said to me: _____.
   - Somebody called me this name once: _____.
   - I saw _____ happen to someone once.
   - My caregiver did _____ once.
   - I heard _____.
   - Someone made me _____.
   - I was very scared when _____.
   - The hardest part about foster care is _____.
   - I feel _____ when I think about my family.
   - I feel alone when _____.
   - I feel broken inside when _____.
   - I wish _____ never happened.
   - I feel sad about _____.
   - I feel embarrassed when _____.
   - I feel different from other kids because _____.
   - Goodbye, _____!
3. Also ask them if there is anything else they want to write down to be flushed down the toilet.
4. Isolate the negative responses and accompany the client to the bathroom (or allow them to go alone, if they are old enough). They can then throw the toilet paper into the toilet and flush it all away.

PHASE 2

Building Coping Skills

This phase provides clients with effective ways to manage and cope with the stressors triggered by their traumatic experiences, with the goal to promote emotional intelligence. Clients will build a basic foundational skillset to handle any emotions and learn tools to prepare for the next phase, which involves psychoeducation and trauma processing. As therapists, we tend to tread water, waiting for the opportune time to dive into the client's story, when the client isn't ready and doesn't have a basic understanding of how to handle the overwhelming number of emotions that telling their story will unearth.

As you uncover which feelings are more profound for the client, you can help them pick and choose how to manage their feelings. The interventions in this phase cover a wide range of emotional experiences—from anxiety, fear, and worry, to anger, frustration, and aggression, to sadness, grief, despair, and heartbreak, to shame, humiliation, and guilt.

When the client has specific strategies to deal with challenges and life stressors, they can mitigate the adverse effects of trauma on their mental and physical health. This reduction in distress not only improves their immediate well-being but also supports long-term mental health. Learning healthy coping skills reduces the likelihood of clients turning to harmful coping mechanisms such as substance abuse or self-harm. When clients can manage their emotions and reactions, they are more likely to approach situations with a positive mindset, are better equipped to overcome obstacles, are less likely to experience prolonged periods of distress, and can recover more quickly from setbacks.

Each of the following chapters targets a specific set of emotions to help clients understand, cope with, express, and release these difficult feelings: stress, anxiety, fear, and worry; anger, frustration, and aggression; sadness, grief, despair, and heartbreak; and shame, humiliation, and guilt. The interventions were inspired by the teachings of Daniel J. Siegel (2010), Violet Oaklander (1978), Elisabeth Kübler-Ross (1969), Holly van Gulden and Charlotte Vick (2005), Angela Hobday and Kate Ollier (1998), and Connie Zweig and Jeremiah Abrams (1991).

CHAPTER 4

Managing Stress, Anxiety, Fear, and Worry

Shadow World

Age Range **8–17**

Goals:

- Help clients to imagine and internalize feelings of safety and fulfillment as well as to externalize, discover, and accept the rejected parts of themselves.
- Reduce anxiety, worry, and fear; strengthen self-awareness, self-esteem, and empathy.

Materials:

- Two large pieces of poster paper: one white and one black
- Coloring utensils, including colors that will show up on the black paper (e.g., gold, silver)

Directions:

Session 1

1. Inform the client that they are going to create a "shadow world" where they are the boss and where they can have everything they have always wanted.
2. Instruct the client to fold the white poster paper into thirds to create a "door." Ask them to think of a secret code that only they know, using words, letters, or numbers. Once the code is made, the client can use it to open the door and enter their new world.
3. Explain the rules within this shadow world, which is a world of light, as the client begins to draw the scene:
    a. The client is the ruler of this world, and they live in a huge castle.
    b. They have three special powers of the client's choosing (e.g., x-ray vision, invisibility, speaking many languages, sensing danger).
    c. They can have five visitors at their castle (e.g., family members, friends, fictional characters, pets).
    d. They also have three storage buildings, which will hold things they need or want (e.g., clothing, toys, video games, ice cream).
    e. Near the castle there is a wishing well where they can throw away something bad in the shadow world (a person, place, feeling, object, etc.) and magically turn it into something good (e.g., butterflies, bubbles, candy bars, toys).
4. Once the rules are established, the client is free to add other items they need to make their shadow light world the most beautiful, perfect place.
5. Process with the client and convey the following messages:
    - In the outside world our needs will not always be met, but we can create a safe place within ourselves.
    - This shadow world is a place you can always go to when you feel unsafe in the real world.
    - There is a king or queen inside of you reminding you that life can be good, beautiful, and fulfilling.
    - You are in control of your world and scary emotions.

Session 2

1. Inform the client that they are now going to create the second part of their shadow world, which is a hidden place in their world that others cannot see.
2. Instruct the client to fold the black poster paper into thirds, creating another door with its own secret code that only they can open.
3. Remind the client of the shadow light world rules listed earlier. Additionally, there are special items to include in this scene of their shadow hidden world:
    a. There are three more storage buildings, which can hold things they need to keep them safe in this shadow world (e.g., armor, weapons, bravery, strength).
    b. There is a jail where the client can hold bad or evil things and feelings prisoner so they can do no harm.
    c. There are three gatekeepers of the jail—which can be people, places, or things—to make sure the bad and evil things never escape without permission.
    d. There is a cemetery to identify people who have passed away as well as people who are still living but the client feels as though they have died.
4. Once the rules are established, the client is free to add other items they need to express what is lurking in the darkness and what protects them.
5. Process with the client and convey the following messages:
    - This shadow world is a hidden place, unseen to our visitors but where we must go to understand and control what's evil or bad and make sure those things can't harm or overpower us.
    - We can create order in the sometimes messy and chaotic shadow world by using our gatekeepers, our powers, our jail, and our cemetery.
    - When your light world inside turns dark, there is always a king or queen inside you with the power to make sure you are safe.
    - You can be in control of your world and scary emotions.

The Stress Bag™

Age Range
5–14

Goals:

- Teach coping skills to help clients problem-solve and self-regulate when they feel stressed emotionally or physically.
- Reduce stress, agitation, and helplessness; increase self-awareness, self-esteem, and self-regulation.

Materials:

- Bag with handles
- Index cards and a writing utensil
- Variety of stress-relief toys and tools (e.g., stress ball, bubble wrap, clacker balls, paper and coloring utensils, play-dough, bubbles)

Directions:

1. Discuss what stress feels like and explain to the client that there are ways to help them control those feelings when they arise so the client is the one in charge, not the stress. They are going to create a "stress bag" full of special items and activities that they can use when they have these feelings and don't know how to express or control them.
2. Introduce each item, exploring and practicing together how the client can use it to help calm their mind and body. Here are some suggestions:
   - **Stress ball:** The client can put all their stress into the ball by squeezing it, sitting on it, flattening it, and so on. You can purchase stress balls or make them by using a funnel to fill balloons with dry rice or corn starch. Wrap two extra balloons around each stress ball for additional strength.
   - **Bubble wrap:** Provide precut pieces of bubble wrap, which the client can stand on to begin popping the bubbles. Explore with the client how the wrap feels beneath their feet. What are they popping away? Where is the stress going?
   - **"Clacker-thinker":** Include a clacker ball toy or another item that takes the client a bit of time and practice to master. They can use this to refocus, think, and center themselves. Let them know this is a game about patience and mastery of their stress.
   - **Paper and coloring utensils:** Create a "stress journal" where the client can draw or write about their feelings and triggers.
   - **Play-dough:** Teach the client the "rip-squish-spaghetti" technique to regulate and externalize their stressful feelings. First, they take the play-dough and say "Rip!" while breaking it into two pieces. Then they say "Squish!" while squeezing their feelings into the play-dough. Finally, they say "Spaghetti!" while separating their fingers so that the play-dough squishes right through them. They should do this five to ten times until they feel more relaxed.
   - **Bubbles:** Instruct the client to sit down and slowly blow one bubble at a time while they imagine seeing their stressful feelings entering the bubble and then disappearing when it pops. Encourage them to focus, feeling the lightness of the bubble gliding within their control, helping them to feel calm.

3. Help the client think of three to eight coping strategies and write them on index cards. These "stress buster cards" are also stored in the bag, and the client can reach in and pick one out anytime they need help figuring out what to do with their stress. Examples include:
   - Stretch my body like a cat. Meow!
   - Fall on my bed backward five times. See if I can bounce back up!
   - Pretend I'm a statue in a museum for 10 seconds.
   - Stand on my tiptoes and walk really, really slow to the count of 10. Shhh!
   - Smile really big in the mirror to the count of three.
   - Take five deep belly breaths.
   - Tighten my body for five seconds . . . and let it go! Do it three more times.
   - Go up to someone in my house and make a funny face!
4. Place all of the items in the bag. You can write on the outside of the bag (or on a label that you affix to it), "Things to do when I feel stressed to help me calm and catch my breath!" Encourage the client to take the bag home and keep it within reach by hanging it on a doorknob or hook in their room.

Five Ways to Hack Your Stress

Age Range
5–10

Goals:

- Teach coping skills to help clients problem-solve and self-regulate when they feel stressed emotionally or physically.
- Reduce stress, agitation, and helplessness; increase self-awareness, self-esteem, and self-regulation.

Materials:

- *Hack Your Stress* handout
- Video player

Directions:

1. Explain to the client that they are going to learn five ways to relieve their stress. They can use these tips anytime to calm their body and mind. You can say, "At times we all feel stress and fear. I want you to know that these feelings are natural. They are our body's way of warning us when we feel strongly and deeply that something is out of our control and we feel helpless to fix it. But the truth is, we can control our feelings. I'm going to teach you a few ways to cope when these feelings arise."
2. Show the client "5 Ways to Hack Your Stress for Kids Video with Jeanette Yoffe" (https://www.youtube.com/watch?v=2gudahyfKSs) to guide them through the steps. Or you can explain and demonstrate the techniques yourself.
3. Encourage the client to congratulate themselves after they practice a technique. Explain to them: "When you congratulate yourself, your brain releases chemicals called endorphins that make you feel good, so you will remember to do this again when you're feeling stressed!"
4. To follow through, give the client the *Hack Your Stress* handout. The hack cards can be cut out and put on a keychain to be displayed in the client's room.

Hack Your Stress

Breathe Mindfully

Put your hands over your nose like a tent. Imagine you are sitting right in front of your birthday cake. Breathe in deep to take in the yummy smell, like you're filling up a big balloon in your belly. See if you can hold it without popping the balloon for 1, 2, 3 . . . and then release the breath like a tidal wave!

Connect Your Mind and Body

Place one hand on your forehead and the other hand on your belly. Close your eyes if you like. Hold for 10 seconds, feeling the connection between your mind and your stomach.

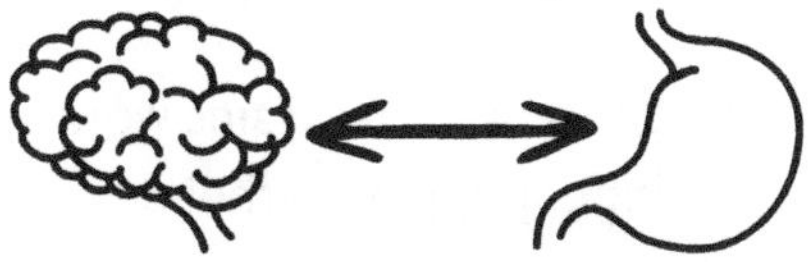

Connect Your Mind and Heart

Place one hand on your forehead and the other hand on your heart. Hold for 10 seconds, feeling the connection between your mind and your heart. End with a deep breath.

Stretch Like a Cat

Stretch from side to side, stretch your arms, stretch your back, stretch your neck, stretch any which way you can! Feel the positive energy flowing through your body.

Tap the Stress Cells Out of Your Body

Tap gently up and down your right arm, your left arm, your neck, your chest, your tummy, your right thigh, your left thigh, then your calves, ankles, and feet. Breathe and imagine that with every tap you are releasing stress and fear, like letting air out of a balloon.

Flip Your Lid

Age Range
7–17

Goals:

- Help clients identify and communicate their big emotions to gain clarity, self-compassion, and self-empowerment.
- Build self-regulation skills and self-control.

Materials:

- Video player
- Hand paints or washable markers
- Googly-eye rings
- Finger puppets
- Index cards
- Writing utensils
- Envelope or small bag

Directions:

1. Explain to the client that they are going to learn how brains work using the "hand model of the brain" (Siegel, 2010). Have the client place a finger puppet on their thumb and a googly-eye ring on their middle finger. Wear your own finger puppet and googly-eye ring as well. Alternatively, use paints or markers to draw the animals on your hands.

2. Show the video "Hand Model of the Brain for Kids" by Jeanette Yoffe (https://tinyurl.com/534mnb6f) or read the script below to demonstrate the hand model:

   The hand model of the brain is a fun way to understand how our brains work, especially when we have big feelings. Imagine your hand as your brain:

   - Your wrist is the brain stem, which controls basic functions like breathing and heart rate.
   - Your thumb, tucked against your palm, represents the "animal part"—the emotional part of your brain called the limbic system, which helps us feel emotions.
   - When you fold your fingers over your thumb, this is the thinking part of your brain, the prefrontal cortex, which acts like a comforting, problem-solving blanket taking care of your animal part.

   The thinking part helps us make good choices and stay calm. But sometimes, when we get really upset, it's like we "flip our lid," and our fingers (the thinking part) go up, leaving just our emotional brain in charge. This can make us act out like animals, doing things like fighting, running away, or freezing because we don't know what to do.

3. Instruct the client to act out flipping their lid and practice stating out loud, "I'm about to flip my lid."

4. Help them brainstorm ways to keep their lid on and recognize when they are about to flip their lid (e.g., taking a break, going for a walk, finding someone to talk to). Write each coping skill down on an index card; on the other side of the cards, write, "When I'm about to flip my lid, do this instead . . ."

5. Place the cards in an envelope or bag for the client to take home. Encourage them to practice using the cards to recognize when they are about to flip their lid and use the coping skills listed.

Mighty Anxiety

Age Range
7–17

Goals:

- Help clients understand, manage, and reduce their anxiety by empowering them with practical coping strategies and fostering a sense of control and resilience.

Materials:

- Several jars of play-dough in the same color
- Googly eyes
- Paper and coloring utensils
- Empty tissue box
- Variety of arts and crafts supplies (e.g., scissors, glue, duct tape, magazine clippings of images that evoke stillness, peace, and tranquility)

Directions:

1. Explain to the client that managing anxiety begins with understanding what it is. Describe "Mighty Anxiety" as a sort of superhero that tries to protect us from harm. You can say:

   Anxiety is a part of us that wants us to survive. It is a natural feeling that is trying to protect us from anything scary, unknown, or dangerous—like when you hear a loud noise and are not sure what it is, or when you have a big event the next day and are worried about how you will look or perform.

   "Mighty Anxiety" is always on the lookout for danger or stressful situations and because it is a natural response that means to protect us from harm or shame, it's hard to turn off or stop—but there are ways to control these strong feelings of restlessness, worry, and fear. The idea is to calm these feelings by understanding that you are not in danger, and to stop Mighty Anxiety from growing to the point where you lose your focus and feel powerless to do anything about it. The truth is, you are* not *powerless!

2. Provide the client with the play-dough and have them imagine, as they take the dough out of each jar, that they are pulling their "Mighty Anxiety" out of their body and mind.

3. Encourage them to squish and knead the play-dough into one big ball of anxiety. Then instruct them to give the Mighty Anxiety some eyes. Ask: "How many eyes do you think they need? They are always on the lookout for you. They must be exhausted too."

4. Process with the client, asking questions like:

   - How old is your anxiety?
   - What's the speed of your anxiety?
   - When was the first time you remember feeling anxiety?
   - What do you think your anxiety is afraid of?
   - Who do you think your anxiety is afraid of?

5. Ask them to think of a dangerous person, place, or thing and draw or write it down. Then encourage them to imagine their Mighty Anxiety taking off in dread at the thought of confronting the danger.

You can prompt them on what to draw to keep the client engaged in the story development. Allow for the re-enactment of avoiding the danger by asking them to draw the following:

- What does the danger look like?
- What does the danger want?
- What is the danger saying?
- What does it smell, sound, and feel like?

6. Encourage the client to say out loud, "Hi, Mighty Anxiety. Nice to meet you. I understand you wanted me to survive. Thank you. I'm not in danger anymore. I was in danger and now I am not." If possible, encourage them to say, "We are not in danger anymore."
7. Next, using the empty tissue box, have the client create a place of safety where their Mighty Anxiety can relax and rest from the danger. Instruct the client to give this place a name (e.g., "Chill Cave" or "Comfy Cove") and make it into a calming place where they can turn off the activation of Mighty Anxiety. They can draw on the box, add duct tape to create security, put calming words in the box, glue magazine clippings on the box, and so forth to surround Mighty Anxiety with images and thoughts of stillness, peace, and tranquility.
8. Congratulate the client for turning their "Mighty Anxiety" into "Tiny Anxiety."

ANTs to ANDs

Age Range
7–17

Goals:

- Help clients identify and reframe their automatic negative thoughts and learn a new coping skill to increase resiliency and self-compassion.

Materials:

- *ANTs to ANDs* worksheet and a writing utensil
- "The Ants Go Marching" or other music (optional)

Directions:

1. Explain to the client that everyone experiences ANTs, which stands for automatic negative thoughts. These thoughts can go on and on like a never-ending trail of ants. But today the client will learn to become aware of these imaginary ants and challenge these thoughts by replacing them with ANDs—automatic new directions—which are positive thoughts that can change the course of the marching ANTs and bring the client's mind some peace.
2. Introduce the *ANTs to ANDs* worksheet and encourage the client to write out some of their ANTs on the left side of the page. They can repeat the same dominant ANT several times, write down multiple different negative thoughts, or both.
3. Instruct the client to place the paper on the floor and stomp on the ANTs for a few minutes. You can play "The Ants Go Marching" or another song that the client finds energizing and empowering while they do so.
4. Instruct them to break the trail of ANTs by using their feet to rip the paper in half, separating the list of ANTs from the space for ANDs. Have them write at least three positive "automatic new direction" thoughts on that half of the paper. You can prompt, "What would your best friend say to you? What would you say to your best friend to help them feel better?" (For more ideas, see the *Affirmation "Me Cards"* intervention on page 282).
5. Have the client practice saying out loud one negative thought and add the word *AND* while introducing three positive thoughts. Brain science research has found that replacing one negative thought with three positive thoughts negates that pesky thought!

ANTs to ANDs

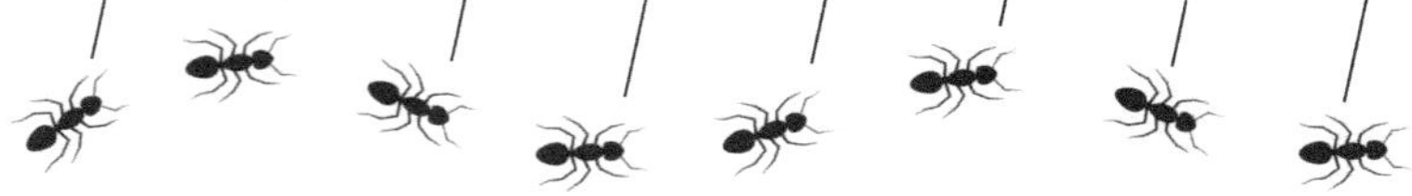

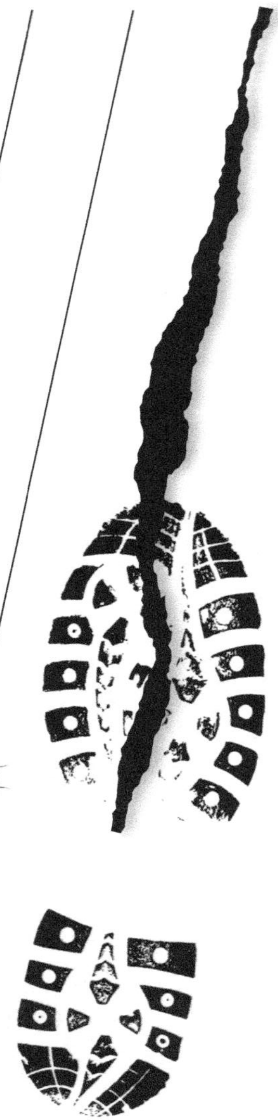

1. ______________________________

2. ______________________________

3. ______________________________

ANTs
Automatic negative thoughts

ANDs
Automatic new directions

Dream Web

Age Range
4–17

Goals:

- Provide an opportunity for clients to externalize, verbalize, and express feelings of fear, worry, and anxiety around sleep.

Materials:

- Pipe cleaners
- String
- Feathers

Directions:

1. Explain to the client that they are going to create a dream web, which can protect them from scary thoughts or dreams. You can say: "Legend has it, a dream web, if truly believed in and made right, can make your fears, worries, and concerns disappear."
2. To build the web, have them form a circle out of pipe cleaners by twisting the ends together. Have them tie a long piece of string to the circle and begin wrapping the string around and across the circle until the string is close to its end, then secure that end as well. Encourage the client to explore what type of pattern they want to create within their dream web. They can undo and redo their pattern, take additional pieces of string, and so on.
3. Once their pattern is complete, take a new piece of string about 12 inches in length. Loop it through the bottom of the circle, so two strings hang down, and tie it securely. Then tie a feather to the bottom of each string. Encourage the client to name each feather as representing one of their fears, worries, or concerns. Add more pieces of string with feathers to match the number of fears the client wants to include.
4. Encourage the client to place their finished dream web in a special area in their room, such as above their bed or above their door, where the web can protect the entire room. Before they go to bed each night, they will activate their dream web by naming each fear and saying, "They will not bother me tonight!"

Note: This dream web can also be used to capture good thoughts and dreams. It is recommended to create two dream webs for capturing both the good and the bad. This way the client is more able to integrate these opposites rather than create a split.

Worry Wart Tree

Age Range
7–17

Goals:

- Help clients visualize, understand, externalize, and manage their worries.

Materials:

- Poster board or large piece of paper
- Coloring utensils
- Sticky notes
- Tape, glue, and scissors
- Decorations like stickers, glitter, and so on
- Model magic clay
- Calm music
- Lavender oil (optional; assess for allergies before use)

Directions:

1. Explain to the client that when we worry, it is usually an imagined fear of something we believe is going to happen in the future, but that does not always come true. As an old saying goes, our life is full of troubles—most of which have never happened to us! Worry has a way of growing bigger and bigger until it feels overwhelming and we become "worrywarts." Explain that they are going to create their own "worry warts" to place on a special tree that will help cancel out any worries they have in their mind.
2. On the poster board, draw a large tree with branches. Encourage the client to decorate their worry wart tree with leaves, flowers, and other features to make it their own.
3. On sticky notes, have the client write down each worry. This can include people, places, situations, doubts, fears, and so on. For younger clients, you can write for them as they express their worries.
4. Then have them use model magic clay to mold a "wart" for each worry. Glue these to the worry wart tree.
5. Encourage them to take a few minutes to see how their worries look when they are placed on the tree. Instill a sense of calm by playing soothing music, inviting the client to breathe in the scent of lavender oil, and guiding the client through some deep breathing. They can imagine that they are walking through a quiet, peaceful forest feeling less burdened by their worries.

Bottled Up

Age Range
7–17

Goals:

- Help clients understand how stress builds up in the body and how to reduce their stress by empowering them with an externalization technique.

Materials:

- Two-liter bottle of a carbonated drink with aspartame in it, with the label removed
- Mentos mints
- Permanent marker
- Outdoor space

Directions:

1. Explain to the client that when people explode in anger and yell, scream, or even physically hurt someone else, it is usually because they never learned how to acknowledge, manage, and express their strong feelings. This leads to a bottling up of emotions that grow and grow, building more and more pressure until it finally explodes like a volcano. Inform them that they are going to learn how to express and verbalize their feelings so that they can manage their stress and don't explode and hurt themselves or others.
2. Instruct them to use the permanent marker to write on the bottle all the things they may have bottled up and have kept deep inside (e.g., leaving their family, witnessing something scary, fears or concerns about their life). Each time they write something, they must shake the bottle to represent that stress. Process with the client, exploring their bottled-up feelings. You can say:
    - When do you have that feeling?
    - What gets repressed must be expressed.
    - Stress incubates over time and will cause pressure on your body, heart, and soul.
3. After the bottle is fully marked, go outside with the client and have them (carefully) open the bottle, letting it release all of this pent-up stress before them. You can also invite the client to drop a minimum of five Mentos into the bottle, which will create a much stronger explosion effect to represent the release of intense emotions.

Stressed-Out Puppet

Age Range
7–17

Goals:

- Help clients identify, express, externalize, and manage their stress.
- Teach clients healthy coping strategies.

Materials:

- *Stressed Out? Yell It Out!* handout
- Two white socks
- Materials to decorate sock puppets (e.g., permanent markers, yarn, googly eyes, fabric glue)
- Paper and a writing utensil

Directions:

1. Explain that today you will be creating puppets to help the client express their feelings and learn ways to manage stress.
2. Give the client one sock and use the other to create your own puppet. Decorate the socks with markers, yarn, googly eyes, and so on. Give the puppets names and personalities.
3. Explain that the client's puppet will be a character who is feeling stressed. Encourage the client to talk about, embody, and act out the stress with their sock puppet, joining in with your own puppet. You can utilize the *Stressed Out? Yell It Out!* handout to give the client examples of what to say.
4. Reinforce that it's okay for the puppet (and the client) to feel stressed. Everyone feels stressed sometimes, and it's important to talk about those feelings before they build up and explode.
5. Work with the client to come up with solutions or coping strategies for their puppet's stress. Write these down and help the client act them out with the puppets.
6. End the session by reminding the client that just like they helped their puppet, they can help themselves manage stress by talking about their feelings before they can build up and explode.

Stressed Out? Yell It Out!

Expressions of Overwhelm

- I can't handle this right now.
- This is too much for me.
- I'm completely overwhelmed.
- I feel like I'm drowning.

Expressions of Anxiety

- I'm so anxious about this.
- I can't stop worrying.
- I have a bad feeling about this.
- I'm so nervous.

Physical Symptoms

- My head is killing me.
- I feel tense.
- I can't sleep.
- My stomach hurts.
- I'm shaking.

Expressions of Time Pressure

- I don't have time.
- Leave me alone!
- I'm running out of time.
- I can't do this.

Expressions of Frustration

- I'm fed up.
- I can't catch a break.
- Nothing is going right.
- This is so frustrating.
- Why does this always happen to me?

Expressions of Helplessness

- I don't know what to do.
- I feel so lost.
- I'm stuck.
- I can't deal with this.

Requests for Help

- I need help.
- Can you take over for a bit?
- I need a break.
- I just need someone to listen.

Expressions of Exhaustion

- I'm so tired.
- I can't keep going.
- I'm worn out.
- I need to rest.
- I'm at my limit.

Negative Self-Talk

- I'm not good enough.
- I can't do this.
- I'm failing.
- I'm a mess.
- I'm falling apart.

Prescription for Stress

Age Range
7–17

Goals:

- Help clients manage stress by identifying stressors and developing healthy coping mechanisms.

Materials:

- *Prescription for Stress* worksheet (multiple copies, cut into cards)
- Writing or coloring utensils
- Clear jar with a lid
- Materials to decorate the jar (e.g., stickers, paints)

Directions:

1. Explain that the client will be creating a special jar as a tool to help manage stress. This jar will hold "prescriptions" for stress relief, which they can use whenever they feel stressed. By doing this they will become the "expert" and "doctor" that helps cure and calm their stressful feelings.
2. Allow the client to decorate the jar to make it personal and inviting to use.
3. Discuss what stress is and what it feels like. Explain that everyone feels stressed sometimes. (You can utilize the "Hand Model of the Brain for Kids" video as described in the *Flip Your Lid* intervention on page 72).
4. Ask the client to think about things that make them feel stressed. Write each stressor on one of the prescription cards that you created from the *Prescription for Stress* worksheet, on the line labeled "problem." If the client has difficulty identifying stressors, provide examples such as homework, changes in the family, or conflicts with friends.
5. Then complete the prescription cards. On the line labeled "treatment," write down a coping strategy that the client would like to try to help them deal with that problem. Have the client sign off on the prescription as the "doctor." Fold the cards and place them into the jar.
6. Remind the client that they now have the power to manage their stress. Encourage them to bring their jar home and to take out and read the various prescriptions whenever they feel overwhelmed. They can also add new prescriptions and coping strategies as they encounter new situations.

Prescription for Stress

Rx for Stress

PROBLEM: ____________________

TREATMENT: ____________________

DOCTOR'S SIGNATURE: ____________________

Rx for Stress

PROBLEM: ____________________

TREATMENT: ____________________

DOCTOR'S SIGNATURE: ____________________

Rx for Stress

PROBLEM: ____________________

TREATMENT: ____________________

DOCTOR'S SIGNATURE: ____________________

Rx for Stress

PROBLEM: ____________________

TREATMENT: ____________________

DOCTOR'S SIGNATURE: ____________________

Rx for Stress

PROBLEM: ____________________

TREATMENT: ____________________

DOCTOR'S SIGNATURE: ____________________

Rx for Stress

PROBLEM: ____________________

TREATMENT: ____________________

DOCTOR'S SIGNATURE: ____________________

River of "Its"

Age Range
7–17

Goals:

- Help clients understand and manage their negative or stressful images, thoughts, and sensations without getting overwhelmed by encouraging mindfulness and emotional regulation.

Materials:

- Large sheets of paper or a roll of butcher paper
- Sticky notes
- Coloring utensils
- Toy boat and a sink or basin of water

Directions:

1. Introduce the idea that thoughts and feelings are like a river. Just as water flows in a river, images, words, and other thoughts constantly flow through our mind and sensations flow through our body. The client can call these thoughts and sensations the "its." Explain that sometimes the river is calm and sometimes it's turbulent. Show how the toy boat floats in calm water and how it bobs and swivels in rough water to illustrate how our thoughts and feelings are ever changing as they float atop the water.*

2. Ask the client to draw a river winding and flowing across the paper. Encourage them to decorate the riverbanks with trees, rocks, or other natural elements.

3. Explain that this river represents their mind and body, and the water represents the "its" they experience every day. Ask them to write down different thoughts and sensations that they constantly feel and think about throughout the day.

4. Once the client's drawing is complete, guide them through a mindfulness visualization:

   Imagine you are having a hard time steering your boat through a choppy river. Up ahead you spot a beach that looks calm and comfortable. You steer your boat onto the shore and discover a comfortable chair that sits on a perch overlooking the river. Amazingly, it has your name on it. As you sit in the chair, you can see images and feel thoughts and sensations, good and bad, flowing by without getting attached to them. Take a few moments and observe them floating past you down the river while you stay far above them. Take a deep breath in . . . hold it for three seconds . . . and now exhale for three seconds. Once more—breathe in . . . hold it . . . and breathe out.

5. Have the client write positive affirmations or coping strategies on sticky notes and place them in their river as "helpful currents" that can guide them through tough times (e.g., "I am flowing through challenging times," "I can handle the currents of my life").

* You can also use the following video to guide clients through this activity: "River of Thoughts: Mindfulness for Children Ages 3 to 11" (https://www.youtube.com/watch?v=LPpUEHWeXpM).

6. Process with the client, asking questions such as:
    - How did it feel to visualize your "its" as a river?
    - Were there any thoughts or sensations that were hard to let flow by?
    - What did you notice about your thoughts and feelings?
7. Remind the client that just like a river flows, their thoughts and sensations will continue to flow. This is part of the healing process. They can observe these thoughts and sensations without letting them take control. Encourage them to use the simple breathing exercise and visualization technique whenever they feel overwhelmed.

Draw Your Breath

Age Range
7–17

Goals:

- Help clients practice mindful breathing and increase relaxation and emotional regulation through art.

Materials:

- Large sheets of paper or a drawing pad
- Variety of coloring utensils (watercolors can be an evocative option)
- Lavender oil (optional; assess for allergies before use)
- Calm music

Directions:

1. Explain that the way we breathe can help us feel calm and centered. Encourage the client to take a few deep breaths with you. Inhale deeply through the nose, hold for a moment, and then exhale slowly through the mouth. Repeat this a few times to help them relax. You can utilize lavender oil to enhance the breath.
2. Ask the client to imagine and draw what their breath looks like to them. Encourage them to continue their mindful breathing as they draw; you can play soothing music to help them focus on their drawing and breathing. Explain that there is no right or wrong way to draw their breath. Encourage them to be creative and expressive, using the mediums, colors, and shapes that feel calming and represent their breathing. They might draw waves, spirals, colors, light, and so on.
3. Process with the client, asking questions such as:
    - How did it feel to draw your breath?
    - Did you notice any changes in your body or mind while you were drawing?
    - What colors or shapes did you choose, and why?
4. Assess whether their breathing is more regulated. If not, continue practicing deep breathing and identify any stressors in the room that could be impacting the client.
5. Encourage the client to keep their drawing somewhere they can see it regularly as a reminder to take deep, calming breaths whenever they feel stressed or anxious.

Grab Fear's Hand

Age Range
7–17

Goals:

- Help clients identify, externalize, and understand their fears to gain clarity and self-compassion.

Materials:

- *Grab Fear's Hand* handout
- Paper and coloring utensils

Directions:

1. Explain to the client that they are going to learn how to befriend their fear. You can say: "Fear develops when it is left alone, when no comfort and nurture is present. Fear can be our friend, and it is important to accept that fear is a part of us that just needs understanding and attention."
2. Ask the client to draw their fear as an image.
3. Ask processing questions like the following:
    - What age is your fear?
    - What does fear do to your body that tells you to be scared?
    - Where does fear live in your body?
    - What do you think your fear is afraid of?
    - Who do you think your fear is afraid of?
    - If your fear had transportation, what would it be (e.g., boat, subway, car, escalator, roller coaster, lightning bolt)?
    - Where does your fear hide?
    - When does your fear hide?
    - What does your fear need to feel better?
    - What can you do to help your fear lessen?
    - What does it want to do other than scare you (e.g., walk, nap, rest, skip, hide, play)?
4. Have the client draw something that indicates a hand to hold on to, like they are holding their fear's hand. Ask if they would be willing to take a walk with their fear, with your help, and give their fear the attention and care it needs by reading any of the phrases on the *Grab Fear's Hand* handout.

Grab Fear's Hand

- I am here with you now.
- You are not alone.
- We can do this together.
- It's okay to feel scared or sad.
- It's okay to cry.
- It's okay to feel numb.
- It's okay to feel angry.
- It's okay to want to kick, scream, or tantrum.
- It's okay to want to run away.
- It's okay to face our feelings.
- It's okay to want to laugh and feel safe.
- It's okay to take this first step toward understanding.
- It's okay to be together for our healing's sake.

Express Your Mind

Age Range
7–17

Goals:

- Help clients express and process their thoughts and emotions through art.
- Foster resilience and self-awareness.

Materials:

- Large sheets of paper or canvas
- Smaller pieces of paper
- Variety of coloring utensils (e.g., markers, crayons, colored pencils, paints)
- Collage materials (e.g., magazines, scissors, glue)
- Clay or play-dough
- Calm, soothing music

Directions:

1. Explain that sometimes it's easier to show what's going on in our minds through art than through words. Discuss common artwork themes that emerge in the mind of a person who is experiencing trauma or challenges like the client's (e.g., a "foster care mind"), such as hope, fear, happiness, or sadness.
2. Guide the client through a brief breathing exercise: inhale deeply through the nose, hold for a moment, and then exhale slowly through the mouth. Repeat this a few times to help them feel calm and centered.
3. Ask the client to close their eyes, if they feel comfortable doing so, and imagine what their mind looks like. Encourage them to think about the thoughts, feelings, and memories that are important to them. What colors, shapes, or images come to mind?
4. Invite the client to express their inner world using the art supplies. Play calm, soothing music while they do so. They can mix and match materials to create a rich, textured representation. Encourage them to create an image that represents their mind and the thoughts and feelings within it. Remind them that their art doesn't have to look like anything specific. It's about expressing what's inside them.
5. Once they are finished, have them write positive affirmations on small pieces of paper. These can be placed around their art as reminders of their strength and resilience.

CHAPTER 5

Managing Anger, Frustration, and Aggression

The Anger Bag™

Age Range
5–12

Goals:

- Help clients utilize various coping skills to lessen feelings of anger and aggression, self-regulate, and problem-solve.

Materials:

- Bag with handles
- Index cards and a writing utensil
- Variety of items to help release anger (e.g., small pillow, paper to rip, paper and coloring utensils, play-dough, bubble wrap, bubbles)

Directions:

1. Explain to the client that they will be learning how to gain control of angry and aggressive feelings with the help of a special "anger bag" that they will create. The bag will contain different items and activities for them to use when they have these feelings and don't know how to contain them.

2. Introduce each item, exploring and practicing together how the client can use it to help release the angry feelings from their mind and body. Here are some suggestions:

    - **Scream pillow:** The client can scream or yell into the small pillow to vent their anger (without hurting anyone else with a loud noise or unkind words). Make sure they breathe between screams. They can shout phrases into the pillow such as "I'm angry!" "It's not fair!" or "I'm so frustrated!"
    - **Paper to rip:** Explain that this paper is available for the client to tear up when they are frustrated or angry—but the rule is, when they are finished they must clean it up. As they rip up the paper, they will verbally express why they are angry. The client can throw the pieces up in the air or directly into a garbage pail. This can be very cathartic and freeing.
    - **Paper and coloring utensils:** The client can use these to draw pictures or write about their triggers and feelings of anger.
    - **Play-dough:** Teach the client the "rip-squish-spaghetti" technique to safely release their angry feelings into the play-dough. First, they take the play-dough and say "Rip!" while breaking it into two pieces. Then they say "Squish!" while squeezing their feelings into the play-dough. Finally, they say "Spaghetti!" while separating their fingers so that the play-dough squishes right through them. They should do this five to ten times until they feel more calm.
    - **Anger buster poppers:** The client can step, stand, sit, or jump on the bubble wrap to project their aggression in a safe, fun way. Encourage the client to tell you a story about what they are doing to the poppers and who or what the poppers represent to them.
    - **Anger buster bubbles:** Instruct the client to sit down and slowly blow one bubble at a time while they imagine putting their angry or frustrated feelings inside each bubble and then watching it float away until it pops and disappears. The client should continue until they regain focus and internalize a sense of calm.

3. Assist the client in thinking of three to eight coping strategies and writing them on index cards. These "anger buster cards" are also stored in the bag, and the client can reach in and pick one out anytime they need help figuring out what to do with their stress. Examples include:
    - Scream as loud as I can in my scream pillow!
    - Punch my scream pillow with all my might 10 times!
    - Take 10 deep breaths in and out of my belly.
    - Say out loud 10 times, "I am the boss of my anger!"
    - Count to 10 like this: 1 chimpanzee, 2 chimpanzee, 3 chimpanzee . . .
    - Go to my mirror and make a funny face!
    - Go outside, find a stick, and hit a tree with all my might . . . then hug the tree!
    - Draw a picture or words about the person or thing I'm mad at, then rip it into pieces!
4. Place all of the items inside the bag and write on the outside of the bag (or on a label that you affix to it), "Things to do when I feel angry to help calm the pain inside me." Encourage the client to take the bag home and keep it within reach by hanging it on a doorknob or hook in their room.

Erupt My Feelings

Age Range
5–17

Goals:

- Help clients externalize and project repressed feelings of anger, grief, loss, and resentment toward others.

Materials:

- Modeling clay
- Aluminum tray
- Thin glass tube or vase
- Baking soda
- Vinegar
- Slips of paper or popsicle sticks
- Writing utensil

Directions:

Session 1

1. Explain to the client that you are going to help them with their overwhelming feelings of anger by creating a volcano to erupt these feelings out of their body.
2. Give the client the modeling clay on the aluminum tray and have them carefully mold the clay around the vase into the shape of a volcano, leaving the top of the vase open as the volcano crater.
3. While the client is creating the volcano, begin to process how the volcano will be used when it is finished by asking questions such as:
   - What thoughts or feelings are boiling within the volcano that may want to erupt out?
   - What lies inside the volcano?
   - Has this volcano erupted before?
   - How old is this volcano?
   - Where did the fire come from?

Session 2

4. Have the client write down the thoughts or feelings that are "boiling inside of them" or making them angry on pieces of paper or popsicle sticks. These can also be used to represent people.* Discuss what they are writing and expressing as they create.
5. Pour the baking soda into the top of the volcano, then add the paper and popsicle sticks. Ask the client if there's anything else they need to get out of their system before pouring in the vinegar and watching the volcano erupt!

---

* In one case, a client put a popsicle stick in the volcano to represent his drug addicted birth father, whom he loved very much but who was abandoning him over and over. The client chose to erupt his father over and over in the volcano while verbalizing his anger and disappointment, which became quite a cathartic experience for him.

My Venom

Age Range
5–17

Goals:

- Help clients identify and understand feelings of bitterness or anger that arise unexpectedly and develop strategies to manage and express these feelings constructively.

Materials:

- *My Venom* and *My Antidote* worksheets
- Writing and coloring utensils

Directions:

1. Introduce the concept of venom (a toxic substance produced by some animals, such as snakes or scorpions) as a metaphor for feelings of bitterness, resentment, or anger that can surface unexpectedly.
2. Provide the *My Venom* worksheet and explain to the client that they are going to create their own unique venom using feelings as ingredients. Discuss how venomous feelings manifest in their body and mind (e.g., tense muscles, negative thoughts, trouble thinking, shaking, racing heart, stomachache). List these on the worksheet under "ingredients," then identify and write the meaning of each one (e.g., for the ingredient of "clenched fists," the meaning may be "ready to fight").
3. Ask what words ignite and spark the venom in their body (e.g., "loser," "stupid," teasing) and how it feels to hear them. Also ask what things other people do that spark the venom in their body (e.g., being pushed, being yelled at, being treated unfairly) and how it feels when this happens. Record these on the worksheet.
4. Invite the client to draw their venom in the jar outline. Encourage them to think about what their venom looks like, what temperature it is, and how it behaves.
5. After that is complete, provide the *My Antidote* worksheet and explain that this will be their remedy to help counteract their venom so they can feel better again. Brainstorm and practice coping strategies (e.g., deep breathing, positive affirmations, talking to a trusted adult). Note the words and actions that help neutralize the client's venom, identify the ingredients in the client's antidote and their meanings, and encourage the client to draw their antidote, parallel to the venom worksheet.
6. Reflect on how understanding and managing their venomous feelings can lead to better emotional regulation and overall well-being. Remind them that an antidote can quickly calm their mind and body, so they should use it as soon as they notice the venom arising.

Variation:

Clients can also create their venom and antidote out of arts and crafts supplies. You can provide two plastic jars with lids, duct tape, and a variety of "ingredients" for this purpose (e.g., water, vegetable oil, lemon, lime, paprika, googly eyes, confetti, glitter). At the end, be sure to seal the jars with duct tape and write "Do not drink" on them.

My Venom

Ingredients	Meaning

What sparks the venom?

Words	Things People Do

My Antidote

Ingredients	Meaning

What calms down the venom?

Words	Things People Do

The Hot Seat

Age Range
7–17

Goals:

- Provide clients with a safe and structured way to express and process their emotions and to work through unresolved anger issues.

Materials:

- Two chairs
- A quiet and private space

Directions:

1. Explain that the purpose of an empty chair exercise is to help the client express and process their emotions by talking to an imaginary or absent person, a part of themselves, or an abstract concept. Ensure the client understands that this is a safe space for them to express their feelings without judgment.
2. Place two chairs facing each other in a quiet, private space. Explain that one chair is for them to sit in and the other chair will be for the person or thing they want to imagine talking to.
3. Guide the client through a brief breathing exercise: inhale deeply through the nose, hold for a moment, and then exhale slowly through the mouth. Repeat this a few times to help them feel calm and centered.
4. Help the client decide who or what they want to address. This could be a person (e.g., a birth parent, a foster parent, a friend), a part of themselves (e.g., their younger self, an angry part of themselves), or a concept (e.g., their future, their fear). Ask the client to imagine that the person, part, or concept is sitting across from them in the empty chair.
5. Encourage the client to speak openly to the empty chair, expressing their thoughts and feelings as if the person or entity were really there. Provide prompts if needed, such as:
   - What do you want to say to them?
   - How do you feel about what happened?
   - What do you wish they knew?
6. Allow the client to switch chairs and respond as the person or entity, if they are comfortable doing so.
7. After the conversation, have the client return to their original chair. Discuss what they experienced during the exercise by asking questions like:
   - How did it feel to express those feelings?
   - Did you learn anything new about yourself or the situation?
   - What do you think will help you moving forward?
8. End by repeating the breathing exercise to help the client relax.

Angry Tar Pit

Age Range
4–17

Goals:

- Help clients process and contain overwhelming experiences by externalizing and managing their emotions.

Materials:

- Black clay
- Clear plastic bowl at least three inches deep
- Small objects (e.g., stones, buttons, toys) to represent experiences
- Paper and coloring utensils

Directions:

1. Explain what tar pits are: deep pools of sticky tar that trap anything that falls or wanders inside of them. Scientists have found many huge dinosaur bones and other animals inside of them when excavating, proving that once something falls into a tar pit, it cannot escape until the time is right for the remains to be dug up. Those dinosaur fossils are similar to huge, overwhelming feelings—the "fossils" of our bad experiences—which need to be trapped in the tar pit and held until we can better make sense of them.

2. Ask the client to write down or draw examples of significant fossils of experiences they have had that they are not ready to deal with yet (e.g., moving to new homes, loss of loved ones, bullies).

3. Provide a variety of small objects (e.g., stones, buttons, toys) and ask the client to choose a few objects that represent their big experiences. Be curious if they are open to share why they chose each object and what it represents.

4. Give the client larges pieces of black clay (to fill the bowl at least three inches deep) and ask them to mold it into the bowl so it represents a tar pit.

5. Have the client place their chosen objects into the clay, pressing them in and covering them to symbolize burying and containing their big experiences. Ask them questions such as:
    - How does it feel to bury your fossil experiences?
    - Do you feel a sense of relief or is the feeling boiling?
    - When do you think you will dig up these experiences again?

6. Reflect on how managing their big fossils of experiences can lead to better emotional regulation and overall well-being.

Anger Dice Game

Age Range
4–17

Goals:

- Help clients recognize and manage their anger and practice coping strategies.

Materials:

- Two dice (standard six-sided)
- *Anger Dice* handout
- Paper and coloring utensils

Directions:

1. Explain that this activity is designed to help the client explore and manage their anger in a fun way. Emphasize that the game provides a safe space to express feelings, learn about anger, and practice coping strategies.
2. Show the client the *Anger Dice* handout and the dice. Explain how the game is played:
    - You and the client will take turns rolling the dice.
    - The numbers rolled will correspond to a specific square on the grid.
    - Each square contains a prompt or an activity related to understanding and managing anger, which the player will complete.
3. During the game, encourage the client to engage fully with each prompt or activity. Practice the coping strategies together, reinforcing their application in real-life situations. Highlight the importance of each strategy in managing anger effectively.
4. Afterward, allow the client to share their overall experience with the game. Discuss which strategies they found most helpful or insightful. Encourage them to reflect on how they can apply these strategies in their daily life.

Anger Dice

Play with a partner and two dice. Roll both dice and complete the prompt or activity that corresponds with the numbers. Play until you have completed all the squares!

	⚀	⚁	⚂	⚃	⚄	⚅
⚀	Tell a story about a time you were frustrated.	If you're angry, can you walk away and let it go?	Practice saying: "I feel ___ because ___ and I want ___."	What was the best holiday you ever had?	Draw anger on paper, then rip it up!	Tell a story about your anger.
⚁	Count to 20 like you are calming down.	What's something that you don't like?	If you're angry, can you tell them to stop?	Tell a story about a time you lost your temper.	What sound annoys you the most?	What's your favorite kind of ice cream?
⚂	What's your favorite food?	If you're angry, should you confront the person?	What is the best surprise you ever had?	You're doing a great job learning about anger!	If you're angry, can you go do another activity?	When's your birthday?
⚃	What makes you smile?	Do a body scan and check your body for tension.	Take four deep breaths.	What are you good at?	Tell a story about a time you were proud of yourself.	If you're angry, can you use an "I" statement?
⚄	If you're angry, can you wait and cool off?	How do you like to have fun?	If you're angry, can you talk it out?	What do you like to do on weekends?	Where are you originally from?	Say out loud: "I am the boss of my anger!"
⚅	Name three good things in your life.	Get a drink of water right now.	When someone threatens you, you can . . .	Punch a pillow or squeeze play-dough!	When someone pushes you, you can . . .	Can you agree to disagree?

Anger Baggage

Age Range
4–17

Goals:

- Help clients identify, understand, and manage their anger by externalizing it and developing healthy coping mechanisms.

Materials:

- 10 large rocks
- Adhesive labels (or duct tape) and markers*
- Index cards and a writing utensil
- Backpack

Directions:

1. Explain to the client that everyone feels angry sometimes and it's okay to have those feelings. However, it's important to find ways to manage our anger so it doesn't feel overwhelming or lead to harmful behaviors. Anger can feel like carrying around heavy baggage. This activity will help them identify their "anger baggage" and find ways to lighten the load.
2. Ask the client to imagine that every time they hold on to the feeling of anger, it's like putting a heavy rock in their backpack, which makes it harder to carry around. Have the client name and label each rock and put it in the backpack (e.g., "my mom's anger"—a rock of hurt; "I feel alone"—a rock of loneliness).
3. Have the client wear the backpack and walk around. Ask: "What do you notice in your body? How does it feel to carry all of that baggage? How are you feeling about this?"
4. Explain that we often carry the backpack of pent-up anger around as if we have no choice, even as a badge of honor—"Look at how much emotional baggage I can carry!" But over time the weight will only hurt us.
5. Discuss coping strategies and/or positive affirmations to help the client manage this baggage and lighten the load (e.g., deep breathing, counting to ten, talking to a trusted adult, physical activity, drawing or journaling). Write these on different index cards.
6. Encourage the client to remove the rocks from the backpack one by one, symbolizing letting go of their anger, and to replace them with the coping tools or affirmations.
7. Instruct the client to walk around the room with the backpack again. Ask: "What do you notice in your body? How does it feel to not carry all of that baggage? What feels different for you?"
8. Reinforce the idea that they are in control of their feelings and that they are not alone in managing them.

* For reuse across sessions and clients, consider dry-erase labels/tape and markers.

Echoes of My Anger Collage

Age Range
4–17

Goals:

- Help clients process their emotions and understand the ripple effects of their anger on themselves and others.

Materials:

- Large poster board
- Images for collaging (e.g., magazine clippings, stickers)
- Scissors
- Glue sticks
- Coloring utensils

Directions:

1. Explain to the client how anger can linger as "echoes" and have ripple effects on themselves and those around them. They will be creating a collage to help them visualize and understand these effects.
2. Provide the materials and encourage the client to use images, words, and colors to represent the echoes of their anger. Offer prompts and processing questions such as:
   - What anger still echoes for you from the past?
   - What words still echo for you from the past?
   - What can repair these echoes?
   - Where do the echoes from the past go to be stored?
   - What are the colors of your anger?
   - If your anger had a voice, what would it say?
   - What is the sound of your anger—a scream, silence, a storm?
   - What's a memory that still fuels your anger today?
3. Ask the client to share their collage and discuss what the different elements represent. Reflect on how creating the collage helped them understand the ripple effects of their anger and how they can manage these effects. Discuss the strategies they find most helpful for managing their anger.

Drum the Day

Age Range
5–17

Goals:

- Help clients manifest their feelings through sound, reflect on how their moods can shift throughout the day, practice introspection, and build self-esteem.

Materials:

- Hand drum

Directions:

1. Introduce the drum and explore how different emotions can be expressed through rhythm, volume, speed, and so on. For example:
    - Excited: short, quick drumbeats
    - Happy: light, airy tones
    - Angry: hard, arrhythmic/scattered beats
    - Scared: fast, rhythmic beating
2. Demonstrate how to "drum your day" by describing what happened on a real or hypothetical day while drumming along to express your feelings. For example, maybe the day started out great, but you became angrier in the afternoon, then had a boring evening, and finally had your favorite dessert after dinner.
3. Ask the client to drum a day of their own, starting in the morning and going through the night. Encourage them to create their own sounds and patterns to express their unique feelings. Depending on the client's comfort, you can encourage them to also describe the feelings and events through words or to simply express themselves through drumming. You can prompt the client to drum days such as:
    - Today/tomorrow/yesterday
    - The best/worst day ever
    - Their angriest day
    - The day they left their birth family
    - An ordinary day with their family
    - Their birthday/Father's Day/Mother's Day
    - Their dream day

Frustration Feeling Smasher

Age Range
5–12

Goals:

- Help clients identify and understand the sources of their frustration and develop strategies for managing and expressing these feelings constructively.

Materials:

- Toy hammer
- Foam blocks
- Masking tape
- Index cards
- Writing utensil
- Small broom and dustpan

Directions:

1. Explain that this activity will help the client identify and manage their frustrations. Discuss the importance of understanding and expressing feelings in healthy ways.
2. Explore common sources of frustration for children with foster care or trauma experiences similar to your client's (e.g., frequent moves and instability, separation from family and friends, difficulty adjusting to new environments, lack of control over their life, feeling misunderstood or unheard, academic challenges due to school changes).
3. Encourage the client to share their own unique experiences and to voice as many frustrations as possible. Write each frustration on an index card for the client. Then tape the index cards to the foam blocks and place them around the floor.
4. Give the client the toy hammer and invite them to smash their frustration triggers to bits. Encourage them to continue to express their feelings verbally as they smash the blocks.
5. Help the client sweep up all the debris and toss it away. Discuss how verbalizing their frustrations can help the client "break down" these intense feelings so they are easier to manage and move through. Explain that their own brain and attitude is a hammer they can use anytime to smash the feelings and sweep them clean.

Break Stuff

Age Range
6–17

Goals:

- Help clients physically release aggression in a safe and controlled environment.

Materials:

- Variety of objects that can be broken safely (e.g., cardboard boxes, balloons, old books, small plastic objects—no glass!)
- Tarp or mat
- Safety goggles
- Garden gloves
- Paper and a writing utensil
- Premade pin that says "You are unbreakable!"

Directions:

1. Introduce the concept of breaking stuff as a metaphor for destroying, releasing, or overcoming powerful feelings of anger and aggression in a safe, controlled way. Emphasize the importance of safety and emotional regulation and that the object they break represents a strong mood that feels hard to control.
2. Discuss common sources of aggression for children with foster care or trauma experiences similar to your client's (e.g., feeling misunderstood or unfairly treated, instability or frequent moves, separation from family and friends, academic or social challenges).
3. Encourage the client to share their own unique experiences and write them down.
4. Provide safety goggles and gloves for the client. Set up the breaking area with protective coverings to catch debris and ensure safety. Explain the safety rules: they can rip, tear, bang, and break stuff in the designated area only.
5. Allow the client to choose the breakable objects that they feel best represent their aggression or sources of anger. Invite the client to express their feelings verbally while breaking the objects if they wish. Supervise closely to ensure safety and provide emotional support as needed.
6. Afterward, help them clean up and dispose of the debris. Discuss how they felt during the process and what they learned about their aggression. For example:
    - Did breaking stuff make them feel better or worse?
    - Did they wish they didn't have to break anything? Did they want to break more? Why?
    - What can they do in real life when having strong feelings?
    - What imaginary things can they break to help them feel better?
7. Brainstorm and practice coping strategies to manage these feelings of aggression in the future (e.g., deep breathing, talking to a trusted adult, engaging in physical activities).
8. Reflect on how understanding and managing their aggression can lead to better emotional regulation and overall well-being.
9. Provide the client with a pin that reads "You are unbreakable!"

Scream Whisperer

Age Range
6–17

Goals:

- Help clients manage and express their intense emotions, particularly anger and frustration, in a healthy and controlled manner.

Materials:

- Poster mailing tube with a closed end
- Paper and coloring utensils
- Images (e.g., magazine clippings, stickers) of emoting
- Glue

Directions:

1. Explain to the client that you understand they have had experiences of intense emotions and it's important to find safe and effective ways to express them. Discuss how bottling big feelings up and keeping them hidden can lead to them building up and exploding in ways that only hurt themselves and those around them.
2. Introduce the concept of the "scream whisperer": someone who can turn a loud scream into a powerful yet controlled whisper. When emotions are high, it's like a volume button has been turned all the way up and no one can hear what you're saying; speaking or shouting louder just makes it even worse. But when the volume is turned down to a whisper, it's much easier to communicate your feelings and for people to hear you, making the situation more manageable and calmer.
3. Invite the client to let out a good scream, letting them know that it's okay to do so in this safe, controlled environment. Cover your ears to emphasize how loud and disturbing the sound is.
4. Have them scream again, this time inside the "scream tube." Note how the scream comes out much quieter. Encourage them to decorate the scream tube with words and images, then let out some more good screams into the tube.
5. Discuss how loud screams drown everything out, even your own feelings, and usually lead to someone screaming back and nobody being heard. Explore how being able to control the scream, letting the pressure out while remaining quieter, allows you to be heard and more quickly get what you need.
6. Suggest that the next time they want to let out a good scream, they use the tube, a pillow, or something similar to muffle the sound so the feelings don't grow but subside, allowing dialogue to take place.
7. As another option, teach the client a deep breathing exercise—inhaling deeply through the nose, holding for a few seconds, and exhaling slowly through the mouth—to help them calm themselves when needed.
8. Offer the coloring materials and ask the client to draw or write about their intense feelings, turning the scream into a whisper on paper. After they have finished, encourage them to share about it. Discuss how it feels to express their emotions in a quieter, more controlled way.

9. Work with the client to create a personalized "scream whisperer" plan. This plan should include steps they can take when they start to feel overwhelmed by their emotions, such as:
    - Identifying triggers that increase emotional volume
    - Safe ways to release energy (e.g., screaming into a pillow or scream tube)
    - Calming techniques (e.g., deep breathing, listening to music)
    - A list of supportive people they can talk to
10. End the session by reinforcing the idea that it's okay to have intense emotions, but finding healthy ways to express and manage them is crucial. Remind the client that they have the power to turn their emotional screams into whispers and that there are people and tools available to help them.

D-anger

Age Range
12–17

Goals:

- Help clients understand the consequences of risky behaviors and develop strategies to make safer choices.

Materials:

- *Risky Behaviors* and *Safe Alternatives* card templates
- Paper
- Index card
- Writing and coloring utensils

Directions:

1. Before the session, copy and cut out the *Risky Behaviors* and *Safe Alternatives* cards. Make some blank cards as well for the client to add their own examples.
2. In session, point out to the client that *anger* is one letter away from *danger* to illustrate how easily risky behaviors can lead to dangerous situations. Explain the importance of recognizing and avoiding danger to stay safe.
3. Discuss common risky behaviors. Have the client choose from the cards or create their own cards with examples of risky behaviors they have experienced, encountered, or heard about.
4. Talk about the triggers and warning signs that can lead to risky behaviors (e.g., peer pressure, feeling angry or sad).
5. Have the client create a chart with two columns: "risky behaviors" and "safe alternatives." Place or write the most relevant risky behaviors for the client in the first column. For the second column, explore strategies the client can use to avoid risky behaviors and stay safe. Offer the premade cards as a starting point and help the client brainstorm their own strategies as well. If possible, practice these strategies with the client in session.
6. Reflect on how understanding and managing risky behaviors can lead to safer and healthier choices.
7. On the index card, write the key strategies the client can use to stay safe. This safety plan card serves as a reminder to use their skills. Encourage them to personalize it with a symbol of safety.

Risky Behaviors

Risky Behavior Running away	**Risky Behavior** Physical fights
Risky Behavior Drugs or alcohol	**Risky Behavior** Skipping school
Risky Behavior Stealing	**Risky Behavior** Hanging out with negative people
Risky Behavior Unsafe online situations	**Risky Behavior** Lying
Risky Behavior Self-harm	**Risky Behavior** Isolation

Safe Alternatives

Safe Alternative Talk it out with a trusted adult	**Safe Alternative** Walk away from the situation and use conflict resolution skills
Safe Alternative Use healthy coping strategies like journaling, art, or talking to someone you trust	**Safe Alternative** Discuss problems with a school counselor or teacher to find a solution
Safe Alternative Earn what you want through chores, a job, or saving allowance	**Safe Alternative** Spend time with friends who make positive choices and support you
Safe Alternative Use the internet safely and talk to a trusted adult about online interactions	**Safe Alternative** Be honest and open about your actions and seek help when needed
Safe Alternative Use techniques like deep breathing, meditation, or listening to calm music	**Safe Alternative** Join a club or team that interests you and is a positive activity

CHAPTER 6

Managing Sadness, Grief, Despair, and Heartbreak

The Sad Bag™

Age Range
5–17

Goals:

- Teach clients how to problem-solve, self-regulate, and use coping skills when they are feeling sad.

Materials:

- Bag with handles
- Index cards and a writing utensil
- Variety of items to soothe sadness (e.g., small pillow, journal, paper and coloring utensils, small photo album, Guatemalan worry dolls, bubbles)

Directions:

1. Discuss with the client how feelings of sadness can be overwhelming and lead to an emotional shutting down that only seems to make matters worse. Explain that they are going to learn how to manage and control these sad feelings with the use of a special "sad bag" they will create. This bag will contain items and skill reminders to help them process and manage intense feelings of sadness so they don't become overwhelmed.
2. Introduce each item, exploring and practicing together how the client can use it to help comfort their mind and body. Here are some suggestions:
    - **Tear pillow:** A small pillow can be used to practice self-comfort and care. The client can place their face in the pillow and express their sadness by sighing or crying into it. They can also say phrases like "It's not fair," "I'm hurt," or "I feel sad."
    - **Magical wish journal:** Explain that this special wish journal can bring magic into their life. Whenever they write their wishes in the journal, amazing things can happen. They will start to feel better and more confident. Their wishes may not all come true in the exact way they'd hoped, but the magic of the journal will always help them care for themselves and find good things in their life.
    - **Paper and coloring utensils:** The client can write and draw pictures to express their pain and sadness, reducing its intensity.
    - **Happy photo album:** Include a small photo album where the client can put pictures of people, places, and things that make them happy. They can use photos as well as magazine clippings, printouts, drawings, and so on to represent their loved ones, cartoon characters, flowers, celebrities—anything that helps them feel happy, loved, or optimistic. This will then be a resource to open whenever they begin to feel sad.
    - **Guatemalan worry dolls:** These dolls allow the client to project their concerns, worries, and fears into an external object. You can introduce the dolls as "powerful friends" who can help us with our feelings, but first we have to tell them what we are upset about so they can understand and help us feel better. Once informed, the client's powerful friends are placed under their pillow at

bedtime and work all night, taking their sadness away and ensuring that when they wake up in the morning they feel better.

- **Bubbles:** Instruct the client to sit down and slowly blow one bubble at a time while they imagine seeing their sadness and pain enter the bubble as it appears and then disappear with the bubble when it pops. Encourage them to focus on putting all their sadness inside, feeling the lightness of the bubble gliding in the air and then disappearing like magic, leaving them feeling relaxed and calm.

3. Help the client think of three to eight coping strategies and write them on index cards. These "sadness buster cards" are also stored in the bag, and the client can reach in and pick one out anytime they need help processing their sadness and stress. Examples include:
    - Cross my arms around my body and give myself a big hug!
    - Say this tongue twister 10 times: "Silly Sally sang dilly-dallies sitting on a swing!"
    - Cry on my tear pillow and let it catch my tears for me!
    - Take five deep breaths slowly.
    - Write my sad feelings in my journal.
    - Ask someone I trust for a hug.
    - Go to my mirror and make a funny face really big!
    - Get my bubbles and blow three wishes into the air!

4. Place all of the items in the bag. You can write on the outside of the bag (or on a label that you affix to it), "Things to do when I feel sad to make my broken heart feel glad!" Encourage the client to take the bag home and keep it within reach by hanging it on a doorknob or hook in their room.

Tracks of My Tears

Age Range
5–17

Goals:

- Help clients process and express their grief and understand the cause and meaning behind their tears.

Materials:

- Kinetic sand in a tray
- Small footprint molds or toy feet
- Coloring utensils
- Multiple sheets of blue paper
- Scissors
- Calm, soothing music

Directions:

1. Explain to the client that it's okay to feel sad and one way to start feeling better is to understand where the sadness is coming from. Discuss the concept of grief and how it can feel like walking through wet sand, leaving footprints that can be traced back to the cause. Understanding this cause is crucial to begin to truly heal.
2. Play calm, soothing music and invite the client to use the footprint molds or toy feet to create a path of footprints in the kinetic sand. They can make as many footprints as they like, representing different moments of sadness or grief in their life, and paths that trace the tracks of their tears. Encourage them to also create a pool with some of the blue paper, a place where the tears can land and are held for safekeeping.
3. Cut teardrop shapes out of the remaining blue paper and ask the client to think about times when they felt sad and cried. Inside the teardrops, they can write or draw the main feeling or cause of each tear and place them one by one on a footprint or in the pool. Explain that tears can also be the same feeling over and over; this is normal and part of the healing process.
4. Sit with the client and go through their "tear reflections." Discuss each instance of sadness and validate their feelings. Ask open-ended questions like "What did you feel when this happened?" or "What do you wish could have been different?"
5. Praise the client for their courage in expressing their emotions. Reinforce the idea that it's healthy to acknowledge and talk about their feelings. Offer a comforting activity afterward, like reading a book together or having a calm moment with a favorite toy.

Blue Day Book

Age Range **6–17**

Goals:

- Create a resource to help clients cope with sadness and grief on difficult days.

Materials:

- Notebook or paper stapled into a book
- Coloring utensils
- Collage materials (e.g., photos, magazine clippings, stickers, glue, scissors)
- Calm, soothing music (optional)

Directions:

1. Explain that the client will be creating a "blue day book"—a special resource that will provide comfort and pathways to feel better on days when they are sad or have a broken heart.
2. Allow the client to decorate the cover of their book. They can draw or add any decorative elements that make them feel happy or calm. Encourage them to write their name and a title like "My Blue Day Book" or "Comfort for My Broken Heart." You can play calm, soothing music during this time.
3. Help the client create different chapters in their book and a table of contents on the first page so they can easily find particular sections or activities. Chapter ideas include:
    - **Positive affirmations:** Encourage the client to write comforting and empowering affirmations such as "I am loved," "I am strong," or "This feeling will pass."
    - **Happy memories:** The client can add photos, drawings, or descriptions of happy memories that make them smile.
    - **Comforting quotes:** These are sayings that the client can read when they need a boost. Print out some quotes or let the client write their favorites.
    - **Calming activities:** List activities that help the client feel better, such as drawing, reading a book, playing with a favorite toy, or listening to music.
    - **Gratitude list:** This can include family, friends, pets, favorite foods—anything the client appreciates. Encourage them to add to this list regularly.
    - **Breathing exercises:** Write and draw instructions for simple exercises (e.g., "Take a deep breath in for four seconds, hold for four seconds, and breathe out for four seconds").
    - **Drawings and doodles:** Leave space for the client to draw or doodle their feelings that are hard to put into words.
    - **Letters to myself:** Encourage the client to write letters to themselves on good days, offering advice and encouragement for when they are feeling down. Write "Dear me . . ." at the top of a few pages.
4. Encourage the client to use their blue day book whenever they feel sad or have a broken heart. They can look through the book, read the affirmations and quotes, try out the activities, and add new entries.

My String of Connections

Age Range **4–12**

Goals:

- Provide an opportunity for clients to acknowledge and reflect on all the connections they have made through their life's transitions.
- Reassure clients that they are not alone and that love continues on even when they are physically separated from loved ones.

Materials:

- Hearts cut out from construction paper (30–50)
- One-hole punch
- Tape
- Yarn or string (3–6 feet)
- Coloring utensils

Directions:

1. Inform the client that they are going to create a "string of connections" to recognize all of the people who have been in their life whom they feel or have felt a connection to.
2. Help the client write one name on each heart. You can start with their birth parents and relatives, then write down adoptive parents, relatives, friends at home and at school, pets, and so on. If a client has a strong connection to places and things (e.g., their birth country or state, a stuffed animal, a special item given to them), they can write a heart for each of those as well.
3. Punch a hole in each heart and help the client string them onto the yarn, leaving space between them so that the names are visible. Tape the ends of the string and hang it up, ideally across a corner or extending from one wall to another so there is space for the client to sit beneath it.
4. Have the client sit down and look up at all the connections while you help them process them in detail. Explain that even when we are physically separated from our loved ones, that love is continuous and ongoing, like an invisible string that connects us across space and time.
5. Encourage the client to take the string home and hang it up in their room as a reminder that they are not alone and are forever connected to their loved ones by the invisible string.

Five Pits of Despair

Age Range
6–17

Goals:

- Help clients understand and process their grief by exploring the five stages of grief in a tangible and interactive way.

Materials:

- Five small containers (e.g., paper cups or bowls)
- Stickers or other decorative items
- Paper
- Coloring utensils
- Clay or play-dough
- Index cards

Directions:

1. Explain to the client that grief can feel like falling into deep pits of emotion, like sadness or anger. Let them know that it's normal to experience these feelings and that this activity will help them understand and better cope with their grief.
2. Use small containers to represent the five "pits of despair." Label each container with one of the five stages of grief: denial, anger, bargaining, depression, and acceptance (Kübler-Ross & Kessler, 2005). Invite the client to decorate the containers with markers, stickers, or other items.
3. Explain each stage of grief to the client in simple terms:
    - **Denial:** Feeling like the loss isn't real or pretending it hasn't even happened.
    - **Anger:** Feeling mad about the loss and looking for someone or something to blame.
    - **Bargaining:** Trying to make deals or promises to change the situation.
    - **Depression:** Feeling very sad and hopeless about the loss.
    - **Acceptance:** Understanding and coming to terms with the loss.
4. Explain that at some point everybody experiences these different aspects of grief and that each person's journey is unique. It's okay and normal to move back and forth between the pits, in any order, even to return to a pit that you've experienced before.
5. Give the client some clay or play-dough and ask them to create a small symbol or object that represents how they feel for each pit of despair. For example, they might make a small heart for acceptance or a storm cloud for depression.
6. Provide the client with coloring materials and ask them to write or draw an experience they've had related to each stage of grief. Encourage them to place these in the corresponding pits. Ask open-ended questions like "Can you tell me more about what you felt during this time?"
7. Brainstorm with the client about coping strategies for each stage of grief (e.g., talking to a trusted adult, journaling, doing a favorite activity, practicing deep breathing). Write the strategies down on index cards and place them near the corresponding pits.

8. On a larger piece of paper, draw a ladder to stretch from the first pit (denial) to the last pit (acceptance). Have the client draw or write on the ladder rungs what steps they can take to move from one stage to the next. For example, "talking to a friend" might be a step from anger to bargaining, and "when I feel like crying, let it out" might be a step from depression to acceptance.
9. Praise the client for their bravery in exploring their grief. Remind them that everybody experiences these stages and it's okay to move back and forth between stages as much as necessary for their own personal journey through grief. Encourage them to take the coping cards and/or ladder home as a reminder of what they can do when they feel themselves sinking into a pit of despair.
10. Offer a comforting activity afterward, such as reading a book together or having a calm moment with a favorite toy.

Missed Connections

Age Range
4–17

Goals:

- Help clients externalize painful and overwhelming feelings of trauma and loss in a creative and constructive way.

Materials:

- Poster paper
- Coloring utensils
- Finger paints (optional)
- Magazine clippings (words, people, places, etc.)
- Glue
- Scissors
- Calm, soothing music

Directions:

1. Play calm, soothing music and provide the client with the collage materials.
2. Introduce the theme of the collage and encourage the client to use any pictures or words they wish to express their feelings and thoughts associated with this theme. Choose from the following prompts, depending on the client's situation and needs:
    - **With and Without You:** Have the client make a collage with two sections: one representing their life before the loss or separation from a loved one and the other representing their life now (e.g., "With Mommy" and "Without Mommy").
    - **Our Family:** This more open-ended prompt allows the client to explore their thoughts and feelings related to their family and the loss or other trauma they have experienced.
    - **Hands Holding Me Yesterday and Today:** The client can draw or use finger paints to create a collage of hands representing the people in their life, past and present. This can include birth, foster, and adoptive family members as well as other loved ones.
3. Process with the client, asking open-ended questions about their collage and letting them know that all of their thoughts and feelings are welcome here.
4. Praise the client for their bravery in exploring these difficult feelings. Follow up with a comforting activity or practice other coping skills as needed.

Grief Friend

Age Range
4–17

Goals:

- Help clients cope with grief by creating a tangible source of comfort and positive reinforcement.

Materials:

- Soft sock*
- Stuffing material (e.g., cotton, polyester fiberfill)
- String or fabric glue
- Fabric markers
- Small drawstring bag
- Scissors
- Paper
- Coloring utensils
- Other decorative materials (e.g., stickers, glitter)
- Box or container
- Calm, soothing music

Directions:

1. Explain that the client will be creating a special companion filled with loving-kindness messages to provide comfort during times of grief. Discuss how creating and using the doll can help them feel supported and remind them of positive thoughts and memories.
2. Play calm, soothing music and help the client create a simple doll or stuffed animal by filling the sock with stuffing material and sealing the bottom with fabric glue or by tying a string around it. They can use fabric markers to add features to their doll if they wish.
3. Cut out slips of paper and brainstorm with the client some loving-kindness messages to write on them. For example: "You are strong and brave," "It's okay to feel sad," "Your loved one is always with you in your heart."
4. Give the client a small drawstring bag and let them know this will hold the loving-kindness messages and will stay with their doll. Have the client fold each message and place it in the bag.
5. Explain that whenever the client feels sad or needs comfort, they can turn to their grief friend for loving-kindness and support. They can hug or hold the doll or take out a message and read it to feel comforted and loved.
6. Ask the client to hold their doll and say three loving-kindness messages to someone they miss and long for, such as a birth parent, foster parent, or sibling. For example: "I hope you are safe," "I hope to see you soon," "I love you." Explain that as they express their messages to others, these same messages will come back to them full circle.
7. Provide the client with a box and explain that it is a safe place to keep their doll and messages. Invite the client to decorate the box. Have them place their doll and bag inside and take them home.
8. Reinforce that it's okay to feel sad, teary, and heartbroken and that the doll can be a helpful tool in their healing journey.

* The style of fluffy sock that has a single, large animal face on it is easy to make into a stuffed animal. You can also buy premade Comfee Dolls at https://griefwatch.com/products/comfee-doll.

Balloon Release Ceremony

Age Range
5–17

Goals:

- Help clients process their grief from losses of loved ones, places, or things.

Materials:

- Large poster board
- Photos and mementos of the loved one (optional)
- Coloring utensils
- Glue, tape, or pushpins
- Rice paper*
- Biodegradable helium balloons (pre-filled)
- Natural twine string or biodegradable paper tape
- Music that evokes letting go

Directions:

1. Explain that this activity is a way for the client to remember and honor the loved ones, places, or things they will not have or see again (e.g., a parent who has left their life, a pet who has died, a home they had to move away from). Discuss how creating a memory board and having a balloon release ceremony can help with the process of grieving. The client can use this opportunity to honor multiple losses in their life or one particular loss.
2. Encourage the client to decorate the poster board with drawings that remind them of their loved one, place, or thing. They can also write messages or memories on the board. If the client has photos or mementos of their loved one, these can be attached using glue, tape, or pushpins.
3. Give the client a piece of rice paper and ask them to write a message to their loved one, place, or thing. Explain that this message will be attached to a balloon and sent up into the sky. Offer to help the client write their message if needed. Provide support and comfort, as this task may evoke strong emotions.
4. Help the client attach the message to a biodegradable helium balloon using natural string or paper tape. Explain that the balloon symbolizes their loved one, place, or thing and that it will carry their personal message. Have them pick a song they would like to play when releasing their balloon.
5. Before going outside, explain how rituals can help people cope with loss by providing a sense of closure and a way to express their feelings. Emphasize that this balloon release ceremony is a special ritual to help them say goodbye and honor their loved one.
6. Go outside with the client and invite them to release their balloon when they feel ready. Play the music as the balloon is released, creating a serene and respectful atmosphere.
7. Spend time after the balloon release talking with the client about their feelings. Offer comfort and validate their emotions. Let them know that it's okay to feel sad and that they are not alone in their grief.
8. Encourage the client to take their memory board home and revisit it whenever they feel the need to remember their loved one, place, or thing.

---

* Ensure the rice paper, string, and balloons are biodegradable to be environmentally friendly.

Grief Mailbox

Age Range
5–17

Goals:

- Help clients process, express, and ease their grief in a safe, tangible way.

Materials:

- Small mailbox or other box
- Stationery or paper
- Assortment of greeting cards (e.g., holiday, birthday, and sympathy cards)
- Envelopes
- Writing and coloring utensils
- Stickers and other decorative items
- Calm, soothing music

Directions:

1. Explain to the client that writing unsent cards and letters to others, as well as to themselves, can be a way to safely express difficult feelings and validate their losses. Discuss how creating a "grief mailbox" can provide a safe place to keep these private letters and help them process their grief.
2. Provide the client with a small mailbox or a box they can decorate to look like a mailbox. They can use markers, stickers, and other decorative items to personalize it. Encourage the client to make the mailbox special, so it feels like a comforting and safe place to store their unsent messages.
3. Give the client a variety of cards, paper, and envelopes. Encourage them to write unsent letters or cards to their loved ones and to themselves, expressing anything they want to say and adding stickers, drawings, or other decorations as they like. Play soothing music and offer support, help, and comfort as the client writes, as this process may evoke strong emotions. Topics they may wish to write about include:
    - Sharing memories or stories of their life right now
    - Expressing feelings of sadness, anger, or confusion
    - Asking questions they wish they could ask
    - Sending love and good wishes
    - Sympathy card to themselves for their loss
    - Cards to themselves for missed holidays and birthdays from their family members
4. Have the client put their letters in envelopes, seal them, and place them in the mailbox. Explain to the client that they can use their grief mailbox whenever they feel the need to. They can add new letters and cards over time and revisit old ones if they wish. Emphasize that this grief mailbox is a special place for their private thoughts and feelings, and it's okay to keep it just for themselves.
5. Offer a comforting activity or items afterward to help the client feel safe and cared for.

Grief Rock Stories

Age Range
7–17

Goals:

- Help clients process and express their grief by chronicling their grief journey.

Materials:

- Variety of smooth, medium-sized rocks
- Quick-dry paint pens
- Large poster board
- Coloring utensils
- Bag or box
- Calm, soothing music

Directions:

1. Discuss with the client how creating and sharing stories about their grief can help them understand and cope with their feelings. Explain that they will be decorating rocks, and each rock will represent a different part of their grief journey.
2. Play calm, soothing music and allow the client to choose several rocks. Encourage them to use the paint pens to decorate each rock in a way that represents their feelings, memories, or messages related to their grief. Examples include:
    - A memory of the day they left their birth family
    - A memory of the day they met their foster family
    - A moment when they felt the deepest grief
    - A message they wish they could tell their birth parents
    - A symbol of hope or healing they have experienced along the way

    They can use symbols, colors, and designs that are meaningful to them. Help as needed and remind them that there are no right or wrong ways to decorate their rocks.
3. Once the rocks are painted and dried, give the client the poster paper and coloring utensils. Instruct them to draw a map with a long path and place the rocks along the path chronologically to symbolize their grief journey.
4. Encourage the client to talk about each rock and the story or message it represents. Offer support and comfort, and validate their feelings, as this process may evoke strong emotions.
5. Provide the client with a bag or box to store their grief rocks. Explain that they can keep these rocks and revisit their stories whenever they need to. Encourage them to add more rocks and stories as they continue their grief journey.

Well of Broken Hearts

Age Range
4–17

Goals:

- Help clients express and process their grief by chronicling their grief journey.

Materials:

- *Broken Hearts* template (several copies)
- Writing and coloring utensils
- Glue stick
- Craft paper tube/canister or other container
- Stickers and other decorative items
- Calm, soothing music

Directions:

1. Explain to the client that this activity is a way to express their feelings of loss and create a visual representation of their grief journey. Discuss how writing and creating art can help them process their emotions.
2. Teach the client how to create the hearts using the *Broken Hearts* template. Make several hearts together, ensuring the client feels comfortable with the process:
    a. Cut out each half of the broken heart, and cut out the horizontal tab.
    b. Glue the ends of the horizontal tab to each side of the broken heart (so that the two halves are reconnected, but at a distance, by the tab).
    c. Flip the heart over and bring the halves together at the seam, folding the tab flat behind the full heart.
    d. Color and decorate the heart shape.
    e. Open up the heart to write on the horizontal tab.
3. On the tabs, encourage the client to express their feelings and thoughts related to the loss (e.g., "I miss you," "Why can't I be with you?" "I'm angry that you're gone," "I remember when we laughed together," "I hope you're at peace").
4. Provide the client with a tube or canister that will be the "well of broken hearts." They can decorate it with markers, stickers, and other items to make it special. Have the client place each heart in the well. Play calm, soothing music as the client creates.
5. Share the following metaphor with the client:

    Imagine the well as a magical place that transforms broken hearts into seeds of hope. When we place our hearts in the well, it's like planting a seed. Just as seeds need time to grow into beautiful flowers, our hearts need time to heal and become stronger. With each heart we place in the well, we are planting a seed of hope and healing within ourselves.

    Over time, these seeds will sprout and grow, symbolizing our healing journey. Just like a garden needs care and attention to flourish, we need to take care of ourselves and be patient with our feelings. Eventually, our garden of hearts will bloom, reminding us of our strength and resilience.

6. Process with the client, asking open-ended questions like:
    - How did it feel to write your messages?
    - Which heart is the most meaningful to you?
    - What do you want to remember about your loved one?
    - Who or what broke your heart the most?
    - What was the hardest goodbye you've ever had to say?
    - What do you wish you could have said before someone left?
    - What is something you have lost that you can never get back?
7. Encourage the client to add more hearts to the well whenever they feel the need to express their feelings or remember the loved ones, places, or things they have lost. Explain that the well is always there for them, holding their memories and emotions.
8. Offer tissues, encouragement, and a comforting activity or item afterward to help the client feel safe and cared for.
9. Ask questions to help the client heal and move forward, such as:
    - What could someone say to help your heart feel lighter?
    - Who or what gives you hope, even when your heart feels broken?
    - What's a piece of your heart that is still whole, no matter what?

Broken Hearts

Candle Ritual

Age Range
8–17

Goals:

- Help clients process and express their grief and honor their losses.

Materials:

- Candle
- Matches
- Decorative materials (e.g., stickers, markers)
- Stationery or paper
- Writing utensil
- Aluminum pan

Note: This intervention must be supervised and granted permission by the parent/guardian, as it involves matches and fire.

Directions:

1. Inform the client that they are going to create a special candle that will represent the loved one they have lost by death or separation (e.g., a birth parent for a client in foster care).
2. Invite the client to decorate the candle. Then, with your supervision or that of an adult parent/guardian, have them light the candle. Ask them to sit and bask in its glow to make a connection.
3. After a few minutes, encourage the client to write a letter to the person the candle represents. Ask them to include everything they didn't get a chance to say or what they want to share with them now. This can include feelings of loss, sadness, regret, guilt, worry, fear, rage, joy, and gratitude. It can be a story of what is happening in their life now or anything they want to share from the past.
4. When they are finished writing, ask them to take a moment and read the letter out loud twice. Then, when they are ready, they can light the letter on fire and quickly place it into the aluminum pan while watching it burn to ash.
5. Take a moment before beginning to process with them the physical action of giving life to their feelings by putting them into words (when they write the letter), hearing their own words (as they read the letter out loud), and offering these feelings to the universe (by tossing them into the fire). Talk about how these actions symbolize the permission they have given themselves to express their truth and then let it go, and how it provides an opportunity for them to share all their deepest unspoken words, wishes, and feelings to the person they lost in an honest, uncensored, sincere way.

Hold On, Let Go

Age Range
4–17

Goals:

- Help clients identify, express, and process their complex emotions.
- Empower clients to choose what they need to hold on to and let go of, increasing self-control and self-esteem.

Materials:

- Large sheet of paper
- Coloring utensils (e.g., markers, crayons, colored pencils, paints)
- Collage materials (e.g., magazine clippings, scissors, glue)
- Calm, soothing music

Directions:

1. Explain to the client that this intervention will help them identify what they need to hold on to for comfort and strength and what they need to let go of to move forward and heal. Discuss the concept of "holding on" and "letting go" in simple terms, relating it to the client's experience (e.g., being in foster care).
2. Play soothing music and have the client draw two large hands on the paper, one on the left side and one on the right side. Label the left hand "Hold On" and the right hand "Let Go."
3. Ask the client to think about things that bring them comfort, joy, and strength—things they want to hold on to. These could be happy memories, caring people in their life, strengths, talents, hobbies, successes, and so on. Help them make choices for themselves. Have the client draw or write these items inside the left hand.
4. Next, ask the client to think about things that cause them pain, sadness, or stress—things they need to let go of. These could be negative thoughts, traumatic memories, feelings of worthlessness, fear of abandonment, resentment or grudges, and so on. Have the client draw or write these items inside the right hand.
5. After the client's artwork is complete, discuss what they have created. Validate their feelings and provide support. Ask open-ended questions like:
    - Can you tell me more about what you decided to hold on to?
    - Why do you hold on to these things?
    - What was it like to think about things you need to let go of?
    - Why do you need to let go of these things?
    - How do you feel about the things you wrote or drew?
6. Reflect with the client on how identifying what to hold on to and let go of can help them cope with their emotions. Discuss ways they can practice holding on to positive things and letting go of negative ones in their daily life.
7. Encourage the client to revisit their "hold on and let go" hands whenever they feel overwhelmed or need to reflect on their emotions.

The Whole Inside Me

Age Range
6–17

Goals:

- Help clients understand feelings of emptiness or incompleteness and develop strategies to address these feelings, promoting a sense of wholeness and self-worth.

Materials:

- Paper
- Coloring utensils
- Collage materials (e.g., magazines, scissors, glue)
- Clear sheet protector
- Paint pens or permanent markers
- Compass or circle for tracing (optional)
- Calm, soothing music

Directions:

1. Explain to the client that we may feel like there is a void or hole inside of us, and this intervention will help them understand and address these feelings of emptiness or incompleteness to feel more whole.
2. Discuss common thoughts and feelings that can lead to a sense of emptiness (e.g., abandonment, uncertainty, lack of control, losses of loved ones, places, and things). Encourage the client to share about their own experiences of emptiness and to journal about them.
3. Play calm music and ask the client to draw or trace a large circle on a piece of paper. Inside the circle, have them add images or words representing their feelings of emptiness.
4. Provide the clear sheet protector and have the client draw or trace another circle of the same size. Explain that this new circle represents wholeness. Ask the client to fill it with images and words representing the things that make them feel whole and complete. Encourage them to think about positive relationships, achievements, hobbies, and so on.
5. When the client's artwork is complete, discuss what each element represents. Reflect on how creating the circle of wholeness helps them understand their feelings of emptiness. Identify some positive activities that can help build feelings of wholeness. For example:
    - Talking to someone
    - Creative expression
    - Physical activity
    - Mindfulness and relaxation
    - Positive affirmations
    - Setting goals
    - Engaging in hobbies
    - Building relationships
    - Journaling
    - Helping others
    - Learning and growth
    - Self-care routine
6. Reinforce the takeaways from this activity. You can say: "Even when we feel like there's a hole inside us, we are still whole and complete. The empty parts are still part of who we are, and realizing this can help us feel better and more in control. By exploring and understanding our feelings, we can fill those empty parts with positive activities that make us feel whole again."

CHAPTER 7

Managing Shame, Humiliation, and Guilt

The Shamewich

Age Range
7–17

Goals:

- Help clients understand and separate their negative inner voice from their self-worth, promoting self-compassion and self-esteem.

Materials:

- *Shamewich* worksheet
- Coloring utensils
- Stickers and other decorative items
- Construction paper, scissors, and glue (optional)

Directions:

1. Explain to the client that people often feel shame because they think they're the one at fault for something bad or difficult in their life. This shame leads to negative thinking—having a negative voice in their head that's always blaming themselves and taking other people's comments or criticism personally. Give examples that are relevant to the client's own experience to show that they are not alone (e.g., how it's common for kids in foster care to blame themselves for not being able to live with their birth family).
2. Use the *Shamewich* worksheet to explore the concept of the "shamewich": a hamburger metaphor to help the client separate their negative inner voice from their self-worth. Explain the parts of the shamewich, starting at the bottom, and have the client write or draw their own examples for each part:
    a. The bottom piece of bread represents their **best friend inner voice**: the type of supportive, understanding, and kind words they would use to talk to a good friend. This is how they should try to talk to themselves too. For example:
        - You are still a good person.
        - You are doing the best that you can.
        - Everyone makes mistakes.
        - This problem doesn't define you.
        - You are loved and valued.
        - I believe in you.
        - You are learning.
        - You have permission to not be perfect.
        - You are lovable.
        - You are worthy.
        - You belong like everyone else.
        - Your feelings matter.

b. The fixings (e.g., ketchup, onions) represent the **negative inner voice**: any feelings of shame, humiliation, or guilt. This might include mistakes they've made or unkind things that other people have said to them. For example:

   - I'm not good enough.
   - Nobody loves me.
   - Everything is my fault.
   - I'll never be happy.
   - No one cares about me.
   - I'm worthless.
   - I'll always be alone.
   - I'm too broken to be fixed.
   - I don't deserve to be happy.
   - I'm a bad person.
   - I can't trust anyone.
   - My feelings don't matter.

c. The top piece of bread represents their **best friend inner voice** again, providing another layer of support and kindness. Have them add more examples as described above.

3. Emphasize that the negative thoughts and feelings are just "fixings" that get stuck onto the client—they are separate from who the client is as a person. The client can surround themselves with kind thoughts and feelings as a reminder of who they really are.
4. Encourage the client to color and decorate the worksheet with stickers and other items to make it personal and meaningful. You can also invite them to cut out the burger pieces and glue or tape them onto a piece of construction paper to reinforce the process of creating a shamewich.
5. Process with the client, validating their feelings and providing support as they talk about their experiences. Ask open-ended questions like:
   - How did it feel to write down your negative inner thoughts?
   - What do you think of the supportive messages from your best friend inner voice?
   - How can you remind yourself of these positive messages when you feel down?
6. Reflect with the client on how separating their negative inner voice from their self-worth can help them view themselves more compassionately. Encourage them to use the shamewich as a reminder that they are more than their negative voice and to practice positive self-talk.

The Shamewich

3. The bread on the top is your **best friend inner voice** again, reminding you of who *you* really are.

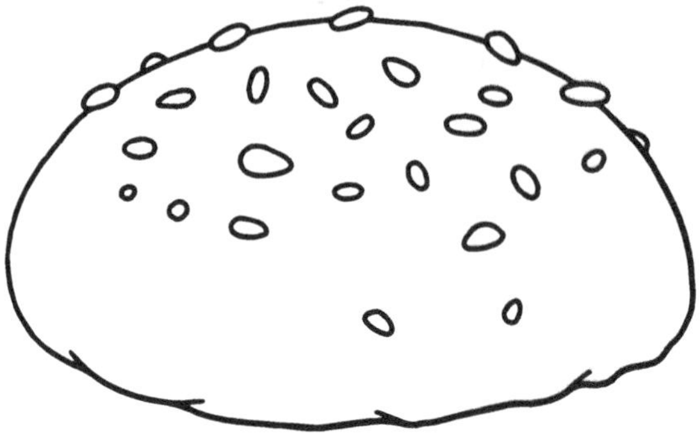

2. The fixings in the middle are your **negative inner voice**—the mistakes, problems, criticisms, feelings, or thoughts that make you feel bad about yourself. Remember that these fixings are *separate from who you are.*

1. The bread on the bottom is your **best friend inner voice**—*you*! What are some kind, supportive things you can say to yourself?

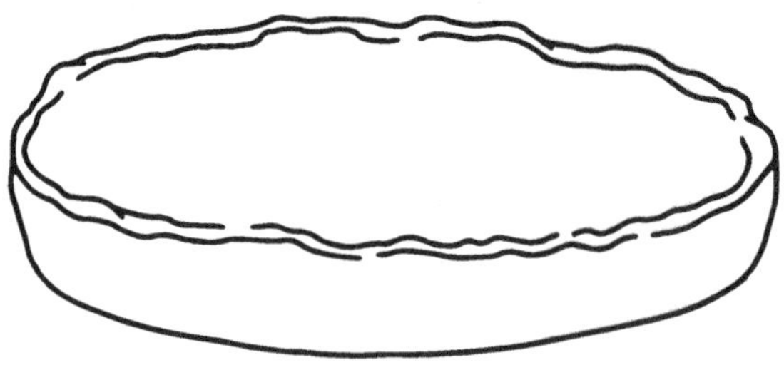

Cloak of Shame

Age Range
6–17

Goals:

- Help clients confront and release feelings of shame and replace negative labels others have placed on them with positive, self-affirming names.

Materials:

- Plain cape or cloak
- Masking tape
- Markers
- Scissors
- Stickers and other decorative items

Directions:

1. Explain that this activity will help the client to identify and let go of shame, humiliation, and negative labels or names others have called them. Discuss how these negative labels can impact their self-esteem and how they can create new, positive names for themselves.
2. Give the client the masking tape and markers. Ask them to write down the negative names or labels others have called them on pieces of tape. These could include hurtful words from peers, family members, or their inner voice (e.g., broken, unwanted, failure, unimportant, a pain, annoying, stupid). Encourage them to be honest and specific but remind them that they will be replacing these negative labels with positive ones.
3. Have the client attach the labels to the outside of the cape, covering it with the hurtful words. Explain that this represents the cloak of shame they have been wearing because of these negative labels. Ask them open-ended questions like:
   - How did it feel to write down the negative names?
   - Does this cape feel comfortable to wear?
   - How heavy is the cape with all of these labels?
4. Then ask the client to write down on pieces of tape some new, positive names and labels for themselves (e.g., strong, kind, brave, loved). Encourage them to think about strengths, talents, and qualities that they like about themselves.
5. Have the client replace or cover each negative label on the cape with a positive one. As they do, discuss why they chose each new name and how it makes them feel.
6. Encourage the client to decorate the rest of the cape with stickers, drawings, or other items to make it personal and meaningful, something they feel proud to wear.
7. Discuss the transformation of the cape. Validate their feelings and provide support as they talk about their experiences. Ask open-ended questions like:
   - How did it feel to write down the positive names?
   - What do your new names mean to you?
   - How do you feel wearing your new cape?
8. Reflect with the client on how recognizing their inherent value and replacing negative labels with positive ones can help them view themselves more compassionately and positively. Encourage them to remember their new names and use them to combat negative thoughts in the future.

You Broke Me

Age Range **7–17**

Goals:

- Help clients process and express their feelings of hurt and betrayal.
- Support healing by helping clients to identify their inner strengths and positive aspects.

Materials:

- Blank puzzle (heart-shaped or with a large heart drawn on it)
- Permanent markers
- Glitter glue
- Gold (or other metallic) paint or markers
- Stickers and other decorative items
- Fan (for drying)

Directions:

1. Explain to the client that this art activity is a way to express and process the feelings of hurt and betrayal they may have experienced from their parents, siblings, caregivers, or others. Discuss how the client may feel broken at times, but it's important to recognize that these experiences can also make us stronger and more resilient.
2. Give the client the heart puzzle already put together. Invite them to take the puzzle apart or throw it to the floor. Explain that the broken-apart pieces represent how they may feel inside because of the actions of the people who have hurt them.
3. Ask the client to use permanent markers to write on the puzzle pieces all the words, feelings, and experiences that have caused them pain (e.g., "my mom leaving me," "betrayal," "worthless"). Encourage them to be honest and specific and remind them that this is a safe space to express their emotions.
4. Introduce the concept of kintsugi, the Japanese art of repairing broken pottery with gold, highlighting that something broken can be made into something even stronger and more beautiful than it was before. Help the client put the heart puzzle back together and fill the seams with glitter glue. Explain that covering the seams shows how they have managed to stay strong despite the pain. Place a fan by the puzzle to help it dry quickly.
5. Once the glue has dried, have the client use gold paint or markers to further fill and cover the cracks. Explain that this symbolizes their resilience and the valuable lessons learned from their experiences.
6. Encourage them to think of strengths and positive aspects within themselves that have emerged despite the hurt (e.g., courage, hope). They can write these words anywhere on the puzzle or on the cracks directly.
7. Process with the client, validating their feelings and providing support as they talk about their experiences. Ask open-ended questions such as:
    - How is it possible for you to put your heart back together and make it even stronger?
    - What do the golden cracks and positive words mean to you?
    - How do you feel about yourself now compared to before?
8. Reflect with the client on how recognizing their strengths and positive aspects can help them view themselves more compassionately. Encourage them to remember their strengths and use them to combat negative thoughts in the future. Emphasize to the client: "The hurt or betrayal you experienced may have broken your heart, but it hasn't broken *you*."

Record of Humiliation

Age Range
9–17

Goals:

- Help clients confront and release feelings of humiliation and pain, replacing them with positive affirmations and self-empowerment.

Materials:

- Vinyl record*
- Metallic markers
- Rubber mallet
- Safety goggles
- Drop cloth or tarp
- Poster board
- Glue or tape
- Coloring utensils
- Other decorative materials (e.g., construction paper, stickers)

Note: Before beginning this exercise, obtain permission and supervision by the parent/guardian as needed for the client to use a mallet.

Directions:

1. Explain to the client that this activity is a way for them to confront and release the feelings of humiliation they have experienced with the metaphor of breaking a vinyl record titled the "record of humiliation." You can say:

    Imagine having a vinyl record that plays a memory of a song in your head that you don't like—a song that makes you feel sad and hurt, and reminds you of bad times. This record keeps playing in your head, just like the negative feelings and hurtful experiences that sometimes make you feel bad about yourself.

    But you can break this record of humiliation. When you decide to stop listening to the hurtful song of humiliation that keeps spinning over and over, it can't play anymore. You are choosing to let go of those bad memories and the negative feelings associated with them. It's a way of saying, "I don't want these sad thoughts and bad experiences to keep bothering me anymore."

2. Give the client a vinyl record and metallic markers. Ask them to write down the humiliating experiences and hurtful words they have endured on the record. Encourage them to be honest and specific and remind them that this is a safe space to express their emotions.

3. Lay down the drop cloth, ensure the client is wearing safety goggles, and invite them to use the rubber mallet to break the record into pieces. Explain that this act symbolizes breaking free from the humiliation and the negative impact it has had on them. Provide support and reassurance during this process, as it may evoke strong emotions.

4. Ask the client to look at the broken pieces and reflect on how they feel now that the record of humiliation is shattered. Discuss how breaking the record of humiliation is a step toward letting go of the negative experiences and reclaiming their self-worth.

* Vinyl records are often available at thrift stores. Alternately, create a record out of cardboard that the client can then cut or tear apart.

5. Help the client create a collage using the broken pieces of the record, the poster board, and the other art supplies. Ask them to write or draw positive, empowering words and images to replace the humiliating experiences. Encourage them to think about their strengths, talents, and positive qualities.
6. Discuss their collage. Ask open-ended questions like:
    - How did it feel to break the record of humiliation?
    - What do the positive affirmations mean to you?
    - How do you feel about yourself now compared to before?
7. Remind them that they have the power to release their negative experiences, thoughts, and feelings and to replace them with self-compassion and positivity.
8. Process the following "you statements" with the client to lessen their humiliation:
    - You were put in a situation where you had no control, and that wasn't fair.
    - You didn't deserve to be treated unfairly. You are valuable and worthy of love.
    - You've carried this humiliation for so long, but it does not define you.
    - You were made to feel "less than," but the truth is, you are enough, exactly as you are.
    - You are the not the words or the actions that humiliated you. That was not yours to carry.
    - You can stand tall knowing your past does not define your future.

Guilt Sandstorm

Age Range
7–17

Goals:

- Help clients express, process, and release feelings of guilt and develop understanding and self-forgiveness.

Materials:

- Large clear plastic jar with a lid
- Sand (different colors if possible)
- Funnel (optional)
- Small pieces of paper
- Writing utensil
- Permanent and metallic markers
- Stickers and other decorative items

Directions:

1. Explain to the client that this activity is a way to express and release feelings of guilt that they might be carrying inside. Discuss how these feelings can sometimes feel overwhelming, like a sandstorm, but there are ways to calm the storm and find peace.
2. Ask the client to think about things they feel guilty about and write them on the slips of paper. These could include actions or words they regret, things they wish they had done differently, or any burdens they carry. Traumatized clients often blame themselves and carry shame for circumstances that are outside of their control (e.g., being in foster care, needing help, their family's troubles, an abuser's actions, escaping a bad situation when their siblings or other loved ones could not). Encourage them to be honest and specific and remind them that this is a safe space to express their emotions.
3. Give the client the jar and sand. Ideally, provide sand in different colors, which the client can use to represent different feelings or types of guilt. Have the client read each of their slips of paper aloud (if they are comfortable), place it in the jar, and pour a layer of sand over the paper using a funnel if needed. Explain that each layer of sand represents the weight of their guilt but also signifies the beginning of the process to cover and transform these feelings.
4. Once all the guilt papers are covered with sand, ask the client to seal and shake the jar. Explain that this represents the "sandstorm" of emotions they might feel inside. Discuss how shaking the jar mixes everything up, just like how guilt can make their emotions feel tangled and overwhelming.
5. Have the client set the jar down and discuss how the best way to calm a storm of guilt and confusion is to not let those feelings get bottled up inside a container, like in their body or brain, so the storm never has a chance to start. The way to do this is to talk about their feelings with you or a trusted friend or family member like they're doing now.
6. Discuss how oftentimes they are feeling guilty about something they had no control over—they're just a kid and have to rely on other people making choices for them. Explain that understanding why they are having feelings of guilt or why what they did felt wrong can help them forgive themselves or others and find peace. Encourage them to think about positive actions they can take or supportive people they can talk to in order to prevent the inner storm.
7. Provide the client with permanent and metallic markers and ask them to write positive affirmations on the outside of the jar (e.g., "I am learning and growing," "I forgive myself for my mistakes," "I am worthy of love and understanding"). Encourage them to further decorate the jar with stickers, drawings, and so on to make it personal and meaningful.

Hard on Myself Puppet

Age Range
5–17

Goals:

- Help clients to recognize and address self-critical thoughts and to develop self-compassion, confidence, and self-esteem.

Materials:

- Two plain socks or paper bags
- Fabric tape or masking tape
- Large sheet of paper
- Coloring utensils
- Arts and crafts materials (e.g., yarn, googly eyes, glue or tape, scissors)

Directions:

1. Explain to the client that everyone has a part of themselves that can be very self-critical. Discuss how being hard on themselves can affect their feelings and behaviors and how learning to be kinder to themselves can improve their well-being.
2. Give the client two plain puppets (socks or paper bags). Explain that one puppet will represent their "hard on myself" part, which includes critical thoughts and feelings. The other puppet will represent their compassionate part, which includes kind and supportive thoughts and feelings.
3. Have the client decorate the "hard on myself" puppet. Encourage them to think about the critical thoughts and feelings they have and represent these on the puppet. They might use colors, symbols, or facial expressions to show sadness, frustration, or other negative emotions. As they decorate, ask them to write down specific critical thoughts on pieces of fabric tape or masking tape and attach these to the puppet (e.g., "I'm not good enough," "I always mess up," "No one likes me").
4. Next, have the client decorate the "compassionate" puppet. Encourage them to think about the kind and supportive thoughts they want to have about themselves and represent these on the puppet. They might show happiness, calmness, or other positive emotions on the puppet. As they decorate, ask them to write down specific compassionate thoughts on pieces of tape and attach these to the puppet (e.g., "I'm doing my best," "It's okay to make mistakes," "I am worthy of love").
5. Once the puppets are complete, let the client know that positive feelings and actions are always stronger than negative ones. It takes much more courage and strength to lift someone up than to put them down. Encourage the client to role-play different scenarios with the puppets:
    a. Have the "hard on myself" puppet act out the critical thoughts, then have the compassionate puppet respond with kind and supportive thoughts.
    b. Encourage the compassionate puppet to try to help the critical puppet feel better.
6. Discuss how the compassionate puppet's responses can help counteract the critical thoughts. On a large sheet of paper, help the client create a chart with two columns: critical thoughts and compassionate responses. Transfer the tape from the puppets to the appropriate columns in the chart. Discuss each critical thought and brainstorm compassionate responses that can help the client feel better and think more positively about themselves.

7. Discuss the client's puppets and self-talk chart, validating their feelings and asking open-ended questions like:
    - How did it feel to create and play with the puppets?
    - What did you learn about your "hard on myself" part and your compassionate part?
    - How can you use what you learned to be kinder to yourself in the future?
8. Encourage them to remember their compassionate part and use it to guide their self-talk in the future.

Mirror of Hurt

Age Range **7–17**

Goals:

- Help clients process and express their feelings of hurt and pain.
- Promote self-understanding, compassion, and healing.

Materials:

- Large mirror
- Wet-erase markers*
- Damp cloth or baby wipes
- Paper and a writing utensil

Directions:

1. Explain to the client that everyone has moments when they feel bad about themselves and that talking to their "hurt self" can help them understand their emotions and feel better.
2. Give the client the wet-erase markers and ask them to draw a line down the middle of the mirror. Have them look at their reflection and, on the left side of the mirror, write down how they feel hurt at times. Encourage them to be honest and write specific feelings (e.g., "I feel rejected," "I feel misunderstood," "I feel unimportant").
3. Then have them respond to those statements to help their hurt self heal and move forward. Ask them to write down compassionate statements on the right side of the mirror (e.g., "It's okay to feel hurt," "It's not your fault," "You are strong and brave").
4. Provide the client with paper and a writing utensil. Ask them to write a letter from their current self to their hurt self, expressing understanding, compassion, and support. Encourage them to acknowledge the hurt feelings and offer words of comfort.
5. Ask the client to look into the mirror again as they erase all the words and lines with a damp cloth. Have them say a couple of positive affirmations to their reflection.
6. Process with the client, validating their feelings and providing support as they talk about their experiences. Ask open-ended questions like:
    - How did it feel to talk to your hurt self?
    - What did you learn about your feelings?
    - How can you use what you learned to be kinder to yourself in the future?
7. Encourage them to remember their self-compassion statements and use them to guide their self-talk in the future.

* Be sure to use a product that is easy to wash off glass.

Me and My Shadow

Age Range
7–17

Goals:

- Help clients explore and express their feelings of shame and guilt.
- Encourage self-reflection, understanding, and self-reliance.

Materials:

- Large sheets of white paper
- Black or dark-colored paint and a brush
- Metallic markers
- Small, bright lamp or flashlight
- Fan (for drying)

Directions:

1. Explain to the client that everyone has a "shadow" part of themselves that carries feelings of shame and guilt. Discuss how these feelings can sometimes become overwhelming, like a dark shadow following them around. This activity will help them explore and express these emotions creatively, shedding light on the shadow and making it fade or disappear.
2. In a dimly lit room, have the client stand in front of a large sheet of paper. Position a small, bright light source (e.g., a lamp or flashlight) to cast the client's shadow onto the paper. Make sure the shadow is clearly visible.
3. Help the client outline their shadow on the paper using a marker or pen. Explain that this outline represents the "shadow" part of themselves—the part that carries shame, guilt, and any aspects of themselves that they keep hidden from others (e.g., shame of being in foster care, shame of abuse or other trauma that happened to them).
4. Provide the client with black or dark-colored paint to fill in the shadow outline. Encourage them to think about the feelings of shame and guilt they want to express as they paint.
5. Dry the paint with a fan. Once it is dry, provide the client with metallic markers to write and draw on the shadow. Ask them to write down specific feelings of shame and guilt they experience and how these feelings affect them (e.g., "I feel ashamed when I make mistakes," "I feel guilty about things I can't change," "I hide my true feelings because I'm afraid people will reject me").
6. In the white space around the shadow (you can attach more paper to the edges or on top of the shadow if needed), have the client write or draw positive affirmations and strengths. Encourage them to think about how they can overcome the feelings in their shadow and embrace their true self (e.g., "I am worthy of love," "I am strong and capable," "I can learn from my mistakes"). Explain how these affirmations bring light and understanding, which makes the shadow grow smaller and even disappear.
7. Process with the client, validating their feelings and providing support as they talk about their experiences. Ask open-ended questions like:
    - How did it feel to paint your shadow and your true self?

- What do the words and symbols in your shadow represent?
- How can the positive affirmations in your true self part help you when you're feeling overwhelmed by shame or guilt?
- If your shadow had a name, what would it be?
- Instead of hiding from your shadow, what do you think about being its friend now?

8. Reflect with the client on how recognizing and expressing their shadow feelings can help them understand and manage these emotions. Encourage them to remember their positive affirmations and strengths and use them to combat feelings of shame and guilt in the future.

9. Process some "you messages" with the client to help integrate their shadow:
   - You have parts of yourself that feel big and messy, and that's okay.
   - You don't have to hide your feelings, even the ones that seem dark or stormy.
   - Your shadow is just a part of you that hasn't been heard, and it needs love too.
   - Even when you feel angry, sad, or scared, you are still a good person.
   - You don't have to be perfect all the time. Every part of you matters.
   - Your shadow doesn't make you bad; it makes you human.
   - Even when you feel dark inside, there is still light in you.

Self-Forgiveness Pool

Age Range **8–17**

Goals:

- Help clients process feelings of guilt and shame.
- Promote self-forgiveness, healing, and self-compassion.

Materials:

- Large bowl filled with water
- Smooth, medium-sized rocks
- Metallic markers
- Rice paper (dissolving)
- Pens
- Comforting music

Directions:

1. Explain to the client that kids tend to blame and shame themselves for their life circumstances and often feel responsible for their family's problems; they have a "shoulda, woulda, coulda" attitude, thinking that they could have done something differently to prevent something bad from happening (e.g., their family breaking up, someone abusing them). Emphasize that kids are not responsible for these things, and learning to forgive themselves is an important step in healing and moving forward from something they had no control of.
2. Place the large bowl filled with water in front of the client. Explain that this is a self-forgiveness pool—a place of forgiveness and healing where they can let go of guilt and shame and embrace compassion and understanding for themselves. Play some calming music.
3. Provide the client with up to five rocks and metallic markers. Ask them to write one of their strengths on each rock. After waiting 20 seconds for the ink to dry, have the client say their strengths out loud and place them one by one on the bottom of the pool.
4. Then provide the client with the dissolving rice paper and ask them to write down specific words or images of guilt or shame. These could include actions, events, regrets, and other burdens the client is carrying. For example:
    - Feeling remorse for conflicts with their parents, caregivers, or siblings
    - Wishing they had asked for help when they were scared
    - Carrying the weight of being judged by others
    - Feeling burdened by being in foster care
    - Struggling with their identity or not knowing where they belong
    - Carrying the burden of taking care of siblings
    - Feeling pressure to be resilient and strong during difficult times
    - Blaming themselves for not being able to meet others' expectations
    - Feeling like a burden to others

- Shaming themselves for having mental health challenges
- Feeling hopeless and helpless

5. One by one, have the client read aloud what they wrote on each piece of rice paper (if they feel comfortable) and gently place the paper into the water. Explain that as the rice paper sinks into the pool, they are symbolically letting go of these feelings and beginning the process of self-forgiveness.
6. Give the client some quiet time to reflect on the experience and what it means to let go of these burdens. Explore if there are any other burdens they want to let go of and place in the forgiveness pool.
7. Process with the client, asking open-ended questions like:
    - How does it feel to let go of your feelings of guilt and shame?
    - What positive affirmations can you say to yourself to instill self-forgiveness?
    - How can you be kinder to yourself in the future?
8. Reflect with the client on how recognizing and letting go of guilt can help them understand and forgive themselves.

PHASE 3

What Happened to You?

Like a tree, a child has many "roots" that support their growth. Trauma can uproot them, cutting them off from resources that would nourish their body, mind, and spirit. Providing clients with trauma psychoeducation helps them make sense of their experiences and see their roots in a new light. It is a vital, and empowering, part of treating trauma.

In this third phase of your work with the client, you will guide them through the narrative of their life journey, starting with their earliest memories and addressing the difficult events and circumstances they have experienced. These might include separations from parents or other caregivers, multiple foster care placements, poverty, neglect, addiction, incarceration, abuse (emotional, physical, or sexual), domestic violence, divorce, accidents, death, or murder.

By helping clients to explore and make sense of their life events, we build resilience and equip them with tools to manage their emotions and reactions effectively. We empower them with the knowledge they need to identify the reasons behind their feelings and actions. They are able to move from "Why is this happening? Why am I feeling this way?" to "I understand now—what I'm experiencing now is because of what happened to me in the past."

Processing their past fosters a sense of control over their emotional responses and behaviors, boosting their self-esteem and confidence in facing life's challenges. This ultimately helps them recover more quickly from setbacks and reduces prolonged periods of distress. As with all mental health interventions, the goal is finding a sense of relief.

The chapters in this phase are designed to help clients transform their traumatic experiences into sources of strength and resilience. Chapter 8 offers general trauma psychoeducation, while the remaining chapters provide targeted interventions for specific circumstances: Chapters 9 and 10 support clients who are in foster care or who have experienced other significant family and home changes (e.g., adoption, kinship care, loss of or abandonment by a parent). Poverty, neglect, addiction, and incarceration are the focus of chapter 11. Clients who have experienced emotional, physical, or sexual abuse can be further supported using the activities in chapter 12. Finally, chapter 13 addresses the impact of death, violence, and accidents.

These interventions were inspired by the work of Bessel van der Kolk (2014), Eitan Kedmy (2023), Ann Hartman (1995), and Peter A. Levine and Maggie Kline (2007).

CHAPTER 8

Trauma Psychoeducation

What Is Foster Care?

Age Range
6–17

Goals:

- Help clients understand and identify the reasons why they are in foster care.

Materials:

- Video player
- Poster board or large sheet of paper
- Sticky notes
- Coloring utensils
- Stickers and other decorative items (optional)

Directions:

1. Explain to the client that they will be watching a video that talks about foster care and the different reasons why a child might be placed in foster care. Assure them that it's okay to have questions and that they can talk about how they feel at any time.
2. Show the client the "What Is Foster Care?" animation by Jeanette Yoffe and Devika Joglekar (https://www.youtube.com/watch?v=HmWIvpv2ktM). Pause the video at key points to discuss and explain what is being shown, making sure the client understands the different scenarios presented.
3. After watching the video, have a discussion with the client about what they saw. Ask open-ended questions like: "What did you learn from the video?" "Can you tell me about some of the reasons why a kid might be in foster care?"
4. Ask the client to think about their own experiences and identify why they are in foster care. Ask them to write or draw their thoughts on the sticky notes. Assure them that it's okay if they are unsure or have mixed feelings.
5. Have the client place the sticky notes on the poster board under headings that match the reasons discussed in the video (physical abuse or neglect, parents lacking housing or resources, parental substance abuse, parental illness, incarceration or detainment, domestic violence, abandonment, or death). This visual representation helps them understand their personal experiences in the context of broader reasons for foster care.
6. Process with the client, offering support and validation of their feelings. Ask open-ended questions such as "How do you feel about the reasons we talked about?" "Is there something you want to share about your own experience?"
7. Provide reassurance and empathy, helping them feel understood and supported. Provide additional sticky notes and ask them to write positive affirmations or messages to themselves (e.g., "I am strong," "I am safe now," "I am loved"). Have them place these affirmations around their chart as reminders of their resilience and worth. They can also decorate and personalize their chart with stickers, drawings, and so on.

My Library of Memories

Age Range
5–17

Goals:

- Provide psychoeducation on how memories are stored in the brain.
- Help clients organize and reflect on their past experiences.

Materials:

- Poster board or large sheet of paper
- Sticky notes (or construction paper, tape, and scissors)
- Coloring utensils
- Stickers and other decorative items (optional)

Directions:

1. Explain to the client that our brains are like a big library where we store all sorts of memories and information from our past. Each book on the shelf is a memory of something that happened to us. Some books are about happy times, some are about sad times, and some are about things that feel scary or exciting. Give examples of these different types of memories:
   - **Happy memories:** Birthdays, playing with friends, family vacations
   - **Sad memories:** Losing a pet, moving to a new place, feeling lonely
   - **Scary memories:** Getting hurt, having bad dreams, experiencing something frightening
   - **Learning memories:** Learning to ride a bike, reading a book, doing a school project
2. Explain that when something happens, our brain takes a "picture" of that moment and stores it away, like taking a photograph and putting it in a photo album. Each memory is like a picture in their brain's album. Some memories are stored very clearly, while others might be a bit blurry or harder to remember. Sometimes, memories pop up on their own, like when you smell cookies baking and remember a time when you baked cookies with someone special.
3. Provide the client with the poster board and ask them to draw a big library, with four sections or shelves that will store the memories: happy, sad, scary, and learning. Encourage them to decorate the library with colors, stickers, and so on to make it personal and meaningful.
4. Ask the client to think about memories they have for each section. Have them give each memory a title and write it on a sticky note (or, to make it more immersive, you can cut book shapes out of construction paper). For example, the client might write, "My Seventh Birthday Party," "The First Day of School," or "I Lost My Pet." Guide and give the client time to self-organize their memories.
5. Process with the client afterward, asking open-ended questions like:
   - Can you tell me about some of the memories in your library?
   - Is there a memory that sometimes makes you feel [*sad, scared, etc.*]?
   - How do you feel when you think about your different memories?
6. Encourage the client to continue cataloging their memories by writing or drawing about them in a journal and marking pages as happy, sad, scared, or learning memories.

Trauma Storms

Age Range
7–17

Goals:

- Help clients understand how different types of traumas can impact their feelings and behaviors.
- Help clients organize and reflect on their past experiences.

Materials:

- Large sheet of paper
- Coloring utensils
- Sticky notes
- Stickers and other decorative items (optional)
- Printouts of different types of storms (optional)

Directions:

1. Explain to the client that everyone experiences difficult moments that make them feel scared, sad, or confused. Sometimes these moments are powerful and overwhelming, like a storm. But the storm will eventually pass, and there are ways to feel safe again and prepare for the next one.
2. Further explain that just like there are different kinds of weather storms, there are different kinds of trauma storms. Each type of storm can have a different impact on how the client feels and behaves. Today you are going to be with them as they share their trauma storms and figure out which type each one is, which will help them feel better.
3. Provide the client with a large sheet of paper and ask them to draw or use printouts of different types of storms to create a "storm map." Encourage them to decorate the map with colors, stickers, and so on to make it personal and meaningful. Describe and have the client draw the following types of trauma storms on their map:
    - **Blizzard:** Just like a blizzard can make everything cold and hard to move around in, some experiences can make us feel really lonely and stuck, like we can't get out or find help (e.g., being separated from family, experiencing bullying, feeling unwanted).
    - **Tornado:** Just like a tornado can quickly cause a lot of damage, some events in our lives happen very fast and can be really intense, making us feel shocked and confused (e.g., a sudden loss, medical emergency, or frightening attack).
    - **Hurricane:** Just like a hurricane can last a long time and affect a lot of things around us, some events in our lives can be big and ongoing, making us feel worried and stressed for a long time (e.g., lacking food or shelter, a long illness, living in a home with ongoing conflict).
    - **Thunderstorm:** Just like a thunderstorm can suddenly appear and be very loud and scary, sometimes things happen in our lives that are unexpected and can make us feel really scared (e.g., a car accident, witnessing a fight, hearing a frightening noise).
4. Ask the client to think about different traumatic experiences they have had and write or draw them on sticky notes. Have them place each note on the storm map in the appropriate area based on how they felt and what happened. This helps them visualize and organize their experiences. Reassure them that it's okay to have different types of trauma and that they are not alone.

5. Process with the client, validating their feelings and providing support as they talk about their experiences. Ask open-ended questions like:
   - Can you tell me about some of the storms on your map?
   - How did you feel during these different storms?
   - What helped you feel better or safe during these storms?
6. Reflect on how understanding and organizing their thoughts about their trauma can help them process their emotions and make positive decisions. Encourage them to think about how they can use this understanding to focus on positive experiences and coping strategies in the present and future.

Fan the Flames of the Five F's

Age Range **7–17**

Goals:

- Help clients understand and recognize their natural coping responses to stress and trauma and develop strategies to manage these responses in healthy ways.

Materials:

- *The Five F's* handout
- Large sheet of paper
- Sticky notes
- Coloring utensils
- Stickers and other decorative items (optional)

Directions:

1. Explain to the client that when we face stressful or scary situations, our brains and bodies have natural ways of responding to help us survive. These are called *coping responses*. Introduce the five main coping responses: fight, flight, freeze, fawn, and flop. Assure them that "when you can name it, you can tame it."
2. Provide the *Five F's* handout and read through each description together.
3. Give the client a large sheet of paper. Ask them to draw a large fan or circle with five sections and label these with the coping responses: fight, flight, freeze, fawn, and flop.
4. Provide the client with sticky notes. Ask them to think about times when they have experienced each coping response. They can write or draw these experiences on the sticky notes and place them in the appropriate sections of the fan. For example, they might write "got really angry at my friend" for the fight section or "ran away when I heard a loud noise" for the flight section.
5. Encourage the client to decorate each section of the fan. They can use colors, symbols, or images that represent their feelings and experiences related to each coping response. This creative expression helps the client externalize their feelings and see them from a different perspective.
6. Discuss each coping response. Ask open-ended questions like:
    - Can you tell me about a time when you felt like fighting back?
    - What do you do when you feel like running away?
    - How do you feel when you freeze up or fawn to please others?
    - What happens when you feel like giving up?
7. Discuss healthy strategies they can use to manage each coping response. For example:
    - **Fight:** Practicing deep breathing or counting to ten before reacting
    - **Flight:** Finding a safe place to calm down and think
    - **Freeze:** Grounding techniques or breathing exercises
    - **Fawn:** Setting boundaries and practicing saying no
    - **Flop:** Breaking tasks into smaller steps or asking for help
8. Have the client write positive affirmations or reminders for each coping response and place these in the appropriate sections of the fan. For example, they might write "I can stay calm and think clearly" for fight or "It's okay to say no" for fawn.

The Five F's: Coping Responses

Flight

When you feel scared or threatened, your instinct is to run away to a hiding spot or another safe place.

Fight

When you feel scared or threatened, your instinct is to fight back to protect yourself—you want to yell or get physical.

Flop

Sometimes when you feel very scared or overwhelmed, your body has no energy and you want to lie down and not move.

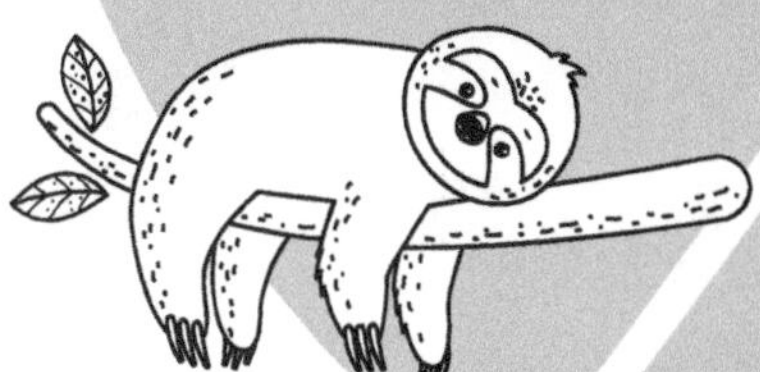

Fawn

When you're scared, you might try to make the person who scares you happy and do what they say so they won't hurt you.

Freeze

Sometimes when you're really scared, your body doesn't move at all. It feels like you're stuck and can't do anything.

Trauma Tsunami

Age Range
7–17

Goals:

- Help clients understand, identify, process, and manage overwhelming emotions resulting from trauma.

Materials:

- Large sheet of paper or poster board
- Sticky notes
- Coloring utensils
- Stickers and other decorative items (optional)

Directions:

1. Explain to the client that emotions from trauma can feel like a powerful tsunami—overwhelming and difficult to manage. You can say:

   A tsunami is a giant, fast-moving wave caused by an earthquake under the sea. Just like that giant wave, you might have intense emotions that were caused by "earthquakes" in your life—the traumatic events or situations you've experienced. These emotions can often feel overwhelming and uncontrollable, like they can drown you in the flood, but there are ways to manage and calm them before they do.

2. Ask the client to think about different emotions they have felt related to their trauma (e.g., fear, sadness, anger, confusion, helplessness). Have them write or draw each emotion on a sticky note.
3. Provide them with a large sheet of paper and ask them to draw a big wave. They can make it as detailed and colorful as they like. Have them place the sticky notes with their emotions within the tsunami, representing the flood of emotions caused by the trauma.
4. Discuss the emotions they've placed in the tsunami, validating their feelings and providing support as they talk about their experiences. Ask open-ended questions like:
   - Can you tell me about some of the emotions in your tsunami?
   - What was the event (earthquake) that caused the tsunami?
   - How do these emotions affect you?
   - What helps you feel better when you have these emotions?
5. Discuss different strategies they can use to calm the tsunami of their emotions when they feel overwhelmed. These might include:
   - **Deep breathing:** Taking slow, deep breaths to calm the body and mind
   - **Grounding techniques:** Focusing on their surroundings or a specific object to bring them back to the present moment
   - **Physical activity:** Engaging in activities like running, dancing, or playing to release pent-up energy
   - **Creative expression:** Drawing, painting, writing, or playing music to express their emotions
   - **Talking to someone:** Sharing their feelings with a trusted adult or friend

6. Reflect on how understanding and organizing their thoughts about their trauma tsunami can help them process their emotions and know how to calm what feels out of control. Encourage them to think about how they can use this understanding to focus on positive experiences and coping strategies in the present and future.
7. Process with the client how they can be "the I in their tsunami" with the following:
    - **Wave breathing:** Breathe in deeply (like a wave rising) and exhale slowly (like a wave crashing).
    - **Body awareness:** Scan the body and ask, "Where do you feel the tsunami in your body?" Then utilize tapping, as described in *My Loving Figure* (page 18) or *My Inner Peace* (page 16).
    - **Move like the tsunami:** Act out swaying like a wave, stomping like crashing water, or curling up like a receding tide to symbolize control over their emotions.
    - **Release ritual:** Safely rip, crumple, or bury their tsunami drawing to acknowledge letting go and putting an end to the storm.

Frozen in Time Capsule

Age Range **6–17**

Goals:

- Help clients understand, express, and process their complicated grief by exploring specific feelings or memories in a tactile and visual way.

Materials:

- Clear slime
- Clear jar with a lid
- Small objects (e.g., beads, buttons, tiny toys) to represent feelings or memories
- Coloring utensils
- Paper
- Freezer
- Stickers and decorative items (optional)

Directions:

1. Explain to the client that sometimes when we experience something sad or traumatic, our feelings can get "stuck" or "frozen" in time like in ice. The sadness and pain from the trauma can stay with us for a long time. Introduce the activity by explaining that they will be creating a time capsule using clear slime to represent their frozen grief and objects to symbolize specific feelings or memories.
2. Provide the client with clear slime, a clear jar, and a selection of small objects. Ask them to place the slime in the jar. Allow them to choose objects that represent different feelings or memories related to their grief that have been frozen in time. For example, a small toy might symbolize a happy memory, while beads may represent tears of sadness. They can also write or draw people, places, and things on small strips of paper.
3. Have the client embed the chosen objects into the clear slime. Encourage them to manipulate the slime to observe how the objects move and change positions. Discuss how, just like the objects in the time capsule, their feelings and memories can shift and change over time but can't escape.
4. Once the client feels ready, they can seal their time capsule. Explain that the jar now symbolizes their feelings that have been stuck inside for a long time.
5. Validate the client's emotions and discuss how the client acknowledging their stuck feelings is the first step in freeing them and letting them go. Talk about different strategies they can use to "melt" their frozen grief and help their feelings to change and heal. These might include:
   - **Talking to someone:** Sharing their feelings with a trusted adult or friend
   - **Creative expression:** Drawing, painting, writing, singing, dancing, or playing music to express their emotions
   - **Physical activity:** Engaging in activities like running, dancing, or playing to release pent-up energy
   - **Mindfulness and relaxation:** Practicing deep breathing or meditation
   - **Creating new memories:** Engaging in fun and positive activities to create new, happy memories with their loved ones
6. Provide coloring materials and ask the client to draw a sunny scene melting the frozen grief. They can use colors and images that make them feel safe and relaxed. Encourage them to think about what helps them feel calm and include these elements in their drawing.

Trauma Thinky Dinks

Age Range
7–17

Goals:

- Help clients understand how trauma can distort their thinking and teach them to challenge these negative thinking patterns.

Materials:

- *Seven Negative Thinking Patterns* handout
- Shrinky Dinks® plastic sheets
- Permanent markers
- Scissors
- Microwave
- Small canvas board
- Quick-dry glue
- Additional decorative items such as paper, coloring utensils, and stickers (optional)

Directions:

1. Explain to the client that trauma can cause negative thinking patterns, which can distort the way they see themselves and the world. Explain that they will create "trauma thinky dinks"—they will use Shrinky Dinks to represent their negative thoughts and then shrink them down to show that they can manage and reduce these thoughts.
2. Use the *Seven Negative Thinking Patterns* handout to discuss the different types of distorted thinking.
3. Ask the client to draw symbols or write words representing each of the seven negative thinking patterns on the Shrinky Dinks sheets using permanent markers. Encourage them to use different colors and decorations to make each one unique.
4. Have the client cut out their drawings or words from the Shrinky Dinks sheets.
5. Microwave the cutout shapes according to the Shrinky Dinks instructions. Have the client watch as their "thinky dinks" shrink, reducing the power of the negative thoughts.
6. Give the client the remaining art supplies and ask them to glue their shrunken thinky dinks onto the canvas. They can also write explanations around their thinky dinks and add drawings, stickers, or other decorative elements. This creates a vibrant and personal art piece that visually represents the client's journey to diminish the influence of negative thinking patterns.
7. Discuss their piece, validating their feelings and providing support as they talk about their experiences. Ask open-ended questions like:
    - How did it feel to watch your negative thoughts shrink?
    - How do these negative thoughts affect you?
    - What positive thoughts can you use to replace these negative ones?

Seven Negative Thinking Patterns

Name Calling

Calling yourself or others names based on mistakes or flaws. Imagine a thorny bush that scratches anything it touches. When you call yourself or others names, you hurt everyone you touch.

Catastrophizing

Expecting the worst-case scenario to happen. It's like imagining that a small snowball will turn into an avalanche. For example, you might worry that forgetting your homework one time means you'll fail school.

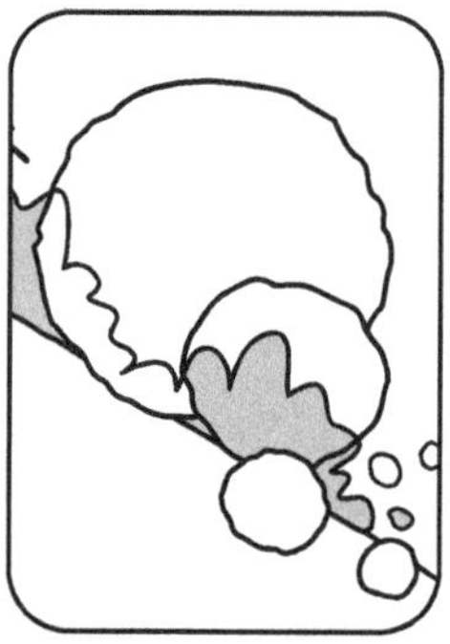

Jumping to Conclusions

Making negative assumptions without evidence. A frog that jumps without looking might land in trouble. Making assumptions without knowing the facts is like being a hasty frog.

Denying the Positive

Focusing on negative experiences and thinking the positive ones don't matter. Imagine you did well in a game but you shrug off people's compliments and think only about the one mistake you made. That's like ignoring the sun and focusing only on the clouds drifting by.

All-or-Nothing Thinking

Seeing things in black and white, with no middle ground. It's like a light switch that is either all the way up (on) or all the way down (off), with no dimmer option. For example, you might think that if you don't get first place in the race you've failed completely.

Exaggerating the Negative

Making broad statements based on a single event. Imagine you fail one test and then think you're terrible at all subjects. That's like seeing one drop of water and thinking it represents the whole ocean.

Seeing Only the Negative

Noticing only the negative aspects of a situation. Maybe you had a fun day at the park but remember only the moment when you fell down. It's like wearing dark sunglasses and only seeing the shadows.

"Trauma may make your thoughts feel big and overwhelming, but like a Thinky Dink, you can shrink them down to a size you can handle. **You've got this!**"

My Protective Wall

Age Range
7–17

Goals:

- Help clients understand how trauma can create emotional barriers between themselves and others, focusing on fears of being hurt or abandoned.

Materials:

- Cardboard bricks
- Coloring utensils
- Sticky notes

Directions:

1. Explain to the client that when we experience trauma, especially from being hurt or abandoned, we sometimes build a wall to protect ourselves. This wall is made of our fears and feelings we are trying to avoid. Explain that they will be building a wall using cardboard bricks to represent the protective barriers they have built to keep themselves safe from being hurt or abandoned again.
2. Ask the client to think of people they are afraid to see again from the past or get close to in the future. Have them write or draw each person or event on a sticky note and attach it to a cardboard brick. Allow them to construct the brick wall as thick or as high as they would like.
3. Discuss how these bricks represent the protective barriers they have built to keep themselves safe. Validate their feelings and provide support as they talk about their experiences. Ask open-ended questions such as:
   - Can you tell me about the different bricks in your wall?
   - How do these bricks make you feel?
   - What do you think might happen if some of these bricks were removed?
4. Explain to the client that they will be taking down their wall, one brick at a time. On more sticky notes, have them write or draw their fears of being hurt or abandoned and other feelings about the person or event (e.g., betrayal, sadness, anger). Tell them to attach these notes to the bricks and, as they do, they can remove them from the wall until all that is left is a pile of bricks. Explain that this represents their resiliency and power over their painful memories.
5. Explain that while the wall can keep them safe, it can also keep them from forming close and supportive connections. Ask questions like:
   - How do you feel when you think about letting others get close to you?
   - What are some things you can do to feel safer about letting others in?
6. Provide some examples of how to let others in:
   - If you feel sad or scared, tell a friend or grown-up you trust. Sharing your feelings can make your heart feel lighter, like opening a treasure chest.
   - Do something nice for a friend, like drawing them a picture or saying something kind. Small acts of kindness can help your relationships grow strong, like flowers in a garden.

- Play a game, do a fun activity, or just talk with someone you want to get closer to. Every moment you spend together helps build a stronger friendship, like adding another layer to a sandcastle.
- When a friend talks to you, listen carefully and ask questions to understand their feelings. Just like a detective solves a mystery, you can solve the mystery of your friend's feelings by listening.
- If you hurt someone's feelings, say sorry. If someone says sorry to you, try to forgive them. Just like fixing a toy makes it fun to play with again, apologizing and forgiving can make your friendship strong again.

7. Practice "you messages" with the client to help them move out of protective mode and begin to lower their emotional walls they've built:
    - You built this wall to keep yourself safe, and now it's keeping you alone.
    - Your wall protects you from hurt, but it also blocks love and kindness.
    - Not everyone wants to hurt you; there are people who want to understand you.
    - You can let people in who show they care and respect your feelings.
    - You are strong enough to let people in without losing yourself.
    - You needed this protection; now you deserve connection.

Trauma Mandala

Age Range
7–17

Goals:

- Help clients recognize their core self while acknowledging the defensive layers they have built around this core due to trauma.
- Increase clients' self-esteem and resilience.

Note: This intervention should be done after the client has identified the types of trauma they have experienced (see *Trauma Storms* on page 154) and their coping responses (see *Fan the Flames of the Five F's* on page 156).

Materials:

- Large sheet of paper or poster board
- *Feelings Map Legend* handout
- Coloring utensils
- Compass or several different-sized circles for tracing (optional)

Directions:

1. Explain to the client that everyone has a core self that is calm, curious, loving, and creative but sometimes, due to difficult experiences or trauma, we lose touch with these characteristics and want to protect them by building layers of protection around our core. Introduce the concept of a mandala—a circular design that represents wholeness and can be used to express different parts of ourselves.
2. On a large piece of paper, draw four concentric circles (like a bull's-eye). Explain that the innermost circle represents their core self, which is calm, curious, creative, centered, confident, and loving. Have the client decorate this core circle with colors, patterns, or symbols that represent qualities like love, joy, and innocence.
3. Explain that around their core self, they have built layers of protection due to trauma. Connect this to the types of trauma and coping responses they have experienced (as you previously explored in interventions like *Trauma Storms* and *Fan the Flames of the Five F's*) so they understand how these layers of protective behaviors have helped them survive and cope with difficult situations.
4. Invite the client to decorate each protective layer. Encourage them to think about the different ways they protect themselves and represent these with colors, patterns, or symbols. For example, they might draw a strong, solid layer for anger, a spiky layer for fear, or a soft, fuzzy layer for sadness. You can use the *Feelings Map Legend* handout (found on page 37) for more ideas.
5. Ask the client to write positive affirmation statements around each defending layer of their mandala (e.g., "I am strong, and I protect myself," "I am cautious because I want to be safe," "I am loving even when I feel scared"). Discuss how they have survived and continue to live despite their trauma.
6. Introduce the mantra: "You are alive, you are living, and you survived ______." Ask the client to complete the sentence with their own words, reflecting their personal journey and experiences. Write this completed mantra in a decorative way around the outermost layer of the mandala.

7. Process with the client, validating their feelings and providing support as they talk about their experiences. Ask open-ended questions such as:
    - Can you tell me about your core self?
    - What do each of these layers mean to you?
    - How does your survival mantra make you feel?
8. Encourage them to put their trauma mandala in a special place in their room to remind them how far they have come in their journey.
9. Process with the client:
    - You have built these layers to stay safe and protected, and now you can choose which ones to keep and which to let go.
    - Every layer tells your story, and you have the power to grow beyond the pain.
    - Your heart is always at the center, strong and protected, and still open to love.
    - When you are feeling safe, you can peel back the layers and let your true self shine through.

CHAPTER 9

My First Family, My Identity

The Roots in Me

Age Range
5–13

Goals:

- Help clients create a chronological narrative about their life, gaining objectivity, empathy, and awareness of their journey.

Materials:

- List of the client's different families/households (foster care placements, kinship care, etc.) with dates
- Photos of the client's family members and/or homes (optional)
- Large sheet of paper or poster board
- Construction paper
- Stencils of leaves and houses (optional)
- Coloring utensils
- Yarn
- Clear packaging tape
- Glue
- Scissors
- Hole punch (optional)

Directions:

1. Before the session, ensure you have as accurate a list as possible of the different families/households the client has experienced (foster care placements, kinship care, etc.), including the dates. In addition, cut the following shapes out of construction paper so they will be ready to use:
    - Houses (enough to represent all the client's placements/households)
    - Leaves (enough to represent all the people in the client's families)
2. In the session, explain to the client that they are going to create a visual narrative of their life using the image of a tree. Ask the client to draw on the poster board a large tree with a tall, thick trunk and thick roots beneath the ground.
3. Tell them the roots represent the beginning of their story: their birth family. Have them write the first names of their birth parents and other members of that family on leaves and glue them down by the tree roots. If they don't know or remember an individual's name, they can use a descriptor (e.g., "my angel," "Mom," "Dad").
4. Ask them to label the roots with the birth family's last name (again, if this is not known, they can use "my birth family" or similar) by writing the name on one of the house cutouts and gluing this by the roots. The client may also like to decorate or draw the house as they remember it (shape, color, etc.).
5. On or near the house, write the dates the client lived there and any important or memorable information about their experience while living there. Ask open-ended questions such as:
    - What do you remember about that home/family?
    - What was the best part?
    - What was the worst part?

6. Continue upward and explain that the trunk represents the other homes and families the client has been a part of. Depending on how much space there is in the drawing, these families can be represented inside the trunk itself or by adding a thick, sturdy branch for each one. Start with the first family after the client's birth parents, and follow similar steps as before:
    - Ask the client to write this family's last name in a house, place it in the appropriate spot, and decorate it as they like.
    - Have the client write the first names of those family members on leaves and add them to the family's branch.
    - Write down the dates the client lived there and other important information they share in response to your open-ended questions about their experience.
    - Guide them to the next family in chronological order by asking questions like:
        - Where did you move to next?
        - What happened that you had to move?
        - What was it like in your new home?
7. Continue upward on the trunk for as many families as the client has experienced, including their current home. Once this is complete, the client can continue to decorate their tree. They might add photos, draw, or write next to each family to further process and express their thoughts and feelings about being there.
8. Write the client's name on a leaf, put clear packaging tape around the leaf so it is laminated, and use a scissors or hole punch to make a hole near the top. Also make two holes in the tree drawing: one at the roots and the other at the top. Cut a piece of yarn long enough to extend between the holes with a little length to spare. Pull one end of the yarn through the first hole and secure it on the back of the drawing with tape. Thread the leaf onto the other end of the yarn before pulling that end through the remaining hole and securing it.
9. Show the client how their leaf can now travel up and down the tree, symbolizing their connection to all of their families. They can fold the paper in half to create a door of privacy about their story.

Faces of Me

Age Range
5–17

Goals:

- Help clients learn about, process, and express their ethnic heritage.
- Increase clients' self-esteem and sense of identity.
- Reduce feelings of isolation and separation.

Materials:

- Large sheet of paper or poster board
- Sticky notes
- Coloring utensils
- Scissors
- Glue or tape
- Mirror
- Magazine clippings of facial features (eyes, lips, etc.) and hair—gather a variety and include plenty of options that are similar to the client's own (considering skin tone, eye color, hair texture, etc.)
- Photos of the client's birth family members (optional)
- Stickers and other decorative items (optional)

Directions:

1. This activity is designed to help the client connect to their ethnic identity and heritage by remembering or imagining the face of the birth parent they have been separated from. Explain to the client that they will be making a collage to represent the face of their birth parent. (Or they may choose to represent a different member of their birth family, such as a sibling.)
2. Ask the client to write the birth parent's name, if known, at the top of one side of the paper. This will help the client focus on them.
3. If the client has photos of their birth parent or other birth family members, place these on the table. If not, provide the client with a mirror and give them some time to look at their own features so they can remember and/or imagine their birth parent's appearance.
4. Provide the magazine cutouts and ask the client to create or choose different features that they feel represent their parent and arrange them to construct a face on the paper. Encourage the client to be creative and assure them that it doesn't have to be an exact match, just something that feels right or similar.
5. Once the client has selected the facial features, have them glue or tape these pieces onto the paper to create a face. They can adjust the placement until they are satisfied with the final look. Encourage them to decorate the collage with drawings, stickers, and other decorations to make it personal and meaningful.
6. Process the client's collage, validating their feelings and providing support as they discuss their choices. Ask open-ended questions such as:
   - Can you tell me about the features you chose?
   - How do you feel when you look at this face?
   - What do you remember most about your parent?

7. Provide the client with sticky notes and ask them to write or draw positive memories or feelings they have about their parent. These can be placed around the face on the collage.
8. Give the client some quiet time to reflect on their connection to their parent and what it means to create a collage to connect with them. They can take their collage home and hang it on their wall to remind them of their birth parent and their ethnic heritage.

My Family Q&A Box

Age Range
4–17

Goals:

- Help clients confront, explore, and organize unanswered questions about their life and provide a container for their anxiety and curiosity.
- Encourage self-reflection and emotional expression regarding their ambiguous loss.

Materials:

- Two boxes of any kind with lids
- Index cards
- Writing utensil
- Decorative items (e.g., colored paper, stickers)

Directions:

1. Introduce the first box to the client as the "question box," which is going to hold all the client's questions about their life and their family that they have been curious about. Introduce the second box as the "answer box," which is going to hold any answers found. Encourage the client to decorate and personalize each special box to create significance and importance.
2. Instruct the client to write their questions down on index cards or other paper and place them into the question box. It is important to tell them, "We may never know all the answers to these questions, but at least you'll have a place to hold them other than inside of you. That way you can share the load and they may not feel as heavy."
3. If the client needs prompts to formulate questions, you might suggest:
    - Why am I in foster care?
    - What happened to my mom or dad?
    - Do I have any siblings?
    - Why can't I stay with my mom or dad?
    - Where is my mom or dad now?
    - Can I get a picture of my mom or dad?
    - What happened to my previous foster family?
    - Am I moving again?
    - Can I write a letter to my foster parents?
    - Why couldn't they keep me?
4. Have the client choose one question from the box and work together with you to determine who in their life might be able to answer it (a parent/guardian, social worker, case manager, attorney, etc.). The client's age, circumstances, and preferences will determine the level of involvement you will have in obtaining the answer to the question.
5. The answers can be placed in the answer box for the client to read, either in their next session or on their own, depending on the client and the content.

Note: This is a longer-term intervention, as it will take longer for some questions to receive answers than others. Be sure to prepare the client for this when you begin the intervention.

Our Pack Roles

Age Range
5–17

Goals:

- Help clients understand, define, and process their roles and experiences within their family dynamics.
- Alleviate the client's sense of being an outsider or someone who doesn't belong.

Materials:

- Large sheet of paper
- Coloring utensils
- Stencils or printed outlines of wolves
- Glue or tape
- Stickers or other decorative items (optional)

Directions:

1. Explain to the client that families, like wolf packs, have different roles that members play. Each role is important for the pack's survival and well-being.
2. Describe the following roles wolves can play:
   - **Alpha:** The leader who makes decisions and protects the pack.
   - **Beta:** The second-in-command who supports the alpha and helps manage the pack.
   - **Caretaker:** The nurturing wolf who takes care of the young and ensures everyone is safe.
   - **Hunter:** The provider who finds food for the pack.
   - **Omega:** The playful, friendly wolf who often defuses tension within the pack.
3. Ask the client to think about the roles they have played in their family. These can include the wolf roles you have described or any other roles they identify with.
4. Provide the client with the art supplies. Have them draw, trace, or glue to the paper one wolf for each member of their family and label it with the family member's name.
5. Have the client identify and write the roles each person has played in their family by the corresponding wolf. Encourage them to color and decorate their wolf pack to make it personal and meaningful.
6. Validate the client's feelings and provide support as they talk about their experiences. Ask open-ended questions such as:
   - Can you tell me about the role(s) you have played in your family?
   - How did these roles make you feel?
   - Which role did you find the most rewarding?
   - Which role did you find the most challenging?
   - What role would you like to play?
   - What role do you not want to play?
   - Do you think your role was meant for you?
   - Why do you think you were given your role?

My Unique Fingerprint

Age Range
6–17

Goals:

- Help clients reflect on their life experiences before foster care, kinship care, or adoption, increasing their sense of self and self-confidence.

Materials:

- *My Unique Fingerprint* template
- Large piece of paper
- Coloring utensils

Directions:

1. Before the session, you may wish to photocopy the *My Unique Fingerprint* template onto a larger piece of paper, creating a fingerprint design with space for the client to write or draw between the lines.

2. Explain to the client that everyone has a unique "fingerprint" of experiences that make up their life. These experiences include the people they've met, places they've been, foods they've enjoyed, holidays they've celebrated, and more. Explain that they will create a visual representation of their life using the concept of a fingerprint.

3. Have the client use the template or draw a large fingerprint design on the paper. Within the ridges of the fingerprint, ask them to write or draw the key experiences they remember from their life before the disruption in their care (e.g., before foster care, kinship care, or adoption). Encourage them to think about each category separately:
   - **People:** Family members, friends, teachers, neighbors, etc.
   - **Places:** Homes, schools, parks, favorite hangouts, etc.
   - **Food:** Favorite meals, snacks, family recipes, cultural dishes, etc.
   - **Holidays:** Celebrations, traditions, special events, etc.

4. Discuss their fingerprint, validating their feelings and providing support as they talk about their experiences. Ask open-ended questions like:
   - Can you tell me about some of the people in your fingerprint?
   - What are some of the places you remember?
   - What were your favorite foods?
   - Which holidays did you enjoy the most?

5. Encourage them to continue to add their memories and feelings to their fingerprint. Ask them to hang it up in their room to remind them of their unique history.

My Unique Fingerprint

Live! Breaking News!

Age Range
6–17

Goals:

- Help clients process and reflect on significant traumatic events in their lives.
- Help clients express their feelings and make sense of their experiences in a more objective, structured way.

Materials:

- Poster board or large sheet of paper
- *News Flash!* template (multiple copies)
- Coloring utensils
- Glue or tape

Directions:

1. Explain to the client that often talking about difficult events can help them understand and process their feelings. To make it easier they will be creating a "news flash" report as a creative way to express what happened and how they felt.
2. Provide the client with the paper and coloring utensils. The poster board will serve as the front page of the newspaper, which the client can title as they like (e.g., "The [*Client's Name*] Times").
3. For each event, ask the client to fill out a copy of the *News Flash!* template. They will give it a headline (e.g., "News Flash: The Day the Police Showed Up") and write or draw about the day, the people involved, the key moments, and how they felt during and after the event. Encourage them to add any other important details they remember, such as sensory details (what they saw, heard, smelled, etc.), actions taken by other people involved, and their own actions.
4. If they are playful, do a mock news reporter interview. Hold a pretend microphone toward the client and begin using prompts like:
    - How did you feel when this happened?
    - What were you thinking at that moment?
    - Were you in danger?
    - How did you get to safety?
    - Who's responsible for this?
    - How do you feel about this now?
5. When each news story is complete, have the client glue or tape it to their newspaper front page.
6. Discuss their news flash reports, validating their feelings and providing support as they talk about their experiences. Ask open-ended questions such as:
    - Can you tell me more about this event?
    - How do you feel now that you've written about it?
    - Is there anything you would like to add or change?

News Flash!

DAILY NEWS

News Flash! The World's Bestselling Newspaper

FIRST EDITION **DATE:**

Headline:

Description of the Event:

Feelings:

Other Important Details:

Missing Person Ad

Age Range
4–17

Goals:

- Help clients process and express their memories and feelings of loss related to a missing birth parent or other family member.

Materials:

- Poster board or a clean, empty milk carton
- *Missing Person Ad* worksheet
- Coloring utensils
- Sticky notes
- Glue or tape
- Scissors
- Magazine clippings for collaging
- Stickers and other decorative items

Directions:

1. Introduce the concept of a missing person ad, which used to appear frequently on milk cartons and continue to be shared through newspapers, flyers, social media posts, and so on. Explain to the client that they will be creating a pretend missing person ad for their birth parent or another family member (e.g., sibling, previous foster parent) who is missing from the client's life.
2. Give them the *Missing Person Ad* worksheet. Ask them to begin the ad with a headline, such as "Missing: My Parent" or "Have You Seen My Parent?" Below the headline, have them write their parent's name (if known) and a description. Encourage them to include details like physical appearance, personality traits, favorite activities, and special memories. Glue or tape the ad onto the milk carton or poster board.
3. Provide magazines or printouts with various pictures that the client can use to represent their parent. This can include images of people, objects, places, and activities that remind them of their parent. Have them cut out these pictures and glue or tape them around their ad.
4. Provide sticky notes for the client to write or draw their feelings about their missing parent. This can include how they feel about the loss, memories they cherish, and things they want to know or miss about their parent. Ask them to place these notes around their ad.
5. Encourage them to continue decorating the ad with stickers or other elements to make it personal and meaningful.
6. Discuss their ad, validating their feelings and providing support as they talk about their experiences. Ask open-ended questions such as:
    - Can you tell me about the description you wrote?
    - What do the pictures you chose represent?
    - How do you feel when you think about your parent?
    - What would you want them to know about you?
    - What do you want to know about them?
7. Reflect on what it feels like for the client to make this missing person ad for their parent. Have the client take this ad home to be a keepsake and token of their connection and desire to find their loved one.

Missing Person Ad

MISSING

HEADLINE: ______________________________

NAME: ______________________

FROM: ______________________

LAST SEEN: ______________________

DESCRIPTION: ______________________

____

____

____

____

____

____

____

____

____

____

____

HELP FIND!

IF YOU CAN IDENTIFY THIS LOST PERSON, PLEASE REPORT ANY INFORMATION TO:

NAME: ______________________ **PHONE NUMBER:** ______________________

Mother's Day or Father's Day Ritual

Age Range
5–17

Goals:

- Help clients process their feelings and honor their birth parents or other parental figures they are missing on Mother's Day and Father's Day through meaningful and supportive rituals.

Materials:

- Poster board or large sheet of paper
- Coloring utensils
- Glue or tape
- Scissors
- Photos of the client's parent (optional)
- Magazines for collaging
- Stickers and other decorative items
- At least one of the following:
  - Mother's and Father's Day cards
  - Pot and a small plant or seeds
  - Tea light and a clear jar
  - Journal or scrapbook

Directions:

1. This intervention is designed to support the client around Mother's Day or Father's Day, when they are missing their birth parent or another parental figure. Explain to the client that this holiday can bring up various emotions, especially for those who have been separated from their parents. These rituals will help the client honor their parent, process their feelings, and create meaningful memories, while mitigating their sense of loss and grief.

2. Provide the client with poster board for creating a tribute board. Follow their lead and let them choose who they want to honor—this could be a birth parent, a previous foster parent, another caregiver, or multiple people (e.g., both birth parents). Encourage the client to draw pictures, write messages, and include photos or cutout images that remind them of this person. They can use stickers and other decorative items to make the board personal and meaningful. Ask them to give their tribute board a title (e.g., "My Cherished Memories," "I Carry My Parents in My Heart").

3. You can choose any or all of the following for the ritual:

   - Encourage the client to write a Mother's or Father's Day card to their missing parent. Have them express their feelings, memories, and any other messages they wish to share. This can be added to the tribute board.

   - Provide a pot and a small plant or seeds for the client to plant in honor of their parent. Explain that caring for the plant symbolizes their love and memories growing over time. The client can decorate the pot and add a label with their parent's name or a special message.

- Organize a candle lighting ceremony where the client can place a tea light in a jar to honor their parent. Explain that the light represents the love and memories that continue to shine, even if their parent is not present.
- Provide the client with a journal or scrapbook to create a memory book dedicated to their parent. They can draw pictures, write stories, and include any mementos or photos they have or magazine clippings that show their experience together. Encourage them to add new memories and reflections over time.

4. Discuss their tribute board and ritual items, validating their feelings and providing support as they talk about their parent. Ask open-ended questions such as:
    - Can you tell me about your favorite memory with your parent?
    - How do you feel about Mother's Day or Father's Day?
    - What do you appreciate most about your parent?

Family Paper Dolls

Age Range
5–12

Goals:

- Help clients identify and process the positive and negative behaviors they experienced from their first family members.
- Provide context to increase clients' understanding of their situation.
- Promote self-esteem and confidence.

Materials:

- Paper
- Coloring utensils
- Scissors
- Glue or tape
- Premade paper dolls with a variety of clothing pieces

Directions:

1. Explain to the client that they will be using paper dolls and clothing to represent their family prior to the change in their care (e.g., before entering foster care or kinship care) to try to better understand their family members' behavior and choices.
2. Provide them with the art materials and the premade paper dolls. Ask them to select or create a doll to represent each member of their first family.
3. Have the client select or create different pieces of clothing to represent specific behaviors or qualities they experienced from their family members (e.g., loving, playful, funny, neglectful, absent, mean). Ask the client to create both positive and negative behaviors or qualities and to label each piece of clothing by writing or drawing what it represents. They might use different colors or patterns to differentiate between positive and negative attributes.
4. Ask the client to place the clothing items on the paper dolls to identify the behaviors and qualities of their family members. They can mix and match the clothing items to show the complexity of their relationships.
5. Discuss their paper dolls and the clothing they chose, validating their feelings and providing support as they talk about their experiences. Ask open-ended questions such as:
    - Can you tell me about the behaviors you chose for each family member?
    - How did these behaviors make you feel?
    - What were you feeling as you picked out the clothes and created these dolls?
    - What are some positive memories you have with your family?

Where We Left Off

Age Range
6–17

Goals:

- Help clients process their feelings and experiences related to a significant relationship that ended abruptly or was unresolved.
- Provide context and help relieve the sense of loss, helplessness, guilt, and unfairness.

Materials:

- Poster board or large sheet of paper
- Coloring utensils
- Fan (for drying)
- Paint (ideally washable)
- Paint tray or pan
- Stickers and other decorative items

Directions:

1. Explain to the client that sometimes relationships end suddenly, leaving feelings and experiences unresolved. Normalize that children (and adults) often experience sadness, anger, confusion, and other difficult, mixed-up feelings when this happens. This activity will help them explore and express those feelings using their left handprint.
2. Pour some paint into the tray and have the client dip their left hand and press it onto the poster board to create a handprint. (If paint is not available, they can trace their left hand with a marker or crayon.) Place a fan near it to help it dry quickly.
3. When the paint is dry, label each finger of their handprint as follows:
    - **Thumb:** The good times we shared
    - **Index finger:** The things I learned from them
    - **Middle finger:** The things that hurt me
    - **Ring finger:** The love or connection we had
    - **Pinky finger:** What I miss the most
4. Ask the client to write or draw their response to each prompt by the corresponding finger to represent their feelings, memories, or experiences related to the significant relationship that ended unresolved.
5. Encourage the client to decorate the handprint and the surrounding area to make it personal and meaningful.
6. Discuss their handprint, validating their feelings and providing support as they talk about their experiences. Ask open-ended questions such as:
    - Can you tell me about each finger and what it represents?
    - How do these unresolved feelings affect you?
    - Do you know why this person went away so suddenly?
    - Do you feel responsible for this loss?
    - Do you understand that it's not your fault?
    - Do you think they miss you too?
    - What do you miss the most about this relationship?

CHAPTER 10

My Journey Through Placement

Foster Care Story Cards

Age Range
5–17

Goals:

- Help clients identify, organize, and process their traumatic and stressful life experiences by expressing them through narrative.

Materials:

- *Foster Care Story Cards* template (multiple copies, cut out)
- Coloring utensils
- Poster board or large sheet of paper
- Glue or tape
- Scissors
- Magazine clippings for collaging
- Stickers and other decorative items

Directions:

1. Explain to the client that the *Foster Care Story Cards* are a tool to help them explore and understand their experiences and feelings related to being in foster care.
2. Show the client the different categories of cards: "What Happened," "I Believe," "I Feel," "I Lived," "I Attach," and "I Miss." Briefly explain each domain and what type of experiences or feelings they represent. Allow the client to look through the cards and select ones that resonate with them.
3. For each selected card, have the client explain why they chose it and what it means to them. Use open-ended questions to facilitate discussion, such as:
    - Can you tell me more about this experience?
    - How did this make you feel?
    - What do you believe about yourself because of this experience?
    - How did you live through this time?
    - How do you feel about attachment and relationships now?
    - What or who do you miss from your past?
4. Provide the client with the art supplies and ask them to create a collage or drawing that represents their foster care journey using the story cards as inspiration.
5. Discuss their visual representation. Validate their feelings and provide reassurance and support as they talk about their foster care journey.

Foster Care Story Cards

What Happened

Parents fighting

What Happened

No attention

What Happened

Drugs or alcohol

What Happened

Arrested

What Happened

Death

What Happened

Accident or fire

What Happened

Not OK touch

What Happened

Other

I Feel . . .

Relieved

I Feel . . .

Sad

I Feel . . .

Frozen

I Feel . . .

Hopeless

I Feel . . .

Angry

I Feel . . .

Stressed

I Feel . . .

Ashamed or guilty

I Feel . . .

Worried

I Lived . . .

Car

I Lived . . .

Motel

I Lived . . .

Apartment

I Lived . . .

House

I Lived . . .

Foster home

I Lived . . .

With strangers

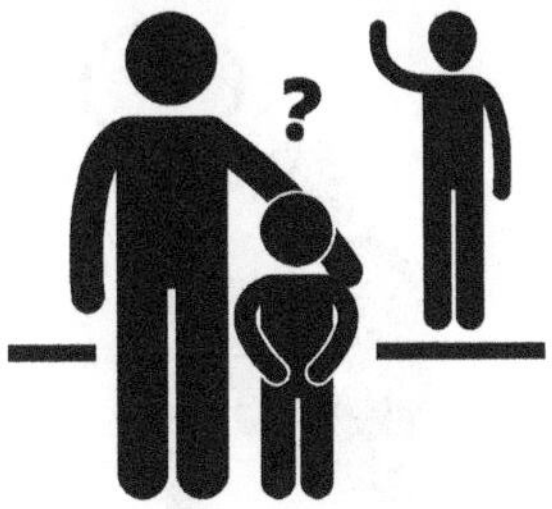

I Lived . . .

Shelter

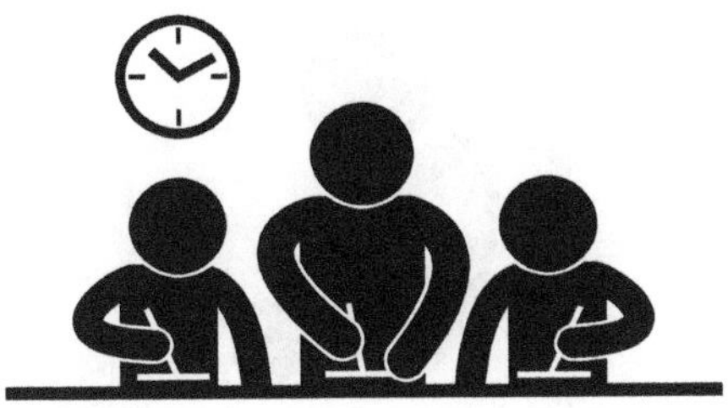

I Lived . . .

With Relatives

I Attach

Crying out for help

I Attach

Clingy

I Attach

Pay attention to me

I Attach

Avoid

I Attach

Talk to me

I Attach

Listen to me

I Attach

Don't leave me

I Attach

Afraid to connect

I Miss . . .

My mom

I Miss . . .

My dad

I Miss . . .

My pet(s)

I Miss . . .

My bedroom

I Miss . . .

My school

I Miss . . .

My neighborhood

I Miss . . .

My siblings

I Miss . . .

My culture

My Foster Pal

Age Range **4–10**

Goals:

- Help clients understand the complexities of foster care by "fostering" a stuffed animal.
- Help clients project and connect with their own feelings of grief and loss.
- Reduce feelings of shame, loneliness, and abandonment while strengthening empathy, self-pride, accomplishment, and the ability to love.

Materials:

- Stuffed animal
- Shoebox (large enough for the stuffed animal)
- Tissue paper
- *Birth Certificate* worksheet
- *Foster Care Certificate* worksheet
- Coloring utensils
- Stickers, stamps, and other decorative items

Directions:

1. Present the client with a stuffed animal and invite them to give it a name. Explain that the animal has been separated from its birth family and needs a home to live in and be fostered. Give the animal a similar backstory to the client's. For example: "This is Max. Max has been separated from his family and needs a loving home. He has been in three foster homes since his birth family was unhoused. Would you like to foster Max and take care of him?"
2. Have the client fill out the *Birth Certificate* worksheet to give their foster pal an identity. Ask the following:
    - **Name:** "What do you want to name your animal?"
    - **Age and date of birth:** "How old is your animal? What is its birthday?"
    - **Siblings:** "Does your animal have any siblings?"
    - **Homes lived in:** "How many homes has your animal lived in? Why is it here? What happened to it?"
    - **Likes and dislikes:** "What foods does your animal like to eat? What are its favorite things to do? What are the things it dislikes the most?"
    - **Needs and feelings:** "What does your animal need the most? How does it feel?"
3. Invite the client to decorate the birth certificate to further personalize it.
4. Show the client the *Foster Care Certificate* worksheet and explain that this document symbolizes their role as a foster parent and their commitment to take care of the animal with love and kindness. Sign and date the certificate; the client can also choose a sticker or stamp as an official seal. Ask the client to give the animal a big hug to officially accept it into their family.
5. Encourage the client to create a place for the animal to sleep using the shoebox and tissue paper. They can decorate the shoebox to make it comfortable and cozy for the animal.
6. Talk with the client about their experience of fostering the animal. Ask how it feels to take care of the animal and relate it to their own experiences in foster care.

Birth Certificate

Name of pal: ______________________________

Date of birth: ______________________ Age: __________

Siblings: ______________________________

____

Homes lived in: ______________________________

____

Likes: ______________________________

____

Dislikes: ______________________________

____

Needs: ______________________________

____

Feelings: ______________________________

____

Foster Care Certificate

THIS IS TO CERTIFY THAT

____

IS OFFICIALLY FOSTERING

____

Officially Fostered

INTO THEIR FUR-EVER HOME, PROMISING TO GIVE THEM LOVE, CARE, ATTENTION, AND KINDNESS.

____________________ ____________________

SIGNATURE DATE

Richter Scale Timeline

Age Range
6–17

Goals:

- Help clients process the emotional journey of moving from home to home.

Materials:

- Large paper clips in various colors
- Yarn or string in various colors
- Poster board or large sheet of paper
- Coloring utensils
- Glue or tape
- Scissors

Directions:

1. Explain to the client that this activity will help them explore the emotional impact of moving from home to home during their time in foster care (or kinship care, etc.). Discuss the Richter scale and how it measures the strength of an earthquake. Explain that the client will be creating a record of the "earthquakes" in their life to show the intensity of their feelings as a result of each move.
2. Provide the client with paper clips and yarn. Ask them to link paper clips together to create a chain, with each paper clip representing a different home they have lived in. The yarn symbolizes the continuity of their journey.
3. On the poster board, draw a large L shape to form the axes of a basic graph. Have the client glue or tape the paperclip chain onto the horizontal axis to represent the timeline of their foster care journey. Create a scale on the vertical axis to represent the emotional intensity, from calm at the bottom to intense at the top.
4. Ask the client to use yarn to plot the emotional impact of each move along the vertical axis. Higher peaks indicate more intense emotional experiences. Encourage the client to use different colors of yarn to represent different types of emotions (e.g., red for anger, blue for sadness, yellow for happiness).
5. Discuss their timeline, validating their feelings and providing support as they talk about their experiences. Ask open-ended questions such as:
    - Can you tell me about each home represented by the paper clips?
    - What are some of the feelings you experienced in each home?
    - How did you cope with moving from one home to another?
    - [*Noting the highest and lowest peaks*] Why do you think this move had the most impact, and this one the least?

My Journey Through Placement

Age Range
8–12

Goals:

- Support clients in creating a narrative about their foster care journey, using the power of acting and storytelling to explore the sequence of their life events while gaining objectivity, understanding, and awareness.

Materials:

- Popsicle sticks
- Pipe cleaners
- Markers
- String
- Stencil or cardboard cutouts of a house (optional)
- Construction paper
- Hole punch
- Scissors

Directions:

1. Explain to the client that together you are going to create a show about their life.
2. Ask the client to make a popsicle stick person that represents themselves, using markers to draw their face, hair, and so on. Wrap one end of a pipe cleaner around the figure's waist and shape the other end into a hook at the top by the figure's head, allowing it to be hooked onto a line of string later.
3. Then have the client make a popsicle stick person for each member of their first family, adding a pipe cleaner hook to each. Give the client a cardboard house to represent this family's home and invite them to color and decorate it as they remember it. Alternatively, the client can draw the house themselves and cut it out.
4. Repeat this process of creating popsicle stick people and a cardboard house for all of the client's placements, including their current one.
5. Punch a hole near the top of each house and place the houses on the string in chronological order. Tie the string between two chairs or similar, creating a string of houses. Ask the client to place the people who belong in each home in front of their house by hooking them on the line. Have the client place their own popsicle stick at the beginning of the line.
6. Invite the client to move their popsicle stick figure through the sequence of placements as they narrate and act out their foster care journey. Guide them through their story by asking questions such as:
   - Where did you begin your journey?
   - What do you remember about that home/family?
   - What was the best part?
   - What was the worst part?
   - Where did you move to next?
   - What happened that you had to move?
   - What was it like in your new home?

Lost and Found Conveyor Belt

Age Range
5–17

Goals:

- Help clients process and reflect on their experiences of loss and discovery.

Materials:

- Long strip of paper or poster board
- *Lost and Found Conveyor Belt* template
- Scissors
- Coloring utensils
- Sticky notes
- Glue or tape

Directions:

1. Explain to the client that we experience loss and discovery throughout our lives. These changes can include people, places, and things that are important to us. Introduce the metaphor of a conveyor belt, such as the baggage claim at an airport: It continuously moves, bringing new items in and taking others away. This will represent their journey of loss and discovery.
2. Provide the client with a long strip of paper or poster board to represent the conveyor belt. Invite them to color and decorate it, making it as detailed and colorful as they like.
3. Provide them with the *Lost and Found Conveyor Belt* template and have them cut out the shapes. Have them write or draw the people, places, and things they have lost on the "lost" cutout shapes and keep these together (do not glue or tape the shapes down yet). Examples of losses include family members, friends, homes, schools, pets, personal belongings, clubs or sports teams, and so on. The more specific, the better.
4. Then have the client create a collection of the people, places, and things they have gained by writing them on the "found" cutout shapes. These might include new friends, foster family members, safe places, supportive adults (e.g., teachers, counselors), new hobbies or interests, positive experiences and memories, and more.
5. Have the client place their lost and found items on the conveyor belt, arranging them in a way that shows the flow of their experiences. For example, the conveyor belt can be divided into sections according to the client's placements or their age like a timeline. They can place losses and discoveries next to each other or in separate sections. Use glue or tape to secure the cutouts.
6. Discuss their conveyor belt. Ask open-ended questions such as:
    - Can you tell me about some of the things you have lost?
    - What are some things you have found or gained?
    - How do these experiences make you feel?

Lost and Found Conveyor Belt

Album Covers of My Life

Age Range
7–17

Goals:

- Encourage clients to reflect on their past experiences, understand their present, and envision their future by exploring significant life events and feelings.

Materials:

- *Album Cover* worksheet (three copies)
- Coloring utensils
- Collaging materials (scissors, glue or tape, magazine clippings, etc.)
- Stickers and other decorative items (optional)

Directions:

1. Explain to the client that they will be creating three album covers representing different parts of their life: past, present, and future. Each album cover will have song titles that describe significant events or feelings from that time, as well as artwork and a title for the album.
2. On the first copy of the *Album Cover* worksheet, ask the client to design a cover that represents their past. This can include colors, images, and symbols that remind them of their previous experiences. Encourage them to think about key events and moments from their past and come up with song titles to describe them, such as "First Day at School," "Family Dinner," or "Moving to a New Home." They should also give the album itself a title, such as "My Past."
3. Ask them to repeat this process to design another album, one that represents their present-day life. Encourage them to think about their current feelings and experiences. Song titles might include "New Friends," "Playing Baseball," or "Feeling Confused."
4. Finally, have the client design an album cover that represents their hopes and dreams for the future. Encourage them to think about what they hope to achieve or experience. Song titles might include "Graduation Day," "Traveling the World," or "Finding Peace."
5. Discuss their album covers. Ask questions such as:
    - Can you tell me about the song titles you chose for this album?
    - Do you have a favorite song on this album?

Album Cover

Album Title ______________________________

Songs

____

____

____

____

Foster Family Eco Map

Age Range
6–17

Goals:

- Help clients better understand the relationships and connections within their foster family and broader social network.

Materials:

- *My Eco Map* worksheet
- Coloring utensils

Directions:

1. Explain to the client that an eco map (Hartman, 1995) is a way to visualize all the important people and connections in their life. Discuss how creating this map can help them see their support system more clearly and understand how different people are connected to them.
2. Provide the client with the *My Eco Map* worksheet. Explain that the circle at the center represents the client; have them label it with their name.
3. Ask the client to draw additional circles on the map to represent their foster family members and any other significant people they wish to include (e.g., birth family members, friends, supportive adults).
4. Use different colors or line styles to represent the quality of each relationship (see the legend on the worksheet). Encourage the client to be honest about how they feel about each person and to represent those feelings visually. The client can also create their own symbols, such as hearts for support, stars for positive influence, or lightning bolts for sources of stress or conflict.
5. Once complete, discuss their eco map. Ask questions such as:
    - Who are the people that you feel most supported by?
    - Are there any relationships that you find challenging?
    - How do you feel about the connections you have mapped out?

My Eco Map

(me)

Legend	
———————	A solid or thick line represents an important, strong, or positive connection.
....	A broken line represents a tenuous or weak connection.
≠≠≠≠≠	Lines with crosses through them indicate a stressful relationship.
→ → →	Arrows along the line show the direction or flow of resources, energy, or interest.

STOP Asking Me

Age Range
6–17

Goals:

- Help clients set boundaries when faced with personal questions they are not comfortable answering.

Materials:

- *STOP* handout
- Paper and coloring utensils (optional)

Directions:

1. If needed, explain to the client what an acronym is. Inform them that they are going to learn an acronym made from the word STOP that can help them set boundaries when people ask personal questions they do not feel comfortable answering. Explain that the STOP method is a respectful way to respond to anyone—whether a peer or an adult—and will help the client protect their own feelings and privacy.
2. Teach the STOP method to the client using the *STOP* handout.
3. Help the client practice using the steps in the acronym. Discuss different scenarios based on the client's experience (e.g., a friend asking if the client's parent is their "real" parent or an adult asking how they are feeling after a recent family event) and brainstorm together how they might use the STOP acronym in each situation. Practice with role-playing activities where you pretend to be an adult or peer asking personal questions and the client uses the STOP steps to respond.
4. You can also create visual aids like posters or bookmarks with the STOP acronym and steps. Encourage the client to decorate these with drawings or stickers.

STOP

When someone asks you a question that you don't feel comfortable answering, you can use these steps to respectfully ask them to STOP asking you that.

S **Say No Politely**

It's okay to say no! You could tell the person, "I'm not comfortable sharing that right now," "I'd rather not talk about that," or "I prefer to keep that private."

T **Turn the Conversation**

It can be helpful to change the subject. You could say, "Let's talk about something else" or ask them a question like "How was your weekend?"

O **Offer a General Answer**

If you feel pressured to respond, you can give a vague or general answer. For example, if your sibling asks about your grades you could say, "School is going fine."

P **Protect Your Feelings**

Remember that you have the right to protect your feelings and privacy. It's important to feel safe and comfortable in conversations. You can remind yourself, *It's okay to keep some things private or It's my choice to share this when—or if—I feel comfortable.*

Going to Court

Age Range
3–17

Goals:

- Explain what clients can expect during a foster care court hearing in order to reduce anxiety and uncertainty.

Materials:

- *Going to Court* handout
- Coloring utensils
- Video player
- Role-play props such as a toy gavel and judge's robe (optional)

Directions:

1. In simple terms, explain to the client why they are going to court. Emphasize that the court is a place where important decisions are made to ensure their safety and well-being. You might say, "Court is a place where a judge helps make decisions about where you will live and who will take care of you. It's all about making sure you are safe and happy."
2. Share the *Going to Court* handout with the client to show what the courtroom looks like and where everyone sits. As you complete the next steps, you can add notes or drawings to the diagram to support the client's understanding. You can also watch the "What is Family Court?" animation on the Jeanette-ically Speaking YouTube channel together (https://www.youtube.com/watch?v=rMCLxlCTghE). Pause the video at key points to explain what is happening and answer any questions the client may have.
3. Explain who will be in the courtroom and what their jobs are:
   - **Judge:** "The judge is like a referee who makes sure everyone follows the rules and who makes the final decisions."
   - **Attorneys:** "There will be attorneys who talk about what's best for you. One might be your attorney, who helps the judge understand your feelings and needs."
   - **Social worker:** "Your social worker will be there too. They know you and can tell the judge about your situation."
   - **Guardian ad litem or CASA (Court Appointed Special Advocate)** (if applicable): "This person is there to make sure the judge knows what is best for you, like another helper."
4. Describe the timeline of a court hearing:
   - **Before court:** "Before court, you might meet with your attorney or social worker to talk about what will happen."
   - **Entering the courtroom:** "When you get to court, you will go through a security check, like at an airport, and then go to the courtroom."
   - **During the hearing:** "You will sit with your attorney. The judge and attorneys will talk, and sometimes they might ask you questions. It's okay to tell the truth and say how you feel."
   - **After the hearing:** "After the hearing, you can leave with your social worker or foster parent, and they will explain what happens next."

5. Encourage the client to ask any questions they have about the process. Ask them questions such as:
   - "How do you feel about going to court?"
   - "Is there anything you're worried about?"
6. Help the client identify who their support people are and write their names on the handout. Encourage the client to bring a comfort item with them to court, such as a favorite toy or blanket. Provide reassurance: "Remember, your attorney and social worker are there to help you. They will be with you every step of the way."
7. After the court visit, talk with the client about their experience. Ask:
   - "How did you feel about going to court?"
   - "Is there anything you didn't understand?"
   - "What was the hardest part about being there?"
   - "Did anything happen that surprised you?"
   - "Did you learn something new about being in foster care?"
   - "Did you have any feelings you weren't expecting?"
8. Ask the client if they have any questions they would like to put in their question box (see the intervention *My Family Q&A Box* on page 172).
9. Continue to provide reassurance and support as needed, keeping open communication about future court visits or changes in their situation.

Going to Court

Timeline:

1. Before court

2. Entering the courtroom

3. During the hearing

4. After the hearing

Judge's Call!

Age Range
4–17

Goals:

- Help clients understand the court process and empower them to express their feelings and desires.

Materials:

- Judge's robe and gavel for role-play (optional)
- *Judge's Call! Scenario Prompts* cards
- Paper and writing utensils

Directions:

1. Before the session, copy and cut out the provided scenario cards or make your own prompts tailored to the client's experience.
2. In session, explain to the client that this activity will give them a chance to express what they would do if they were the judge in the courtroom. Provide a robe and gavel for the client to use during the role-play and have them sit in a special "judge's seat."
3. Read one of the scenarios out loud to prompt the role-play. Encourage the client to decide what to do as the judge and to announce their decision by completing the phrase "I hereby rule that . . ."
4. After each scenario, ask them questions as if you are a reporter. For example:
    - Judge, why did you make that decision?
    - Judge, how do you think this decision will help the child?
    - How does it feel to make these big decisions for the family?
5. Explain to the client that judges always try to make the best decision for the benefit of the child and these decisions are not always simple or easy. Remind them that even though the judge makes the final call, the client's voice matters. They are strong and can make a difference in how the judge rules.

Judge's Call! Scenario Prompts

Judge's Call!

You are the judge deciding on visitation rights for a child in foster care. The birth parents want to see the child every weekend, but the child feels overwhelmed by this. How often should the visits be, and where should they take place?

Judge's Call!

You are the judge setting rules for a child's birth parents. The parents need to show they can provide a safe and supportive home. What rules or requirements would you set for the parents to follow?

Judge's Call!

As the judge, you need to decide whether a child in foster care should go back to live with their birth parents. The parents have completed a parenting course and made some changes, but the child still has concerns. What conditions must be met for the child to return home?

Judge's Call!

As the judge, you are responsible for ensuring the safety of children in foster care. There have been concerns about the safety of the current foster home. What steps would you take to investigate and ensure the child's safety?

Judge's Call!

As the judge, you need to decide whether a child should receive therapy or counseling. The child has experienced trauma and needs support to cope with their feelings. What type of therapy or support would you recommend, and how often?

Judge's Call!

You are the judge deciding on contact between siblings who are in different foster homes. The siblings miss each other and want to spend time together. How often should they meet, and what arrangements would you make for their visits?

Foggy Future

Age Range
5–17

Goals:

- Help clients navigate the uncertainty of their future by visually distinguishing between what they are uncertain and certain about.

Materials:

- Poster board
- 8.5 x 11" piece of paper
- Sticky notes
- Sheet protector
- Coloring utensils
- Glue or tape
- Scissors
- Cotton balls or spiderweb decorations
- Random puzzle pieces

Directions:

1. Explain to the client that it's common to feel unsure about the future, especially when they don't know if they will go back to their first home or stay in foster care (or kinship care, etc.). This activity will help them understand and visualize what they are certain about and what feels uncertain.
2. Give the client a sheet of paper and coloring utensils. Ask them to write or draw things they are certain of in their life (e.g., "I am cared for," "I have a comfortable bed," "I have food when I need it," "I go to school," "I have friends"). When complete, place the paper into a sheet protector.
3. Provide the client with the remaining art materials, aside from the puzzle pieces, and encourage them to create a "foggy" scene on the outside of the sheet protector that makes it hard to see the certainties beneath. They might create clouds, spiderwebs, and so on. Glue or tape the sheet protector to the poster board, making sure to leave the opening clear so the paper can be removed later.
4. Ask the client to write or draw things they are uncertain about on the random puzzle pieces (e.g., "Where will I live?" "When will I see my family next?" "What school will I go to?" "Who can I trust?" "What happened to my things?"). Add these to the poster board.
5. Discuss their artwork, validating their feelings and providing support as they talk about their experiences. This may evoke big feelings, so have tissues ready. Ask questions such as:
   - What are some things that make you feel unsure about the future?
   - How do you feel about the things you are certain of?
   - What do the puzzle pieces represent?
6. Gently lift the paper from its "foggy" overlay (sheet protector) to reveal the certainties. Remind the client, "Even though it feels foggy sometimes, know that what you are certain of is always there beneath the fog." Reflect on the client's trauma and identify the needs that are being met for them in foster care.
7. On sticky notes or directly on the poster, ask the client to write positive affirmations and messages of hope (e.g., "I am strong," "I can handle this," "I have people who care about me," "I am certain of me," "I am certain of where I am right now"). Have them place these affirmations around their visual representation as reminders of their resilience and strength.

Transition Tree

Age Range
7–17

Goals:

- Help clients understand and navigate the transition from one home to another and identify their sources of support.

Materials:

- Poster board or large sheet of paper
- Construction paper
- Coloring utensils
- Glue or tape
- Scissors
- Stencils or cutouts of tree branches and leaves (optional)

Directions:

1. Introduce the concept of the "transition tree" to the client. Explain that their journey from one home to another is like a tree, with the trunk symbolizing their core self and the branches representing different sources of support.
2. Ask the client to draw or use construction paper to create a tree trunk on the poster board, emphasizing how strong it—their core self—is.
3. Next, help the client identify different sources of support in their life. These can include people, activities, or places that help them feel safe and supported (e.g., their social worker, therapist, caregivers, school, friends). Create a branch on the tree for each support and label it.
4. Give the client paper leaves and ask them to write or draw specific ways each support helps them. Encourage them to be as detailed as possible. For example, on the caregiver limb, they might attach leaves saying, "They listen to me," "They make me feel safe," or "They help me with my homework." Help the client attach these leaves to the appropriate limbs.
5. Discuss how the tree supports them as they move from one home to another. The strong trunk represents their resilience and core self, while the limbs and leaves provide stability and nourishment.
6. Create a pathway from the base of the tree to a small drawing or symbol of their new home at the top of the poster. Explain that just like a tree grows toward the sun, they are growing and moving toward a brighter future.
7. Discuss the client's transition tree. Ask questions like:
    - Which support limb do you feel is the strongest?
    - How do the leaves of support help you feel more secure?
    - Is there any support you wish you had more of?
8. Encourage the client to decorate the tree with colors, symbols, or additional drawings that make it feel personal and special to them. Leave space for the client to add new limbs or leaves as they identify more supports in their life. This helps them see that their support system can grow and change over time.

Transition Visit Books

Age Range
3–12

Goals:

- Help clients understand and navigate the experience of court-ordered visitation with their birth parents while reassuring them about their return to their foster home, thereby mitigating confusion, anxiety, and separation trauma.

Materials:

- Blank scrapbook or notebook
- Photos of the client, birth parents, and foster parents (optional)
- Coloring utensils
- Stickers and other decorative supplies
- Glue or tape

Directions:

1. Introduce and explain the purpose of the transition book: "This book is about the special visits you have with your parent. It will help you understand what happens before, during, and after the visit, and remind you that you will return to your foster home after each visit."
2. Ask the client to title their book (e.g., "Visits with Mom/Dad") and design a cover that includes photos or drawings of the client, the birth parent(s) they have visits with, and their current foster parent(s).
3. Prompt the client to create the following pages in their book, using photos or drawings, written descriptions, and any decorative elements they wish to add:
    a. **Preparing for the Visit**
        - **Text:** "Before the visit, you and your foster parent get ready. You might pack a bag with some toys or a special item to take with you."
        - **Visuals:** Include space for the client to draw or write about what they like to bring on visits. They can also draw or include a photo of themselves and their foster parent preparing for the visit.

    b. **Saying Goodbye to the Foster Parent**
        - **Text:** "You say goodbye to your foster parent. They remind you that you will come back home after the visit."
        - **Visuals:** Provide space for the client to write or draw their feelings about saying goodbye. They can also draw or include a photo of themselves saying goodbye to their foster parent.

    c. **Arriving for the Visit**
        - **Text:** "When you arrive, you see your Mom/Dad! It's okay to feel excited, nervous, or any other emotions."
        - **Visuals:** Ask the client to include a photo or drawing of the place where they visit their birth parent.

d. **Activities During the Visit**
    - **Text:** "During the visit, you might play games, read stories, or just talk. These moments are special."
    - **Visuals:** Encourage the client to write or draw their favorite activities they do with their birth parent. They can also include a photo of themselves with their birth parent.

e. **Checking the Time**
    - **Text:** "Sometimes, you might check the time to see how long the visit will last. Remember, your foster parent will come to pick you up when it's time to go."
    - **Visuals:** Provide space for the client to draw a clock and indicate the time the visit ends.

f. **Saying Goodbye to the Birth Parent**
    - **Text:** "When the visit ends, it's time to say goodbye to your Mom/Dad. It's okay to feel sad, happy, or any other emotions about the visit ending."
    - **Visuals:** Encourage the client to express their feelings about saying goodbye and to include a photo or drawing of themselves saying goodbye to their birth parent.

g. **Returning to the Foster Parent**
    - **Text:** "After the visit, your foster parent comes to pick you up. They are happy to see you and hear about your visit."
    - **Visuals:** Ask the client to draw or write about their reunion with their foster parent.

h. **Talking About the Visit**
    - **Text:** "When you get back home, you can talk to your foster parent about your visit. Sharing your feelings can help you feel better."
    - **Visuals:** Provide space for the client to write or draw what they like to share with their foster parent. They can also include a photo or drawing of themselves talking to their foster parent.

i. **Understanding the Visits**
    - **Text:** "Remember, these visits are special times to see your Mom/Dad. Your foster home is where you live and where you will come back to after each visit."
    - **Visuals:** Encourage the client to draw or include a photo of each home and to draw or write about their feelings of having two homes.

j. **Looking Forward to the Next Visit**
    - **Text:** "Look at the calendar to see when your next visit will be. Knowing when you will see your Mom/Dad again can make you feel more secure."
    - **Visuals:** Provide space for the client to draw a calendar and mark visit dates.

4. Regularly review the book with the client. Discuss their feelings before and after each visit, reinforcing the concepts of safety and continuity.

House, Suitcase, and Keys

Age Range
10–17

Goals:

- Help clients build analytical skills to further explore their internal lives.

Materials:

- Colorful construction paper
- Large piece of paper
- Coloring utensils
- Scissors
- Tape or glue
- Dictionary

Directions:

1. Ask the client to use the art materials to make a house on one piece of paper, a suitcase on another piece of paper, and a key on a third.
2. Have the client add two more of each shape—house, suitcase, and key—onto their pieces of paper. Ask them to choose the one drawing they like the best from each page. Have them cut it out and tape it to a large piece of paper.
3. Next, give the client a dictionary and have them flip through the pages until you tell them to stop. When they do, turn the dictionary so the client cannot read the words and explain that you will point to random words on the page until the client tells you to stop, thereby selecting a word.
4. Tell the client to write their chosen word at the bottom of their picture. If the client does not know the meaning of the word, read the definition. Tell the client to look at their picture with their word and ask:
    - What does this mean to you in your life right now?
    - Does this word mean anything to you?
    - Have you heard it before? When?
    - What is the relationship between your picture and your word?
    - If your image could speak, what would it say?
    - Does this image represent your past, present, or future?
5. Encourage the client to keep this picture within view during the week and see what new meanings or changes come forth.

CHAPTER 11

Poverty, Neglect, Addiction, and Incarceration

Add to Cart

Age Range
7–17

Goals:

- Help clients process and express their experiences of having limited food, shelter, and resources and explore the needs that would have helped their family stay together.

Materials:

- Large sheet of paper or poster board
- Coloring utensils
- Magazine clippings or printouts
- Scissors
- Glue or tape
- Sticky notes

Directions:

1. Explain to the client that they will be creating an "Add to Cart" artwork to visualize the items and resources they needed that could have helped their family stay together.
2. Ask the client to draw a large shopping cart in the center of the paper. They can decorate the cart to make it personal and meaningful.
3. Brainstorm with the client what they needed most during their time with their first family. Have the client write or draw these needs on the sticky notes. These might include love, safety, food, shelter, a car, counseling, education, health care, a babysitter, and so on.
4. Have the client draw or use the images provided for collaging to represent the resources or items they have identified. Ask them to glue or tape these pictures inside the shopping cart. Have them also place the sticky notes with their identified needs around the cart or inside it, mixing them with the images.
5. Discuss with the client how each item or resource could have helped their family stay together. Validate their feelings and provide support as they talk about their experiences. Ask questions such as:
    - What are the most important things you needed?
    - How do you think these resources could have helped your family?
    - What feelings do you have when you think about these needs and resources?
    - How does it feel to be able to fill your cart with whatever you wanted?
    - Was there a time you would have wished you could have these items? What do you remember?

Garbage Collection

Age Range
5–17

Goals:

- Help clients process and express their experiences of living in a neglected and unclean environment and dilute these negative memories with context and positive ones.

Materials:

- Large sheet of paper or poster board
- Coloring utensils
- Sticky notes
- Small trash can or box

Directions:

1. Explain to the client that this activity will help them talk about the negative things they experienced in their living situation and replace them with positive things. Reassure them that it's okay to share these difficult memories and that this activity will help them feel better.
2. Ask the client to draw a picture of their home, including the rooms and spaces where they experienced neglect and uncleanliness.
3. Ask the client to write or draw on sticky notes things they saw, smelled, and felt in their neglected home (e.g., trash piles, hoarded items, piles of dirty clothes, bad smells, dirty dishes, feeling scared, being cold). Have the client place these in the appropriate rooms or spaces in their drawing.
4. Provide a small trash can and explain that it's time for "garbage collection." Ask the client to take each piece of "garbage" from their home drawing and place it into the trash can. As they do this, encourage them to talk about each item and why it's important to let it go.
5. Discuss their feelings about collecting and removing the garbage. Validate their feelings and provide support as they talk about their experiences. Ask questions such as:
   - What are some things you decided to throw away?
   - How did it feel to put those things in the trash can?
   - What do you think your home would have been like without this garbage?
6. Ask the client to think about positive things they would like to bring into their home to replace the negative ones. These could be happy memories, positive emotions, supportive helpers, or activities they enjoy, as well as physical objects. Have them write or draw these positive replacements on sticky notes and place them in the appropriate rooms or spaces in their home drawing. Examples might include cleaning products, new appliances, more closets, pleasant smells, a comfortable bed, feeling content, or being nice and warm.

Jail Time

Age Range
5–17

Goals:

- Help clients understand and process their feelings about a parent's incarceration and explore ways the parent might be able to repair their relationship.

Materials:

- People figures and LEGO bricks or other toys to create a jail scene
- Paper
- Coloring utensils
- Sticky notes
- Glue or tape
- Scissors
- Books or resources about incarceration

Directions:

1. Explain to the client that this activity will help them understand what it means for a parent to be in jail and allow them to freely express their feelings about it. Reassure them that all of their feelings are valid and it's okay to talk about these difficult experiences.
2. Use age-appropriate language to explain what incarceration means. For example, "Incarceration is when someone is sent to jail because they broke a law. They must stay there for a certain amount of time as a consequence."
3. To help them understand better, share a simple book or story about incarceration, such as *The Night Dad Went to Jail: What to Expect When Someone You Love Goes to Jail* by Melissa Higgins or *What Do I Say About That?: Coping with an Incarcerated Parent* by Julia Cook. Ensure the book is suitable for the client's age and comprehension level.
4. Provide the client with people figures and toys. Ask them to build a jail and designate figures to represent their parent and other characters (judge, guards, their siblings, their other parent, etc.).
5. Provide a list of reasons why someone might go to jail (e.g., stealing, using illegal drugs, hurting someone). Discuss these with the client and have them place sticky notes with these reasons around the jail scene they created.
6. Explain to the client that they will now use the figures to role-play as the judge who helps their parent understand what they need to do to get out of jail and repair their relationship with their child. Have them tell the incarcerated parent figure three things they must do:
    - **Write an apology:** Have the client write or dictate what they would like their parent to apologize for. This should include what the parent did that resulted in their going to jail (if known) and what the client would like their parent to say to them.
    - **Do the opposite:** Ask the client what the parent can do to make up for their crime. Identify the opposite of what the parent did wrong. For example, if the parent stole, they could give something back or help someone.

- **Do a never-ending chore:** Let the client choose a chore or helpful action the parent should do to make amends, such as cleaning the client's room or helping with homework. The client can enact the parent doing the chore over and over. (This can be changed to any chore they choose).

7. Process with the client, asking questions like:
    - Why do you think your parent did the crime in the first place?
    - What are some of the things your parent needs to learn?
    - How do you feel about teaching your parent these things?
    - What do you think will happen once they learn these lessons?

Addiction Magician

Age Range
6–17

Goals:

- Help clients understand and process their feelings about their parents' substance abuse and develop healthy coping strategies.

Materials:

- Magician's hat or wand (optional)
- Small carpet or blanket (optional)
- Shiny stone or decorative jewel
- Coloring utensils
- Sticky notes

Directions:

1. Explain to the client that this activity will help them talk about their feelings regarding their parent's drinking or drug abuse. Reassure them that it's okay to share these difficult experiences and that doing so will help them understand and cope with their feelings.
2. Explain there are three ways people use drugs and alcohol:
    - **Use** is when someone drinks alcohol or uses drugs occasionally, but it doesn't necessarily cause problems.
    - **Dependency** happens when a person starts needing the substance to feel okay. They might feel sick or unhappy without it.
    - **Addiction** is when a person cannot stop using the substance, even if they know it causes problems and they really want to stop. They feel helpless and use it all the time, affecting their mood, relationships, and daily life.
3. Check in with the client and discuss reasons why people become addicted, such as stress, trying to escape problems, feeling peer pressure, or having a family history of addiction. Emphasize that it's not the client's fault and that addiction is a disease that needs treatment. Explain that treatment means going to a special place, like a hospital or addiction treatment center, where people learn not to take drugs or drink.
4. Discuss their feelings about their parent's substance abuse. Validate their feelings and provide support as they talk about their experiences. Ask questions such as:
    - What are some of the things you remember happening when your parent was drinking or using drugs?
    - How did it make you feel?
    - Did they seem like a different person from when they were not on drugs or drinking?
5. Introduce the concept of being an "addiction magician" who can magically transform the negative aspects of substance abuse into something positive. You can provide a magician's hat or wand to make the activity fun.

6. Ask the client to think of ways to transform their parent's drinking or drug use into positive actions (e.g., by turning bottles into books, drugs into healthy snacks, or a pill into a dollar). Write or draw these transformations on sticky notes and place them around the room as if they are magically appearing following the addiction magician's lead.
7. Next, tell the client they are going to take a magic carpet ride:
    a. Have them sit cross-legged on the small carpet or on the floor with their eyes closed, if that is comfortable for them.
    b. Ask them to imagine sitting on a magic carpet that will lift them up in the air and take them to a golden castle in the clouds.
    c. Tell them that somewhere in the castle they will find a treasure chest full of shiny jewels and gold. They can take a piece of treasure with them as a memory of their strength and resilience.
    d. As they return to earth on the carpet, have them lean left, right, forward, and backward as if steering the carpet through the sky and land somewhere that makes them feel peaceful, happy, and content.
8. Provide the client with a stone or decorative jewel to represent the treasure they took from the castle. Encourage them to take it home to remind them of their strength.
9. Process with the client:
    - You are not responsible for your parent's choices. Their addiction was not your fault.
    - Even when people have let you down, you are not alone anymore.
    - You deserve to be taken care of with love and compassion.
    - You now hold the magic. You are the magician in your life who is in control of your story, and you have the power to create something new.

Not My Fault Line

Age Range
6–17

Goals:

- Help clients understand that they are not responsible for their parents' addiction, neglect, incarceration, or life circumstances, promoting self-compassion and emotional healing.

Materials:

- Large sheet of paper or poster board
- Coloring utensils
- Sticky notes

Directions:

1. Explain to the client that this activity will help them understand that they are not responsible for their parents' actions or difficult life events. Reassure them that their feelings are valid and that this activity will help them cope with those feelings.
2. Explain that sometimes negative and challenging things happen in families, and it's not the client's fault. Use the metaphor of an earthquake: "Imagine a huge, scary earthquake happens and shakes the whole house. Did you cause it? No, you didn't. Just like you didn't cause the problems that your parents have or the situation you find yourself in."
3. On the poster board, ask them to draw the earth with an earthquake and a big fault line running vertically down the middle. Have them label it as the "Not My Fault Line." Explain that this line divides the things they are not responsible for from the positive things they have the power to draw on for support during difficult times.
4. Ask them to write or draw on sticky notes the uncontrollable events or actions of others that have affected them (e.g., parents arguing, moving to a new place, parents' addiction). Have the client place these notes on one side of the fault line.
5. On the other side of the fault line, ask them to write or draw their personal strengths, positive attributes, resources, and affirmations (e.g., "I am kind," "I am strong," "I am not responsible for everything," "I can handle this," "I have people who care about me"). Encourage them to decorate this side with positive colors and symbols.
6. Discuss their drawing, validating their feelings and providing support as they talk about their experiences. Ask questions such as:
   - What are some things that have happened that you couldn't control?
   - How did these events make you feel?
   - What are some of the positive things about you that help you cope with these events?

Disappearing Acts

Age Range
7–17

Goals:

- Provide context to help clients process and understand the impact of people who have come in and out of their lives.
- Foster emotional healing and resilience.

Materials:

- Large sheet of paper or poster board
- *Disappearing Acts* worksheet (multiple copies)
- Coloring utensils
- Glue
- Scissors

Directions:

1. Explain that the client will be creating an inventory of "disappearing acts": people who have come in and out of their life. Explain that talking about the people they have connected with can help them make sense of their past and build resilience.

2. Provide the client with the *Disappearing Acts* worksheet and encourage them to complete a copy for each significant person who has disappeared from their life. This can include parents, relatives, friends, foster parents, social workers, and so on. Ask the client to write or draw the following details:
    - **Who:** The name or identity of the person
    - **What:** The nature of the client's relationship with this person
    - **When:** The time period when this person was present in their life and when they disappeared
    - **How:** The manner in which this person disappeared (e.g., moved away, stopped visiting, passed away)
    - **Why:** The reasons or circumstances behind the person's disappearance (if known)

3. Once complete, they can cut out the people who have disappeared and create a collage on the poster board. They can also write or draw about their feelings and thoughts related to these events. Facilitate discussion, encouraging them to share as much or as little as they feel comfortable. Ask questions such as:
    - How did you feel when this person was in your life?
    - How did you feel when they disappeared?
    - What impact did their disappearance have on you?
    - What do you wish you could say to this person now?

Disappearing Acts

Who

What

When

How

Why

Shelter Ups and Downs

Age Range
6–17

Goals:

- Help clients process memories of living in a shelter, understand how shelters are designed to help families, and build resilience.

Materials:

- Large sheet of paper or poster board
- Coloring utensils
- Sticky notes
- Glue or tape
- Scissors
- Yarn

Directions:

1. Explain to the client that this activity will help them talk about their feelings and memories of living in a shelter. Reassure them that it's okay to share these difficult experiences and that the activity will help them understand and cope with their feelings.
2. Explain that shelters provide a safe place for families who need help, offering essentials like food, shelter, and support. Discuss how shelters help families stay together and find resources to improve their situation.
3. Provide them with a large sheet of paper or poster board and draw a line all the way across the middle. Cut a long piece of yarn, about four feet, and have the client glue the yarn going up and down across the line, like a wave. Write "ups" above the line and "downs" below it.
4. Ask the client to write or draw their positive memories (ups) of living in the shelter above the line. Examples might include making new friends, having a place to sleep, or feeling safe.
5. Have them write or draw their negative memories (downs) below the line. Examples might include missing their home, feeling crowded, or lack of privacy.
6. Discuss their ups and downs, validating their feelings and providing support as they talk about their experiences. Ask questions such as:
   - What are some things you liked about living in the shelter?
   - What are some things that were hard about living in the shelter?
   - How do these memories make you feel?
7. Work with the client to create a "safe space" area on the poster, identifying healthy ways to cope with difficult times and memories or things they can do to make their current environment feel more comfortable and secure (e.g., talking to a trusted adult, spending time with friends, drawing, engaging in a favorite activity). Have the client write or draw these activities on sticky notes and place them in the "safe space" area.

Clock of Loneliness

Age Range
7–17

Goals:

- Help clients process and express their feelings about being alone and uncertain about when, or if, their parent will return.
- Promote emotional healing and a sense of self-reliance and safety.

Materials:

- Large sheet of paper or poster board
- Coloring utensils
- Sticky notes

Directions:

1. Explain to the client that this activity will help them express their feelings and memories of being alone and not knowing when their parent would return. Reassure them that their feelings are valid, and that this activity will help them understand and cope with those feelings.
2. Provide the client with a large sheet of paper or poster board. Ask them to draw a large clock face, marking the hours from 1 to 12. Encourage them to make the drawing colorful and expressive.
3. Ask the client to write or draw on sticky notes things that represent the times they felt alone and unsure when their parent would return (e.g., feeling scared, waiting by the door, hearing strange noises, crying). Have the client place these notes around the clock face at the times of the day when these events occurred.
4. Discuss their clock, validating their feelings and providing support as they talk about their experiences. Ask questions such as:
    - What were some of the hardest times when you felt alone?
    - What did you do to feel better during those times?
    - How do these memories make you feel now?
5. Ask the client to write or draw on sticky notes things that represent moments of comfort and safety and healthy coping skills (e.g., hugging a teddy bear, calling a trusted adult, thinking of their peaceful place, reading a book, using body-up moves). Have them place these notes around the clock as reminders of positive ways to handle moments or memories of loneliness.

Down in a Hole

Age Range
6–17

Goals:

- Help clients understand and process their experiences of overcoming dark times.

Materials:

- Play-dough in dark and light colors
- Large clear bowl
- Slips of paper
- Coloring utensils
- Lighthouse figure or toy that lights up
- Ladder or bridge figurine or twine

Directions:

1. Explain to the client that this activity will help them understand that even in the darkest times, when they feel like they are stuck in a deep dark hole, it is possible to find their way out into the light. Reassure them that their feelings are valid and that this activity will help them understand and celebrate their strength and resilience.
2. Ask the client to make the large clear bowl into a deep dark hole using the dark-colored play-dough. Describe the deep hole as a place that feels dark, scary, and overwhelming, much like the difficult experiences they have been through.
3. Introduce the lighthouse figure and explain that it represents hope, guidance, and safety, much like the positive outcomes and survival they have achieved. Help them attach the lighthouse to the top edge of the bowl using play-dough as an adhesive.
4. Give the client the slips of paper and ask them to write or draw things that represent the dark times they have experienced (e.g., feeling scared, being alone, being hit or yelled at, being bullied, not knowing what would happen). Have the client place these into the deep hole and bury them in the play-dough.
5. Ask the client to write or draw things that represent light, hope, and positive outcomes (e.g., finding a safe place, making new friends, feeling loved). Encourage them to place these in or around the lighthouse, decorating it with bright colors and symbols of hope. They can fan the slips of paper like "waves of hope" around the lighthouse.
6. Next, ask the client to place the bridge or ladder figurine, or create a rope ladder out of twine, leading from the deep hole to the lighthouse. Discuss the steps they took in their life to move from the darkness to the light (e.g., talking to a trusted adult, staying strong, believing they could get through the difficult times). Have the client write or draw these steps on slips of paper and place them along the bridge.
7. Once completed, discuss their artwork. Validate their feelings and provide support as they talk about their experiences. Ask questions such as:
    - What were some of the hardest things about being in the deep hole?
    - What helped you find your way to the lighthouse?

- Who or what did you find at the lighthouse?
- How do these experiences make you feel now?

8. Help the client identify healthy ways to cope with future challenges and climb to the light the next time they feel like they are stuck in a deep dark hole (e.g., talking to a trusted adult, doing an activity they enjoy, writing or drawing a picture to express their feelings, using a code word or signal to let someone know they need help). Write these coping strategies on additional paper that the client can take home with them as reminders.

9. Process with the client to deepen the experience of overcoming:
   - There is a light inside you that never goes out. It knows the way and is your greatest guide.
   - You are not what happened to you; you are what you choose to become.
   - The storms in your past may have been strong, but you are stronger. Look at how far you've come.

Life Savers and Suckers

Age Range
6–17

Goals:

- Identify individuals who have been supportive and those who have been unhelpful or hurtful in the client's life.
- Help the client express and cope with their feelings about these individuals.

Materials:

- Life Saver® candies (different colors)
- Yarn cut into one long necklace string
- Rolling pin
- Small plastic bags
- Permanent marker
- Coloring utensils
- Thank-you cards
- Paper

Directions:

1. Explain to the client that this activity will help them identify the people who have been supportive and those who have been hurtful in their life. Introduce the metaphor: Life Saver candies will represent the people who have been "life savers" to them and their family, while crushed candies will represent the "life suckers" who have been hurtful to them and their family.
2. Ask the client to think about people who have been supportive and helpful to them and their family—the "life savers." Have them write these individuals' names or descriptors on a piece of paper and place a Life Saver candy next to each one.
3. Have the client string each person's candy onto a long piece of yarn and tie it into a necklace. Encourage them to wear the necklace so they can keep their life savers close during the next part of the activity.
4. Then ask the client to think about people who have been hurtful or unhelpful to them and their family—the "life suckers." Have them write each person's name on a plastic bag, place a Life Saver candy inside, and seal the bag.
5. Allow the client to crush the life sucker candy gently with the rolling pin, symbolizing letting go of that person's negative impact. Encourage them to say whatever it is they need to say to this life sucker out loud (e.g., "You are a life sucker," "Stay away from my family," "I am in charge now," "Leave me alone," "You can't hurt me anymore," "Go away and never come back!").
6. Process with the client, validating their feelings and providing support as they talk about their experiences. Ask questions such as:
    - How have these life savers helped you?
    - Who are some of the life suckers, and what did they do to you and your family?
    - How do you feel about these people now after saying their names and remembering them?
7. Encourage the client to write thank-you cards or draw pictures for the life savers to express their gratitude. These cards can be sent or unsent.
8. Help the client identify healthy ways to cope with their feelings related to the life suckers (e.g., doing body-up moves, talking to a trusted adult, spending time with friends, engaging in a favorite activity).

CHAPTER 12

Emotional, Physical, and Sexual Abuse

My Safety Plan

Age Range
4–17

Goals:

- Provide clients with a safety plan and emergency kit to help them feel secure, empowered, and prepared.

Materials:

- *My Safety Plan* worksheet
- Coloring utensils
- Box or bag
- Flashlight
- Comfort item (e.g., small toy or blanket)
- Whistle
- Small jar with a lid
- Clay
- Calming aromatherapy oil (optional; assess for allergies before use)
- Basic first aid supplies (e.g., bandages)
- Journal and a writing utensil
- Nonperishable snacks
- Water bottle

Directions:

1. Explain to the client that you will be creating a safety kit together to help them prepare for and know what to do if they ever feel scared or in danger. Reassure them that this kit is designed to help them feel protected and supported. It provides instructions for what to do and where to go if they feel unsafe, as well as items that will help them handle such situations and feel better.
2. Provide the client with the *My Safety Plan* worksheet. Ask them to start by drawing or writing about places where they feel safe (e.g., a specific room in their house, a relative's home, a trusted friend's house).
3. Next, have the client identify and write down the names and phone numbers of trusted adults they can go to or call if they feel scared or in danger (e.g., family members, neighbors, teachers, family friends).
4. Write down emergency numbers the client can use. Teach them how to dial emergency services (e.g., 911) and explain that this number connects them to the police, who will ask the client where they are, who they are, and what the danger is. Emphasize that they should only use this number if there is a true emergency that is putting the client or others in immediate danger, such as a fire or being physically threatened with violence or abuse—not something like being yelled at or being told to do their homework. Help them understand the different levels of danger and how, if they are not in immediate physical danger, avoiding or defusing conflict should be their first choice; calling or talking to a trusted adult should be their second choice; and calling you, as their therapist, should be their third choice.
5. Create a secret code word that the client can use to signal to a trusted adult that they feel unsafe and need help without alerting others.

6. Assist them in drawing a simple map of their home, highlighting escape routes from different rooms in case of emergency. Discuss and practice these escape routes with the client.
7. Invite the client to decorate and label a bag or box that will serve as their safety kit. Then have them add the following items to their kit:
    - Their safety plan
    - A flashlight for visibility in dark or scary situations
    - A comfort item of theirs, such as a small toy or blanket, to help them feel secure
    - A whistle for signaling for help
    - Basic first aid supplies (e.g., bandages)
    - An aromatherapy stress ball (add a few drops of a calming scent to some clay and store it in a small jar)
    - A journal and a pen or pencil for writing messages
    - Nonperishable snacks and a water bottle
8. Role-play different scenarios with the client to practice using their safety kit and plan. For example:
    - What would you do if you feel scared at home?
    - Who would you call first?
    - What would make you want to dial 911?
    - How would you use your code word?
9. Reinforce that it's okay to use the plan whenever they feel unsafe and that they have the right to feel safe and protected. They can keep it right next to their bed.
10. Update the safety plan and kit as needed, adding new safe places, trusted adults, and strategies.

My Safety Plan

Remember: Help is always available.

Places I Feel Safe	Adults I Trust

Emergency Numbers	Code Words
Parent: ______________________	
Therapist: ____________________	
Emergency: ___________________	

Escape Route

My Cocoon

Age Range
5–17

Goals:

- Help clients who have experienced sexual abuse to process their feelings and create a sense of safety and protection around their core self.

Materials:

- Play-dough in six different colors
- Small figurines (people, animals, symbols)

Directions:

1. Explain to the client that they will be using play-dough to create a protective cocoon around their core self. Emphasize that this activity is designed to help them feel safe and empowered. Reassure them that the abuse was not their fault and that they have protective resources within and around them. While they cannot control the actions of the people who hurt them, they can take steps to help protect themselves and take loving care of themselves.
2. Ask the client to choose a figurine (or create one using play-dough) to represent their core self. This figurine can be a person, animal, or any object that they feel connected to.
3. Prompt the client to create the following layers of protection around their core self using the play-dough. Have them use a different color for each layer. Encourage them to reflect on what each layer represents and how it contributes to their overall sense of protection:
    - **Safety:** Their immediate sense of safety and security
    - **Trust:** Trust in themselves and others
    - **Boundaries:** Personal boundaries and the ability to say no
    - **Support:** The support of friends, family, therapists, and others
    - **Strength:** Their inner strength and resilience
    - **Calmness:** Their sense of calmness and peace in their mind and body
4. Encourage the client to reflect on their feelings and experiences. Discuss what they found comforting and any new insights they gained about their emotions and healing process.
5. Encourage the client to use the cocoon as a visual reminder they can hold on to that represents the many protective layers they have to help keep themselves safe.
6. Process with the client:
    - What happened to you was not your fault. You did nothing wrong.
    - You are safe now, and you deserve to feel safe in your body.
    - Your feelings are valid. It's okay to feel sad, angry, confused, numb, or any other emotion.
    - You didn't deserve what happened. You deserve kindness, healing, and love.

Wounds Heal, Scars Remain

Age Range
7–17

Goals:

- Help clients process and heal their feelings of hurt and betrayal following abuse.
- Explain how forgiveness can coexist with the lasting impact of the hurtful actions.

Materials:

- Large sheet of paper or poster board
- Coloring utensils
- Sticky notes
- Bandages or adhesive strips (optional)

Directions:

1. Explain to the client that just like a deep cut on their body might leave a scar that remains even after the wound has healed, hurtful experiences often leave emotional scars that remind them of what happened. The memory and impact of the hurt may stay with them.
2. Take a few minutes to discuss various types of hurt, covering both physical and emotional pain. Define physical, sexual, and emotional abuse in simple, developmentally appropriate terms. Explain that when any of these things happen, we are wounded physically or emotionally and sometimes both. Yes, we can heal and recover, but it brings forth huge feelings that will leave scars.
3. Ask the client, "What do you think about this and how do you feel? What is your level of distress right now before we move forward?"
4. Ask the client to draw an image of a wound (e.g., a cut, bruise, or part of their body that was touched inappropriately) to represent the hurt they experienced.
5. Then, have them draw a scar over the wound to represent the lasting impact of that hurt. They can use bandages or adhesive strips to add a tactile element.
6. Ask the client to write or draw on sticky notes their feelings about the hurt they experienced (e.g., sadness, anger, confusion, betrayal). Have the client place these notes around the wound on the paper.
7. Check in with them. Discuss the concept of forgiveness, including self-forgiveness, explaining that it's a personal choice and a process that can help them heal. Emphasize that forgiveness is a way of letting go of the anger, sadness, or hurt they feel because of what someone did to them. It doesn't mean forgetting what happened or saying it was okay. You can say:

    First, you should think about forgiving yourself. What happened to you was not your fault. You did nothing wrong; you simply did not have the power or resources you would have needed to stop the abuse from happening. Forgiving yourself is like using a bandage—it's the first step to healing and it is so important. Forgiving the person who caused the abuse is much harder and isn't something you need to do now, or ever. When you forgive, you are healing yourself and freeing yourself from the burden of negative feelings like anger, guilt, and shame. Forgiving can help you feel stronger and move forward, even though the memory of the hurt remains.

8. Invite the client to write or draw on sticky notes what forgiveness means to them and place these notes around the scar on the paper. If they refuse and don't want to forgive, reassure them that this is okay too.
9. Suggest ways of expressing their feelings and practicing forgiveness, such as talking about their feelings, writing a letter they don't have to send, or expressing their emotions through art, music, writing, or other creative activities.
10. Encourage the client to further decorate and personalize their scar drawing. Then discuss their artwork, asking questions such as:
    - Can you tell me about the wound you drew?
    - How does the scar make you feel?
    - How long do you think it will take to heal?
    - What do you think you can do to help it heal faster?
    - What do the feelings you wrote or drew represent?
    - How do you feel about the concept of forgiveness?

Hands That Hurt Me

Age Range
5–17

Goals:

- Help clients process and express their feelings about physical abuse, identify perpetrators, and identify ways to protect themselves from future harm.

Materials:

- Paper
- Coloring utensils
- Sticky notes
- Glue or tape
- Sheet protectors

Directions:

1. Explain to the client that this activity will help them talk about their feelings and experiences related to physical abuse. Reassure them that their feelings are valid and that this activity will help them understand and cope with those feelings.
2. Draw, trace, or print out the outline of a hand on a piece of paper. Make or copy several more of these hand pages (up to six). Inside each hand, have the client write or draw a person who has physically hurt them. Encourage them to use different colors to express their emotions related to each person.
3. Process with the client, validating their feelings and providing support as they talk about their experiences. Ask questions such as:
    - Who are some of the people who have hurt you?
    - How did these experiences make you feel?
    - What do you wish you could say or do to these people?
    - Do you think it was your fault that they did this to you?
    - How does it feel to talk about it?
4. Place each sheet of "hands that hurt me" inside its own sheet protector. Explain that the sheet protector symbolizes a barrier of safety between the client and the people who have hurt them. Encourage them to write and draw on the sheet protector to provide another barrier of safety, using whatever words and images come to mind (e.g., jail bars, chains, a dark color, "No!" "Stay away from me!" "That touch is not okay!")
5. Discuss ways the client can help protect themselves and stay safe. Write these on sticky notes and have the client place them on top of the sheet protectors. These strategies could include:
    - Talking to a trusted adult when they feel unsafe
    - Avoiding situations or places where they might encounter the perpetrator
    - Learning and practicing assertiveness skills to say no
    - Using a code word with a trusted adult to signal when they need help

Out of Body

Age Range
9–17

Goals:
- Help clients understand and manage experiences of depersonalization.

Materials:
- Large sheet of paper or poster board
- Coloring utensils
- *Body-Up Moves* handout
- Paper

Directions:

1. Using simple, developmentally appropriate language, explain to the client what depersonalization is: a feeling of being detached from one's body or viewing oneself from an outside perspective. Reassure them that this a common response to trauma and stress, emphasizing that it is a protective mechanism of the brain during extreme stress or trauma. You can say, "Depersonalization is our brain's way of detaching or separating our mind from our body when something is happening to us that we cannot stop or control, like someone touching us or hurting us. This way it becomes more bearable."
2. Ask the client to draw a picture of themselves sleeping in their bed in the middle of the paper. Around this central figure, have them draw or write what it feels like when they experience depersonalization, using words, symbols, and images to express these feelings.
3. Ask them to draw an image of their spirit or silhouette of their self rising above the bed and looking down at their sleeping body.
4. Discuss their drawing. Validate their experiences and feelings, emphasizing that it's okay to feel this way and it's not something that's wrong with them—it's about what happened to them. Ask questions such as:
    - What does it feel like when you see yourself from outside your body?
    - When do you usually feel this way?
    - What thoughts or feelings come up during these times?
    - What is your level of distress right now?
5. Teach grounding techniques to help the client cope with their feelings and manage depersonalization episodes. Give them the *Body-Up Moves* handout and practice with them. You can also brainstorm other strategies with the client, such as identifying safe people they can talk to or writing down positive affirmations and reminders that they are safe.

Body-Up Moves

5-4-3-2-1 Technique

Name 5 things you can see, 4 things you can touch, 3 things you can hear, 2 things you can smell, and 1 thing you can taste.

Deep Breathing

Focus on taking slow, deep breaths to bring attention back to the body.

Tree Grounding

Imagine you're a tree. Take deep breaths and feel your roots going into the earth, helping you feel strong and connected to the ground.

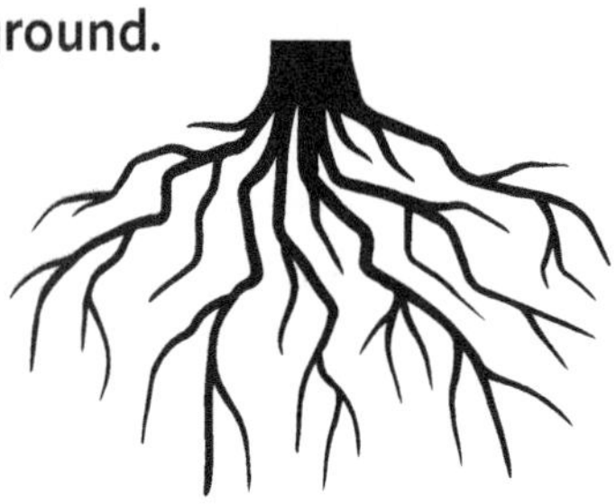

Shake It Off

Shake your hands, arms, and whole body. Pretend you're shaking off negative feelings, like shaking water off your hands after washing them.

Physical Sensations

Hold a comforting object, such as a stuffed animal, or use a stress ball.

Butterfly Hug

Cross your arms over your chest in a hug. Gently tap your shoulders with your hands in a pattern from left to right, like a butterfly flapping its wings, while taking deep breaths.

Affirmations

Move your body while saying good things to yourself. You might stretch your arms up high and say, "I am strong" or place your hands on your heart and say, "I am loved."

Grounding Stomp

Stand up and gently stomp your feet on the ground like a dinosaur. Feel how the ground supports you, giving you strength and keeping you steady.

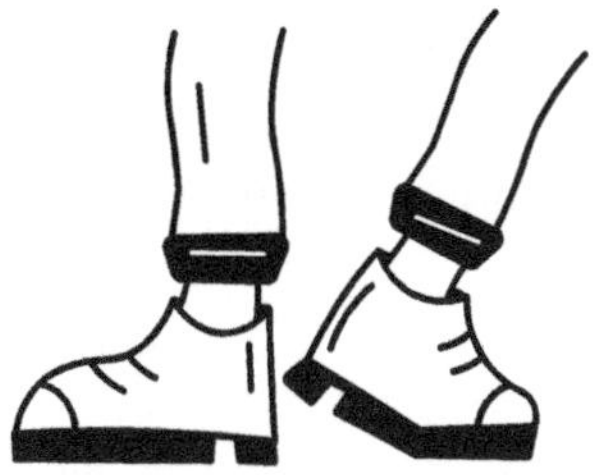

Body Scan

Close your eyes and imagine you are a detective looking for clues in your body. Start at your head and slowly move down to your toes. If you find any spots that feel tight or uncomfortable, take a deep breath and imagine sending a relaxing breeze to those areas.

Squeeze Release

Pretend you are a robot and make your feet really tight . . . then let them go floppy like a noodle. Do this with each part of your body, from your feet up to your face. Notice how different it feels when you go from tight to relaxed.

Sunlight Heart Opener

Stand in sunlight (or imagine the sun). Put your hands over your heart, take a few deep breaths, and pour in the warm, bright light so it spreads from your heart to the rest of your body, making you feel cozy and safe.

Cold Water Splash

Gently splash cool water on your face or wrists, noticing the temperature and sensation. You can also hold an ice cube for a few seconds. Say to yourself, "This water helps me feel awake and present. I am here, in my body, right now."

Maze in Me

Age Range
9–17

Goals:

- Help clients understand and express the extent of their need for protection and safety following physical or sexual abuse.

Materials:

- Large sheet of paper or poster board
- Coloring utensils
- Ruler or straight edge (optional)
- Paper

Directions:

1. Explain to the client that this activity will help them understand and communicate their need for protection and safety after experiencing abuse. Introduce the concept of a maze that represents the barriers they have built to protect themselves.
2. Ask them to draw a complex maze, with the center representing their inner self. They can use a ruler to help with straight lines if desired. Encourage them to make the maze as intricate and challenging as they feel necessary to show how much protection they need.
3. In the very center of the maze, have the client draw a figure or symbol that represents themselves. Have them write words or draw symbols along the various pathways moving out from the center that represent the barriers they have put up to protect themselves (e.g., trust issues, fear, anger, silence, self-isolation).
4. Discuss why these barriers are important and how they help the client feel safe. Ask questions such as:
    - What does each barrier represent?
    - How do these barriers help you feel safe?
    - Are there any parts of the maze where you feel particularly trapped or protected?
    - Do you feel like it's possible for someone to make their way through the maze and hurt you again?
    - Do you feel it's possible for you to find your way out when you're ready?
    - What might make you feel ready?
5. Validate their experiences and feelings, emphasizing that it is okay to need these protections. Talk about the possibility of creating safe pathways through the maze, or giving clues to trusted people (e.g., caregivers, friends, therapists).
6. Ask them to draw a few potential pathways into the center of the maze and identify who they might trust enough to let inside. Also discuss who they don't trust and why.
7. Encourage them to think of ways to gradually reduce some barriers as they feel safer and more supported. Write these strategies down and discuss how they can use them to feel more secure without needing as many protective barriers.

Before, During, and After

Age Range
4–17

Goals:

- Help clients process and express their feelings related to their emotional, physical, or sexual abuse.

Materials:

- Large sheet of paper or poster board
- Coloring utensils
- Images and words related to the client's trauma, printed out or cut from magazines
- Blank puzzle pieces
- Scissors
- Glue or tape
- Calm music

Directions:

1. Explain that this activity will help the client express and understand their feelings about a traumatic event. This is especially helpful for the client to compartmentalize and work through the narrative of their traumatic event to decrease overwhelming stress, begin to create emotional distance from the experience, and promote healing.
2. Play calm music and reassure them that this is a safe space to share their experiences. Ask, "What is your level of distress right now before we move forward?"
3. Ask the client to choose an event or trauma and give it a title (e.g., "The Kidnapping," "My Mom Hurt My Sister" "My Dad's Drinking") at the top of the paper.
4. Fold the paper into three sections and label them "Before" (left), "During" (middle), and "After" (right).
5. Ask the client to draw, write, or paste pictures that represent their feelings and experiences before, during, and after the event. Give them time and support as needed. Encourage the use of words, symbols, and images to fully express their emotions and thoughts. Gently ask them to identify the following:
    - Who was there with you?
    - What happened?
    - Was it just one time?
    - Where were you?
    - When did this happen? (Month, day, year?)
6. Check their level of distress before continuing to encourage them to fully express their emotions and thoughts. Then say, "Take a moment and see if you can remember sounds, smells, or how your body felt and include those images or words too."

7. When the client has finished, check their level of distress and discuss each section, encouraging them to share their thoughts and feelings about the event. Ask open-ended questions such as:
    - What do you notice that is different from before, to during, to after?
    - What did you do during those times?
    - How do these memories make you feel now?
    - How do you feel about this person or place now?
8. Finish by thanking them for sharing and reassuring them that they are in a different place now. They are supported and getting help and they have a bright future ahead, made even brighter by being brave and sharing their experiences.
9. Fold the paper closed and seal it shut with tape or glue to contain the experience.
10. Ask the client if they would like you to store this experience for them by holding it with them.

My Escape Plans

Age Range **6–17**

Goals:

- Help clients process and understand their experiences of terrifying situations from their past.

Materials:

- Paper
- Coloring utensils

Directions:

1. Explain to the client that this activity will help them process and understand their terrifying experience by imagining they had the ability to escape before it happened. Reassure them that this is a safe space to share their experiences and that they can express themselves freely. Before beginning, ask, "What is your level of distress right now before we move forward?"
2. Ask them to think of a specific time in the past when they felt threatened and needed to escape a dangerous situation.
3. Encourage them to write a play-by-play movie script or draw each scene to represent their imagined escape plan, including their thoughts, feelings, and actions. Given them the following prompts:
    - **The threat:** Have them detail the moment they realized they were in danger and needed to escape.
    - **The place:** Ask them to describe the location.
    - **The villain:** Have them identify who the villain was and give them a name (this could be metaphorical, such as "the evil witch").
    - **The plan:** Have them create a step-by-step plan to imagine their escape, including any preparations they made.
    - **The execution:** Ask them to imagine what they would have done to carry out their escape plan, what their thoughts would have been, and how they would have felt during the escape.
    - **Aftermath:** Reflect on what would have happened after they escaped, how they would have felt, and what they would have done next.
    - **Movie title:** Have them give their script a title (e.g., "Running Scared," "Dad's Rage," "The Getaway").
4. Once completed, discuss their script. Ask questions such as:
    - What would have been the most challenging part of your escape?
    - How did you feel while you were planning and executing your imagined escape?
5. Validate their experiences and feelings, emphasizing their bravery and resourcefulness.
6. Remind them of the importance of their safety plan (see *My Safety Plan* on page 232) and how they can help themselves in future situations. Encourage them to think of additional safety measures they can take or people they can trust to help them.

The Kid Who "No's"!

Age Range
4–17

Goals:

- Provide clients who have experienced sexual or physical abuse psychoeducation on setting boundaries.
- Empower the client to say no when necessary and to protect their body.

Materials:

- *"No" Statements* handout

Directions:

1. Describe what boundaries are: limits we set with others to feel safe and respected. Explain different types of boundaries (physical, emotional, mental). Emphasize the importance of setting boundaries to protect oneself and maintain healthy relationships. Identify the signs that indicate it's necessary to set a boundary, such as feeling uncomfortable, stressed, bullied, or overwhelmed. Discuss how saying no is a crucial part of establishing these boundaries.
2. Guide the client through the following embodiment exercise, modeling it for them as needed:
   a. First, settle into a comfortable position.
   b. Take a few deep breaths to center yourself. Settle into the present moment.
   c. Bring your hands up by your shoulders, palms open and facing forward, elbows pointing toward the ground.
   d. Now extend your arms and hands straight out in front of your body, as if you are pushing something away.
   e. Say the word "NO!" with as much force and volume as is comfortable.
   f. Repeat this practice four to five times. Find a rhythm and intensity that feels right for you.
3. Discuss the exercise with the client, asking questions such as:
   - How did it feel to say no with your body?
   - What did you notice about your feelings or thoughts during the exercise?
   - Do you understand how setting boundaries and saying no can protect you?
4. Go through the *"No" Statements* handout and help the client practice saying no in different situations where they need to set boundaries, seek help, or report unsafe situations.
5. Validate their experiences and emphasize the importance of practicing this skill. Encourage regular practice of the embodiment exercise and "no" statements to build the client's confidence in setting boundaries.

"No" Statements

To Say No:	To Clarify Consent:
• No, thank you. • I said no. Please listen to me. • I need to leave now.	• I don't want to do that. • I am not okay with this. • I want to stop now.
To Assert Boundaries: • I don't like that. Please stop. • I need some space right now. • That makes me uncomfortable. Please don't do it.	**To Express Feelings:** • I feel scared when you do that. • That makes me sad. • I feel angry when you say that.
To Seek Help: • I need help right now. • Can you please stay with me? • I don't feel safe. Can you help me?	**To Deflect Unwanted Attention:** • Please leave me alone. • Stop following me. • I don't want to talk right now.
To Report Unsafe Situations: • Something happened, and I need to tell you. • I saw something that made me scared. • I feel unsafe with [*person's name*].	**To Ask for Privacy:** • I need to be alone right now. • Please knock before entering. • This is my private space.
In an Emergency: • Call 911! I need help. • There's an emergency. Please come quickly. • Help! I need help right now.	**To Request a Safe Environment:** • Can we go somewhere else? • I want to be where I feel safe. • Can we stay together?

My Picket Sign to the World

Age Range
6–17

Goals:

- Empower clients to express their feelings and advocate for themselves and others.

Materials:

- Large sheet of cardboard or poster board
- Wooden stick or handle
- Coloring utensils
- Paint and brushes (optional)
- Strong glue or tape
- Craft decorations (stickers, glitter, etc.)

Directions:

1. Explain to the client that this activity will help them express their feelings and advocate for their own safety and well-being. Discuss the importance of standing up against violence and abuse and how their voice can make a difference. Inform them how people make picket signs when they want to make their desires known in public at rallies or protests.

2. Encourage them to think about what they want to say to the world. Provide examples like "Stop Hurting Me!" "Protect Kids," "Every Kid Deserves Safety," "Parents Need Classes Too," or "My Feelings Matter Just as Much as Yours!" Have the client choose a message that resonates with them personally.

3. Have them write their chosen message in big, bold letters on the sign. Encourage them to add drawings and craft decorations that emphasize their message.

4. Help them attach a wooden stick or handle to the back of the sign using glue or tape, making sure it is secure and comfortable to hold. Encourage the client to stand and proudly hold up their sign. Ask questions such as:

    - How does this message make you feel?
    - Why did you choose this message?
    - What do you hope people will understand when they see your sign?

5. Validate their feelings and encourage them to think about how they can safely share their message, such as participating in awareness events or sharing their sign with trusted adults. Support the client in any safe advocacy efforts they wish to participate in.

CHAPTER 13

Domestic Violence, Accidents, Death, and Murder

Cracks in the Wall

Age Range **8–17**

Goals:

- Help clients process and express their feelings about and chronicle incidents of domestic violence that led to the breaking apart of their family.

Materials:

- Large sheet of paper or poster board
- Coloring utensils

Directions:

1. Explain to the client that this activity will help them understand and express their feelings about the incidents of domestic violence in their home. Reassure them that this is a safe space to share their experiences and that they can express themselves freely.
2. Introduce the metaphor: "A family is like a wall, strong and sturdy, but episodes of violence and terrifying anger are like earthquakes that cause cracks. If you get enough cracks, the wall will crumble, just like a family can be broken into pieces. Sometimes it only takes one good crack to make it fall."
3. Ask the client to draw a wall to represent their family and then put as many cracks (incidents of violence or terrifying anger) as they can remember. Ask questions such as:
   - Was it one big crack? Or was it many cracks of different sizes?
4. Then have them draw a pile of rubble next to the wall that represents their broken family. Inside the rubble, ask them to write or draw their feelings. Ask them, "Do you think it's possible to ever rebuild this wall, or will you have to find a new one?"
5. Finally, have them number the incidents in chronological order. Draw a horizontal line under the wall to serve as a timeline. For each crack (incident), draw a line down to the appropriate place on the timeline. Label each incident with the date or time period, if the client can remember. Help them describe what happened during each incident, their feelings, and any other important details. They can also draw an image or symbol that represents the incident.
6. Discuss their timeline. Ask questions such as:
   - What happened during this incident?
   - Who do you think was to blame and why?
   - How did you feel when witnessing the incident?
   - What do you wish could have been different?
   - What caused this crack?
   - Did you or anyone else in your family try to fix the cracks? How?

Walking on Eggshells

Age Range
5–17

Goals:

- Help clients express and cope with their anxiety regarding an explosive caregiver who is prone to domestic violence.

Materials:

- Plastic bags of crunchy crackers
- Mat or rug
- Large sheet of paper or poster board
- Coloring utensils

Directions:

1. Explain to the client that this activity will help them understand and express what it felt like to be very careful at home to avoid upsetting someone and the impossibility of being quiet enough to stop someone else's dysregulation. Reassure them that the therapy room is a safe space to share their experiences and feelings.
2. Place plastic bags full of crunchy crackers under a mat or rug.
3. On a blank piece of paper (or multiple pieces of paper), have the client write or draw their "eggshells" (other people's actions or behaviors they are worried or scared to activate). Examples of "eggshells" might include yelling, being threatened, bullied, being hit, humiliated, trapped, or not receiving food or comfort.
4. Spread the sheets of paper on top of the mat or rug.
5. Ask the client to try to walk over the mat without making a sound to simulate the feeling of "walking on eggshells." If they make a sound—which they will, as this is designed to be a no-win situation—they must try again.
6. Discuss the client's experience, asking open-ended questions such as:
   - How did it feel to walk on the mat?
   - How did you feel while trying to walk and remain silent?
   - How did it feel to hear the crackers breaking?
   - Can you think of times when you felt like this at home?
   - Do you understand it was not your fault?
   - What do you think made your parent/caregiver so angry?
   - What would happen to you if you didn't walk carefully?
7. Provide scenarios for the client to think about and discuss (e.g., waking up in the morning, coming home from school, when their parent/caregiver came home, late at night). For each scenario, ask the client to describe what happened and how they felt.
8. Discuss the overall impact of these experiences. Emphasize that they were in a no-win situation and are not to blame for someone else's actions. No matter how much they tried to make it peaceful around their home, it was futile. Encourage the client to think of ways to cope with their feelings and manage stress in the future (see Phase 2: Building Coping Skills).

Behind Closed Doors

Age Range
6–17

Goals:

- Help clients process and express their feelings about terrifying events that happened behind closed doors in their home.

Note: It is recommended to complete the interventions *Wounds Heal, Scars Remain* (page 236) and *My Safety Plan* (page 232) before this.

Materials:

- Poster board
- Coloring utensils
- Paints, brushes, and fan for drying (optional)
- Magazine clippings or printouts of images and words representing emotions
- Scissors
- Glue or tape

Directions:

1. Explain to the client that this activity is designed to help them process and cope with the frightening arguments, fights, and tension that went unseen in their home by expressing their thoughts and feelings about the experience. Reassure them that the therapy room is a safe space to share their emotions and that they can express themselves freely.
2. Ask the client if they have ever heard loud noises, arguments, or fighting behind closed doors inside their home that scared or hurt them. Have them talk about one specific incident that was particularly scary. Encourage them to think about what was so frightening and how they felt while it was happening.
3. Fold the poster board in half to create a door that opens. On the front of the door, have the client write words or draw images that represent "Keep Out," "Danger," or "Restricted Area."
4. Have them open the door (unfold the poster board) and on the inside create a visual representation of the event by drawing and collaging. Encourage them to express their feelings about the event through their artwork.
5. Once complete, discuss their artwork. Ask questions such as:
   - What does each part of your picture represent?
   - How did you feel during this event?
   - Why do you think it was happening?
   - Did you think it was your fault?
   - If you had a magic word that could have stopped it, would you have said it?
   - What do you wish could have been different?
6. Validate their experiences and feelings. Let them know they are not to blame for what adults do—it's the adults' responsibility to remain calm and work out their problems without shouting or violence.

Discuss ways to defuse arguments before they get loud and scary, such as staying calm, listening to what the other person is saying, trying to find a compromise, and taking a break if things get tense. Encourage them to take notes or journal about these strategies for use in the future.

7. On the back of the poster board, have the client write words of closure such as "Exit," "The Past Is Over," or "This Door Will No Longer Be Opened." Explain that these words represent their decision to leave the past behind and move forward. Remind them that they are not to blame and that they have resources and strategies available to them.
8. Process with the client:
    - What happened behind closed doors was not your fault. You did not deserve it.
    - It was scary because it wasn't safe, but you are safe now.
    - You don't have to keep what happened hidden. Your voice matters.
    - The fear you felt was real, and so is your strength for making it through.
    - You are not alone; there are people who believe in you and want to help.
    - You did what you had to do to get through it. Your survival shows how strong you are.

Origami House

Age Range
8–17

Goals:

- Help clients express and process their experiences before they entered foster or kinship care.

Materials:

- *Origami House* handout
- Paper
- Coloring utensils
- Stickers or other decorative items

Directions:

1. Explain to the client that they will be creating origami houses to represent different parts of their life before entering foster or kinship care. This will help them express and understand their feelings and experiences.
2. Use the *Origami House* handout to show the client how to fold the paper into a house. Do it for them if it is challenging.
3. Encourage the client to draw or decorate the outside and inside of the house with images and symbols that represent what their life was like during the daytime in their first home. Guide them to reflect on their experiences at different times of the day. For example:
    - What did your family do in the morning?
    - What did you usually do?
    - What was usually for breakfast?
    - Who was there?
    - How did you get to school?
4. Next, ask the client to create and decorate another origami house to represent their nighttime experiences in their first home. For example:
    - What did your family do in the evening?
    - What did you usually do?
    - What was usually for dinner?
    - Who was there?
    - How did you get home from school?
5. You can also ask the client to create additional houses for other categories relevant to their experience, such as:
    - When their parent was home
    - When their parent wasn't home
    - When a stranger came over
    - When the police showed up

- When their parent did drugs
- When their parents fought
- When their parent hurt them
- When the power went out

6. Encourage them to talk about their artwork and what each house represents. Conclude the intervention by having the client place all of their origami houses in a safe, designated area to contain and manage their past experiences.

Origami House

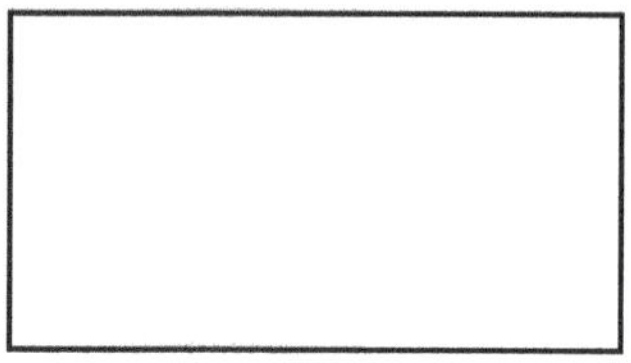

1

Begin with your paper in this position.

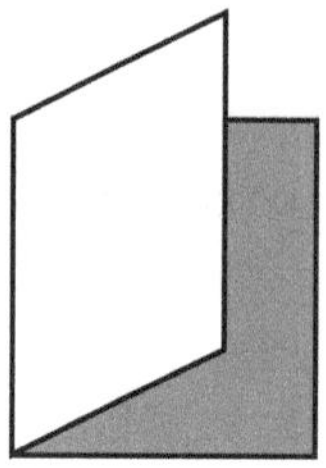

2

Fold it in half from left to right.

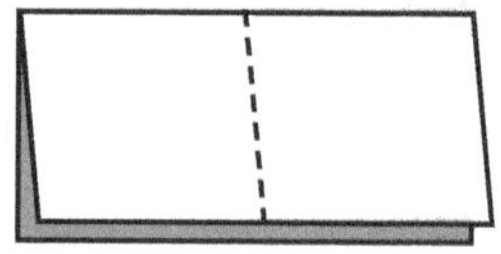

3

Turn your paper so the fold edge is up and fold the right side over to the left side.

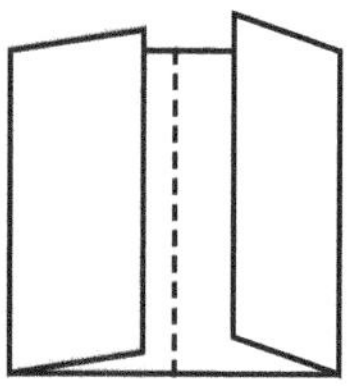

4

Then fold each side into the midline fold.

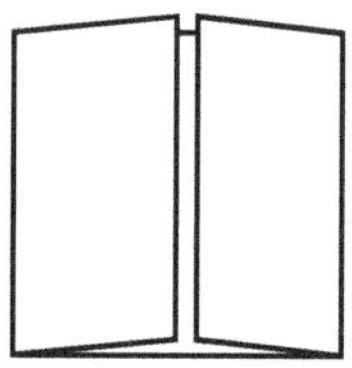

5

Your paper should look like this now.

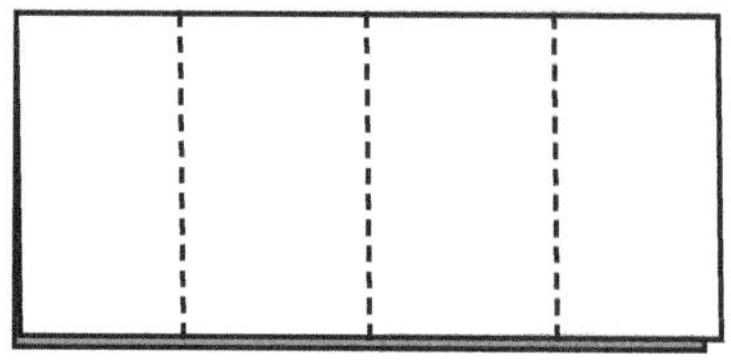

6

Unfold the paper to lay flat with the folds shown this way.

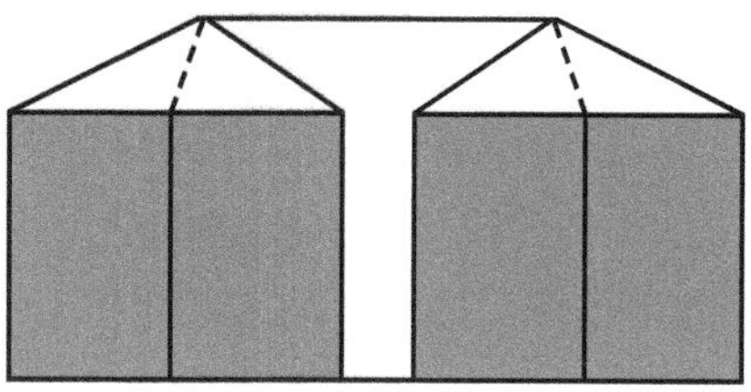

7

Open and collapse the top folds into themselves to create the peaks of the roof.

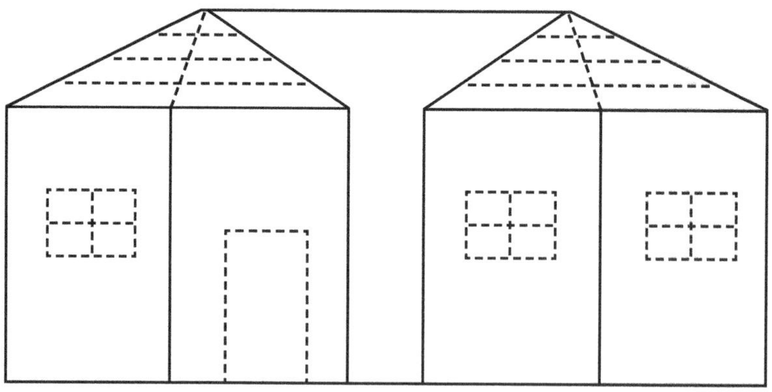

8

Decorate and display your house as desired.

Unfinished Goodbye

Age Range
6–17

Goals:

- Help clients process and express their feelings about relationships that ended abruptly, providing a way to memorialize and honor the person they did not have a chance to say goodbye to.

Materials:

- Large manilla envelope
- Cards or paper with envelopes
- Coloring utensils
- Foam hearts, stickers, and other decorations

Directions:

1. Explain to the client that when they lose a person they really cared about, it can leave a kind of hole in their heart or feel like a dark storm cloud hanging over them that just won't go away. It can be especially difficult if the parting happened fast and abruptly before they could even say goodbye. Tell them this activity will help them blow away the storm and let the sun shine again by helping them express their feelings, understand why and how the person left, and know that it was not the client's fault. Reassure them that the therapy room is a safe space to express their feelings and thoughts.
2. Have them write the name of the person they couldn't say goodbye to on the outside of a large manilla envelope. Encourage them to add drawings and decorations that remind them of that person.
3. Next, ask the client to create messages for this person. They can draw pictures or write a letter, short notes, or single words to describe how they felt and what they wished they could have said to that person before they left so suddenly. These can be messages of love, memories, or anything else the client wants to express.
4. Have them put the messages inside the manilla envelope and seal it. Discuss how it felt to write and draw these feelings. Encourage the client to reflect on positive memories and meaningful moments they shared with this person, regardless of the circumstances of their relationship or the incident that caused the separation. Validate their feelings and provide support. Ask questions such as:
   - What do you wish you could have said to this person?
   - How do you think they'd feel if they opened this envelope and saw what you wrote inside?
   - How did this person impact your life?
   - What are your favorite memories with them?
   - What do you hope happens to this person in the future to make them happy?
5. On the back of the envelope have the client write words of closure, such as "Goodbye," "I Remember You," or "You Will Always Be in My Heart." Discuss how these words represent their decision to honor the person and find closure.
6. Have them journal about this activity and their experiences of losing the person. They can also add new thoughts and reflections as they continue to process their feelings and add new messages to the envelope.

Arms Wrestling

Age Range
5–17

Goals:

- Help the clients process and express their feelings about witnessing domestic violence.

Materials:

- *Arms Wrestling* worksheet
- Coloring utensils
- Sheet protector

Directions:

1. Explain to the client that this activity will help them process their feelings about witnessing their parents, siblings, or other people fighting in their home. Reassure them that the therapy room is a safe space to share their experiences and that they can express themselves freely.
2. Provide them with the *Arms Wrestling* worksheet. Explain that the arms represent the people they saw fighting. Ask them to draw or write the name or designation of each person at the bottom of each arm.
3. Within or around the arms, have them draw or write some of the feelings they had while witnessing the fight. This can include single words, sentences, symbols, or illustrations. Encourage them to be as detailed as they can.
4. Discuss their drawing. Ask questions such as:
    - What did you see happening between these people?
    - Do you know what they were fighting about?
    - What was so scary about the fight?
    - Did you want to try to stop it?
    - How did you feel?
5. Take a few moments to validate their experiences and feelings. When they are ready, have them place a sheet protector over the worksheet. Ask them to draw or write on the sheet protector what they wish had happened instead. This could include peaceful resolutions, kind words, or actions that represent love and understanding (e.g., talk calmly, compromise, hug it out, take a break, agree to disagree).
6. Discuss how they felt when the fight ended and how they might be able to prevent more arguments in the future by using I statements such as:
    - I feel scared when you fight.
    - I need to feel safe at home.
    - Can we talk about what happened?
    - It hurts me to see you hurt each other.
    - I love both of you and want us to be happy.
7. Encourage the client to think of ways to create peace in their own life and how they could respond to any incidents of violence they might witness in the future (e.g., journal their feelings, tell a trusted adult).

Arms Wrestling

My Own Air Bag

Age Range
7–17

Goals:

- Help clients develop strategies for emotional regulation and prevent violent or destructive outbursts.

Materials:

- Large sheet of paper
- Coloring utensils
- Balloons
- Tape
- Permanent markers
- Sticky notes

Directions:

1. Discuss the concept of an airbag in a car. Explain how airbags protect people in case of an accident by cushioning the impact. Relate this to emotions, particularly anger and rage, explaining that just like cars can have accidents, people can have "emotional accidents" if they don't have protection. Although we, as humans, don't have physical airbags, we can create invisible ones out of feelings and strategies like calmness, music, friends, or happy memories.
2. Ask the client to draw themselves in the center of the paper.
3. Talk about how airbags in cars deploy when there is a danger signal. Blow up some balloons and have the client identify what their personal danger signals might be that they are about to "blow up" (e.g., feeling hot, clenched fists, raised voice, feeling the urge to insult or hurt someone). Write these on the balloons and tape them to the poster around the image of the client.
4. Use real-life, age-appropriate examples to illustrate how uncontrolled anger and rage can lead to devastating outcomes, including severe aggression or violence. Emphasize the importance of having protective strategies in place to avoid such extreme reactions. Encourage the client to try to recognize their danger signals early and deploy their "airbag" before things get out of control.
5. Discuss methods of deploying the airbag to defuse tense situations. As the client identifies a tool they could use, a balloon can be popped (if this feels comfortable for the client) or pulled off the poster and thrown away. Write the coping strategies on sticky notes and use these to replace the balloons on the poster, forming a protective layer around the image of the client. Examples include:
   - Walking away from the situation
   - Taking deep breaths
   - Listening to calming music
   - Talking to a friend or trusted adult
   - Accepting blame if appropriate
   - Recognizing when to call for help
   - Doing jumping jacks
   - Squeezing a stress ball
6. Discuss how using these strategies can help them avoid accidental emotional blow-ups. Reinforce the idea that it's important to protect ourselves from intense emotions just like we protect our bodies in physical accidents.

Rock and a Hard Place

Age Range
6–17

Goals:

- Help clients understand the difficult choices they face when witnessing someone they love doing something traumatic (e.g., domestic violence or abuse) and the importance of getting help despite the fear and loyalty that may hold them back.

Note: It is recommended to complete the interventions *My Library of Memories* (page 153), *Trauma Storms* (page 154), and *My Safety Plan* (page 232) before this one.

Materials:

- Play-dough in two different colors
- Large sheet of paper
- Coloring utensils
- List of supportive resources and contacts

Directions:

1. Explain the metaphor of being "stuck between a rock and a hard place," which represents the tough choices we sometimes have to make, especially when it involves people we love. Talk about how witnessing someone we love doing something traumatic can make us feel trapped between two difficult choices: staying silent or getting help.
2. Discuss the emotions involved in this situation, such as fear, loyalty, love, and concern. Have the client choose an emotional memory they want to focus on for this intervention (such as an event they identified during *My Library of Memories* or *Trauma Storms*).
3. Give the client two pieces of play-dough in different colors and ask them to shape each piece into a rock. Explain that one rock symbolizes the pain and suffering of staying silent, and the other rock symbolizes the fear and uncertainty but ultimately the relief of getting help.
4. Ask them to place the rocks on the paper and draw themselves stuck between these two rocks.
5. Around the rock representing silence, have them draw or write the negative feelings and consequences of staying quiet (e.g., fear, suffering, repeated trauma).
6. Around the rock representing help, have them draw or write the potential positive outcomes (e.g., safety, support, relief, getting the help their family needs).
7. Talk about the difficult position of feeling loyalty and love for their family member but also recognizing the need for help. Discuss the benefits of getting help despite the initial fear and uncertainty, such as the potential for safety, healing, and support for their family. Explain that asking for help is a sign of strength and courage. Reinforce the idea that getting help is better than staying quiet, even when it feels difficult.
8. Review the client's safety plan, which includes a list of supportive resources and contacts they can reach out to if they ever find themselves in a difficult situation. Encourage the client to keep their drawing and rocks as a reminder of the importance of seeking help.

Flashback Switch

Age Range
7–17

Goals:

- Help clients identify and manage flashbacks of an incident by recognizing triggers and developing strategies to reduce their intensity.

Materials:

- *Flashback Switch* worksheet (folded)
- Cordless light switch
- Coloring utensils

Directions:

1. Explain to the client that the purpose of the intervention is to help them understand their flashbacks (disturbing memories of a troubling incident) by discussing the incident and learning ways to manage the feelings that come up.
2. Describe how and why flashbacks occur. You can say:

   Traumatic incidents can leave an imprint on the brain, which sometimes "replays" these events in the form of dreams or flashbacks. These flashbacks can happen out of the blue and without warning. They are the leftovers from the shock of the event, like ripples emanating outward in the water after you throw a stone or the aftershocks of a huge earthquake. Healing takes time, and these flashbacks are your brain's way of telling you there is still more healing to do. It is showing you the event repeatedly until you can understand it better and make sense of it. In short, it is like the brain's way of saying, "Something scary happened and I'm still not over it."

3. Discuss how these flashbacks and sudden memories can feel overwhelming and intense like the event is happening all over again.
4. Show the client the cordless light switch and ask them to turn it on and off. Explain how this is like a flashback:

   When something triggers a memory from your mental library, it's like an "on" switch that sends the image right to your brain, startling you. The problem is you have no control over the switch—your brain is triggered by something and throws it on its own, forcing you to see the image whether you want to or not. Remember, it's your brain's way of saying you haven't made sense of it yet.

5. Explain that they are going to begin to train their brain's "off/on" switch with a dimmer switch that they can control. They can use this dimmer switch to help slow down and identify what may have triggered the memory as well as to dim the memory, making it less intense.
6. Provide the client with the *Flashback Switch* worksheet, already folded. Have them open the top half of the paper, representing the trigger "on" switch. Ask them to draw or write the images, thoughts, or

sensations that keep popping into their brain during the flashback. Discuss what they think might be triggering the bad memories (they may not know) and validate their feelings. Ask questions such as:

- Do you remember what you were you doing when the flashback happened?
- Is it always the same images?
- Can you describe them to me?
- Why do you think the brain is replaying them?
- How does it make you feel?

7. Take a moment before having the client open the bottom half of the worksheet, representing the "off" dimmer switch. Ask them to think of at least three ways to "dim" or reduce the intensity of these flashbacks. These could be activities or strategies they have learned from their coping skills sessions, such as deep breathing, listening to music, playing a game, talking to a trusted adult, or engaging in a favorite hobby.
8. Encourage the client to practice the chosen activities whenever they feel a flashback coming on. Role-play or demonstrate these strategies if needed to ensure the client feels comfortable using them.

Flashback Switch

My Cemetery

Age Range
7–17

Goals:

- Help clients process and express grief, loss, and unresolved feelings by symbolically laying to rest the people they have lost to death.

Materials:

- Paper
- Poster board or large sheet of paper
- Coloring utensils
- Glue
- Scissors
- Stickers or other decorative items (optional)

Directions:

1. Explain to the client that they will be creating a symbolic cemetery to honor and remember those who have passed away, which will help the client process their grief and loss.
2. Ask them to think about the people they want to lay to rest. Instruct them to create a paper tombstone for each person. Ask them to write the person's name on the tombstone and decorate it so it is personal and meaningful.
3. Once the tombstones are completed, have the client arrange and glue them onto the poster board to create a cemetery. Encourage them to give their cemetery a name and decorate the area around the tombstones, making it a peaceful and respectful space.
4. Provide a safe and supportive environment for the client to share about their tombstones and the stories behind them if they feel comfortable. Ask questions such as:
    - If this was their funeral, what would you say to them?
    - Do you have any unanswered questions you wonder about?
    - Do you know what happened that led to their death?
5. Discuss the importance of honoring the people laid to rest while also understanding that this symbolic act of creating a cemetery is a step toward healing and finding peace.
6. End the session with a reflective activity, such as a guided meditation or a moment of silence.
7. Process with the client:
    - It's okay to feel sad, angry, confused, numb, or anything else. Grief doesn't have just one feeling.
    - Grief comes and goes like waves. Some days it feels big, and other days it's quieter.
    - You don't have to be strong all the time. It's okay to cry and sit with your feelings.
    - Even though they are gone, the love you shared with them will always stay with you.
    - You can still talk to them in your heart, write them letters, or remember them in special ways.

From Fear to Heroism

Age Range
4–17

Goals:

- Help clients process and express their trauma.
- Empower clients to protect and care for themselves and others.

Materials:

- Music player queued with both dramatic, fast classical music and inspirational, uplifting music
- Doll
- Inflatable punching bag
- Open space for movement
- Costumes or props (optional)

Directions:

1. Explain to the client that this activity will help them express their feelings and experiences without words, using music and dramatic play. Discuss how acting out the traumatic or frightening events they've experienced can help them process their emotions and feel empowered.
2. Ask them to think about the person who did something scary or hurtful to them. Explain that this person is called a *perpetrator*, which is a term for someone who did something wrong or harmful to another person.
3. Explain that the client will be acting out the role of this perpetrator using dramatic movements, gestures, and scary faces. Play dramatic, fast classical music (e.g., "In the Hall of the Mountain King" by Edvard Grieg or "O Fortuna" by Carl Orff). Provide a doll to represent the victim and ask the client to show what happened to them or others through the perpetrator's actions. Give the client permission to fully immerse themselves in this part, and emphasize that this is a safe space to express their feelings.
4. When the song is over, take a moment to pause. Encourage the client to take deep breaths and shake off any remaining tension.
5. Explain that they will now act out the role of the hero who comes in to save the victim from the perpetrator. Play inspirational, uplifting music (e.g., "Eye of the Tiger" by Survivor or "Fight Song" by Rachel Platten). Present the inflatable punching bag as the stand-in for the perpetrator. Encourage the client to act out the hero's role, using strong, confident movements to fight the perpetrator and rescue the doll. Guide the client to use the punching bag to physically release any remaining anger or frustration, imagining they are protecting the victim and vanquishing the villain.
6. After the activity, sit down with the client and discuss their experience. Ask open-ended questions like:
    - How did it feel to act out the perpetrator?
    - How did it feel to become the hero and save the victim?
    - What was it like to use the punching bag?
7. Reinforce the idea that they have the power to overcome their fears and protect themselves and others. Encourage them to use the memory of becoming the hero whenever they feel scared or powerless. If needed, emphasize this is pretend acting and a way to help them repair what happened to them. Remind them that the physical actions of the hero should not be done in real life.

PHASE 4

Regaining Control, Self-Esteem, and Acceptance

It is crucial to help clients regain control, self-esteem, and acceptance, as these elements are foundational for their emotional and psychological well-being. Traumatized youth often experience instability and a lack of agency in their lives, leading to feelings of powerlessness, learned helplessness, and hopelessness. By helping them regain control, we empower them to feel more secure and capable of influencing their circumstances, which is essential for their mental health and development.

I know firsthand that self-esteem is one of the first emotional states that becomes compromised. I kept asking my new foster mother at age 8, "When are you going to give me away?" All that I knew disappeared in a flash and my self-worth went with it. I felt like a piece of garbage. I was stuck in a catastrophic maze of rejection and unlovability in my own young eyes, losing sight of just how resilient I was. It took me years of therapy to open up that crumpled piece of garbage and write the words "You are valuable."

Children in foster care and those who have experienced other forms of trauma *must* restore their self-worth, reinstall their self-value, and believe they are stronger because of the climb. This newfound resilience prepares them for the adventure of discovering their capabilities and thriving despite their adverse childhood experiences. As Jon Kabat-Zinn (1994/2023) wisely said, "You can't stop the waves but you can learn to surf" (p. 30).

The chapters in this phase focus on developing impulse control, self-mastery, and self-control; building self-esteem and self-acceptance; and raising resilience. The interventions were inspired by the works of Deb Dana (2020), Larry Rosenberg (1998), Jon Kabat-Zinn (Williams et al., 2007), Daniel P. Brown (Boston Center for Contemplative Practice, 2019), and Peter A. Levine (2007, 2010).

CHAPTER 14

Impulse Control, Self-Mastery, and Self-Control

Lion Mind, Snake Mind

Age Range
7–17

Goals:

- Help clients understand, practice, and develop a felt sense of impulse control.

Materials:

- Paper
- Coloring utensils
- Pictures of lions and snakes (optional)
- Sheet protectors
- Pipe cleaners

Directions:

1. Explain to the client that the purpose of this activity is to help them understand and manage their impulses. Introduce the metaphors of a "lion mind" and a "snake mind" to illustrate different ways of thinking and reacting. Show the client pictures of these animals and describe them as follows:
    - The lion mind is focused and in control. Lions think before they act and are able to stay calm in tense situations.
    - The snake mind is impulsive, easily distracted, and reactive. Snakes might hiss, bite, and "snap" at any opportunity without thinking.
2. Have the client draw a picture of their snake mind, showing all its impulsive behaviors and reactions (e.g., snapping at somebody, acting before thinking). Then provide the client with a sheet protector to place over the snake mind drawing.
3. Ask the client to draw their lion mind on the sheet protector, symbolizing the transformation. They can add what makes a lion mind calm and in control (e.g., deep breathing, considering consequences before acting).
4. Provide six pipe cleaners that represent the whiskers of the lion (three on each side). For each whisker, help the client create a positive affirmation about their ability to control their impulses (e.g., "I can stay calm like a lion," "I can think before I act"). Write these affirmations on strips of paper and add them to the transformation drawing along with the whiskers by piercing the pipe cleaners through the sheet protector.
5. Discuss their drawing. Ask questions such as:
    - Can you describe a time when you used your lion mind?
    - What about a time when you had a snake mind reaction?
    - How did it feel in each situation?
6. Guide the client through a snake mind exercise: Have them stand up and slither their whole body, moving around as if they are a hyperactive snake. Encourage them to make hissing sounds and move quickly to simulate impulsive energy. After about a minute, ask them to stop and notice how their body feels—likely excited, restless, and energized.

7. Then guide them through a lion mind exercise: Ask them to stand still and take slow, deep breaths while imagining they are a calm, majestic lion. Have them focus on their posture, standing tall and proud. Have them slowly extend their arms, stretching like a lion, then bring them back to a resting position. After a few minutes, ask them to notice how their body feels—likely calm, focused, and relaxed.
8. Role-play with the client to practice using their different states of mind. Give them some scenarios, such as "A bully calls you a name at school" or "Your mother tells you to stop playing video games and do your homework right now." For each scenario, ask:
   - What does your snake mind want to do?
   - What would your lion mind do?
9. Remind them that the lion always takes a few moments to think about the consequences first and tries to respond calmly rather than reacting loudly and with anger. Encourage them to keep practicing their lion mind strategies in their daily life.

"I Can" Can

Age Range
7–17

Goals:

- Help clients transform an "I can't" (fixed) mindset into an "I can" (growth) mindset.

Materials:

- Empty tin cans (cleaned and safe to handle)
- Coloring utensils
- Stickers and other decorations
- Popsicle sticks
- Strips of paper
- Glue or tape

Directions:

1. Inform the client that this activity will help them change their "I can't" mindset into an "I can" mindset. Explain how shifting from a negative or pessimistic outlook to a positive and optimistic one can help them cope with their emotions, take control of their responses, and change everything they experience.
2. Give the client an empty tin can. Ask them to think about times they have said or thought, "I can't." Have them write these thoughts on strips of paper and place them inside the can.
3. Discuss why they might feel like they can't do certain things. Encourage them to share their "I can't" thoughts and explore the reasons behind these feelings.
4. Then ask them to think of ways they can change their "I can't" statements into "I can" statements. For example, "I can't do math" can become "I can learn new things" or "I can keep practicing." Write these new "I can" statements on popsicle sticks.
5. Have the client decorate their "I can" can to make it personal and positive. Place the popsicle sticks inside the can so they stick out and visually take over the "I can't" statements.
6. Have the client stand up, take a deep breath, and strike a can-do pose in a confident stance. Encourage them to say one of their "I can" statements out loud while holding the pose. Repeat this a few times to reinforce a positive mindset.
7. Encourage the client to take their "I can" can home and practice their personal and positive statements.

River of Thoughts

Age Range
7–17

Goals:

- Help clients learn to observe and separate from their thoughts, understanding that thoughts are temporary and that with patience, negative thoughts can change into more comforting and soothing ones.

Materials:

- LEGO or other small figurines of a boat and a person
- Poster board
- Coloring utensils

Directions:

1. Explain to the client that this activity will help them learn to observe their thoughts without getting overwhelmed or taking immediate action they may later regret. Introduce the metaphor of being on a raging river, like whitewater rapids, to describe the rapid flow of thoughts.
2. Ask the client to draw a fast-moving river on the poster board, including details like waves, rocks, and rapids. Then have them draw a peaceful area on the shore with a sandy beach and a big, comfortable chair.
3. Have the client place the person figurine in the boat and the boat on the raging river. Ask them what it feels like trying to navigate the choppy water filled with dangerous rocks they are trying to avoid. Ask them to imagine looking over the side of the boat and seeing their fast-moving thoughts. On the far side of the river, across from the beach, have them write down any negative thoughts they have been having in their life (e.g., "I'm not good enough," "I'll never be happy," "I'm not wanted").
4. Explain that even though the water is rough and fast, they have the ability to steer the boat toward the beach. Have them move the boat to the peaceful shore and place the person on the drawing of the comfy beach chair. Ask them to imagine sitting there, watching all their negative thoughts flow past them in the river. Encourage them to take a few deep breaths and relax.
5. Discuss how it felt to be in the rapids versus on the beach. Emphasize that thoughts, like waves, come and go; they do not last forever. Sometimes just taking a moment to relax and observe our thoughts make them pass even faster. However wild, dangerous, or painful our river of thoughts may be, pausing can keep us from being swept away by the current of an unhelpful impulse. Instead, we have the freedom to choose our response, like steering to the safe, calm beach. We can watch the unhelpful thoughts drift away and replace them with more positive and helpful thoughts and actions.
6. Review the following with the client:
   - Thoughts won't last forever.
   - Thoughts will come and go.
   - You don't have to believe everything you think.
   - You are strong and have overcome.
   - You have the power to turn negative thoughts into helpful ones.
   - You are safe now.

My Regulation Cards

Age Range
4–18

Goals:

- Help clients identify their needs, receive sensory input, and create a sense of safety, control, attachment, and bonding with their caregiver.

Materials:

- Instant camera (or digital camera and printer)
- Cardstock
- Coloring utensils
- Glue or tape
- Scissors

Directions:

1. Explain to the client that this activity is intended to help them contain and cope with their big feelings that can sometimes make them react in ways that only make things worse. They will do this by creating cards that will tell them what to do in certain situations. Knowing what to do will help them feel safer and more regulated in that circumstance and in their day-to-day life.
2. Teach the client the broad meaning of the words *regulation* and *dysregulation*. You can say, "When you are regulated, you are calm and able to make the best choices for yourself and others. When you are dysregulated, you are letting the emotion of the moment—like anger, sadness, or indifference—make the choices for you."
3. Ask the client to think about times when they are very angry or very sad. Ask, "What do you think you need when you are having your big feelings?" This might include getting a hug, having a snack, punching a pillow, and so on. Encourage them to consider how these actions could help them regulate and get their needs met.
4. Have them take photos of themselves demonstrating some of their chosen coping actions. Print out the photos and have them glue each one onto a piece of cardstock that is cut to be a bit larger than the photo. Have them label each card with the name of the action and decorate it if they wish. It is a good idea to laminate these cards for longevity. Or, if using an instant camera, the photos themselves can be the cards and the labels can be written in marker.
5. Explain to the caregiver how these cards are to be used:
   - The cards should be kept safe and available for times when the client becomes dysregulated and needs a reminder of what they can do to help calm themselves down and make better choices.
   - In the moment, the caregiver should get the cards and meet the client on their level, asking them what it is they need to help them regulate their feelings so they can discuss the issue calmly.
   - If the client cannot use their words, the caregiver should show them one card at a time—"Do you need this right now?"—and wait for the client's response. They should go through each card until the client chooses.
   - If the client refuses all of the cards, the caregiver should stop, leave the cards face up where the client can see them, and stay with the client until they are able to calm down. They should not force the client to choose a card, though after a while the client may do so on their own.

Stop, Relax, and Think

Age Range
8–17

Goals:

- Teach clients how to utilize coping skills when they are feeling out of control emotionally or physically so they can problem-solve and regulate themselves.

Materials:

- Circles cut from red, yellow, and green paper
- Large sheet of paper
- Glue or tape
- Coloring utensils

Directions:

1. Inform the client that this activity is designed to help them learn how to stop, relax, and think before they act. They will be creating a stoplight that shows what steps they can take when they feel overwhelmed or out of control.
2. Have them draw a rectangle that is big enough to hold the colored circles. Ask them to glue the red circle inside the top of the rectangle, the yellow in the middle, and the green at the bottom, creating the image of a stoplight. Have them label the circles with "STOP" (red), "RELAX" (yellow), and "THINK" (green), leaving room below each word for additional writing.
3. Ask the client to think of three things they can do to help themselves pause when they feel out of control and write these in the STOP circle. Provide examples if needed (e.g., freeze where they are, stop talking, imagine a plate of their favorite food or place to go). It is important to check with the client to see if the action you have suggested sounds appealing and helpful to them before having them write it down.
4. In the RELAX circle, have the client write down three things they can do to help calm themselves (e.g., count to 10, take five deep belly breaths, play their favorite song).
5. In the THINK circle, have the client write down three things they can do to help themselves articulate their thoughts and feelings and consider their course of action (e.g., say exactly what they are feeling, call a friend, ask themselves if this outburst is helping or hurting).
6. Reiterate what was learned and go through a drill. This step is very important, as it helps the client internalize the intervention, gain self-awareness, and begin to master how to gain a sense of self-control. Have the client role-play being out of control and have them choose and practice a strategy from each circle of their stoplight when you prompt them by calling out "Stop! . . . Think . . . Relax." You can also switch roles and be the actor while the client prompts you.

United Parts of Me

Age Range
7–17

Goals:

- Help clients externalize and manage overwhelming feelings related to trauma and loss and develop impulse control.

Materials:

- Poster board or large sheet of paper
- Small envelopes
- Index cards
- Glue or tape
- Coloring utensils

Directions:

1. Explain to the client that they will be creating a collage to help them understand and manage their different feelings and impulses that can sometimes feel confusing or overwhelming.
2. Ask them to draw an outline of their body. It should be large enough to cover the entire poster board.
3. Have them draw a circle representing the part of themselves that is happy and fill it in with a color that represents their happiness. Ask them to write on index cards what their happy part says (e.g., "I am happy because I love my mom," "I am happy because I got a good grade"). Have them glue an envelope to the happy part and place the index cards inside.
4. Next, have them draw a separate circle representing their unhappy part and fill it in with a color that represents their unhappiness. Ask them to glue an envelope to this part and fill it with index cards showing what the unhappy part says (e.g., "I am unhappy because I don't like where I live," "I am unhappy because I'm being teased or bullied").
5. Have them draw another circle on the body somewhere in between the happy and unhappy circles. Encourage them to fill this circle in with a color that is neutral or a mix of the happy and unhappy colors. Glue an envelope to this part.
6. Discuss with the client how their happy part can actually help their unhappy part manage their negative feelings by balancing them out. Help them come up with affirmations and coping strategies that use their happy and unhappy statements to counterbalance each other (e.g., "People can be happy and sad at the same time," "Happy feelings are stronger than unhappy ones," "When I'm sad I can think of the new friend I made"). Have them write these down on index cards and place them in the balanced part's envelope.
7. Show the client a simple somatic exercise, such as clenching their fists and then slowly releasing them, to symbolize letting go of impulses. Encourage them to do this when they feel a strong impulse coming on.
8. Discuss their body collage and how everyone has parts that can feel different emotions—even many emotions—at the same time. Emphasize that there is always a part that can help manage the other feelings. Reinforce that they can choose how to act on their feelings and that their wise, calm, balanced part can guide them to make better choices.

Adjust the Sail

Age Range **7–17**

Goals:

- Help clients understand that while they cannot control all aspects of their lives, they have the power to adjust their responses and attitudes to navigate through challenges more effectively.

Materials:

- Poster board or large sheet of paper
- Paper
- Coloring utensils
- Sticky notes
- Glue or tape
- LEGO pieces
- Scissors
- String or yarn (optional)

Directions:

1. Explain to the client that life can be like sailing a boat. While they cannot control the wind (external circumstances), they can adjust their sails (responses and attitudes) to help them safely navigate their journey. Tell them they are going to explore how they can adjust their sails to better handle the challenges they face.
2. Ask the client to build a boat out of the LEGO bricks. Encourage them to get creative and design a boat that makes them feel safe on the water. Have them create a paper sail, which they can decorate and personalize before they attach it to the boat. For added realism, you can attach string to represent the rigging, explaining to the client that sailors use these ropes to change the position of the sails, which allows them to control the boat's direction and speed.
3. On sticky notes, ask the client to write or draw different winds (challenges or external factors) they have faced or are facing (e.g., moving homes, changing schools, feeling alone). Have them attach these notes to the left side of the poster board.
4. On additional sticky notes, ask the client to write or draw ways they can adjust their sails (responses and coping strategies) to navigate these challenges (e.g., talking to a trusted adult, engaging in a hobby, practicing mindfulness). Have them attach these notes to the right side of the poster board.
5. In the center of the poster board, have them draw a large sailboat. They can decorate it however they would like. Glue or tape the LEGO sailboat on top of the sailboat drawing, with the winds on one side and the adjusted sails on the other, illustrating how the client can navigate through challenges.
6. Discuss their visual representation. Ask questions such as:
   - Can you tell me about some of the winds you have faced?
   - How did you adjust your sails to handle these winds?
   - Do you see how it's possible to sail in between and stay on course?
   - What are some different ways you can adjust your sails in the future?
7. Validate their feelings and provide support as they talk about their experiences. Help them write positive affirmations or messages of hope, such as "I am capable," "I can adapt," and "I can navigate my journey." Have them place these affirmations around their visual representation as reminders of their resilience and strength.

Pause, Stop, and THINK

Age Range
7–17

Goals:

- Help clients develop more effective impulse control by using cognitive and somatic techniques.

Materials:

- Skin-safe markers

Directions:

1. Explain to the client that this activity is designed to teach them how to pause and think before acting, which will allow them to determine whether they want to follow their impulse or make a different choice.
2. Introduce the acronym THINK* and explain that it can help the client ensure they're making a positive choice for themselves and others:
    - **T:** Is it thoughtful?
    - **H:** Is it helpful?
    - **I:** Is it inspiring?
    - **N:** Is it necessary?
    - **K:** Is it kind?
3. Have the client write the letters T-H-I-N-K on the tips of their fingers.
4. Teach the client about the pressure point between the thumb and index finger. Explain that pressing this point can act as a "pause" button to help calm their body and mind.
5. Have the client write the word STOP in the middle of their palm. Guide them to practice opening and closing their hand while saying "Pause, stop, and think."
6. Discuss how using the THINK acronym and the pause button can help them make better decisions. Role-play different situations where the client can use these techniques.
7. Reinforce the functions of these techniques and encourage the client to practice them regularly for greater self-control.

* The THINK acronym for use before speaking (or acting) is often attributed to pastor Alan Redpath.

The Ripple Effect

Age Range
6–17

Goals:

- Help clients understand the consequences of their actions on themselves and others.
- Foster self-awareness, empathy, and responsibility for their behavior.

Materials:

- Shallow, wide bowl of water
- Small pebbles
- Large sheet of paper or poster board
- Coloring utensils
- Clay or play-dough
- Wood peg doll

Directions:

1. Explain to the client that our actions create "ripples" that radiate outward, affecting ourselves and others. Demonstrate this concept by having the client drop a small pebble into a bowl of water. Encourage them to observe the ripples that form and spread out from the point where the pebble entered the water.
2. Explain that our words and actions can have both positive and negative ripple effects. Emphasize that even when we are impacted by the negative ripple effects of people who have hurt us, we can still create our own positive ripple effects to help ourselves and others. Provide some examples to illustrate this, such as:
   - **Positive actions:**
     - Helping a friend with homework can make the friend feel supported and valued, strengthening the friendship.
     - Complimenting someone boosts their confidence and can make them feel happier.
     - Sharing creates a sense of community and trust among peers.
   - **Negative actions:**
     - Bullying can make someone feel scared, sad, and isolated.
     - Lying breaks trust and can lead to conflicts and misunderstandings.
     - Ignoring someone can make them feel unimportant and hurt their feelings.
3. Ask the client to draw or use clay or play-dough to sculpt a small pond with ripples emanating from the center. Have them place a wood peg doll in the middle of the pond to represent themselves.
4. Around the pond, have the client write or draw examples of how their actions have caused ripples. Discuss both positive and negative actions and their effects on the client and other people in their life.
5. Emphasize that their actions matter and they have the power to create positive ripples. Discuss ways they can make positive choices that will create beneficial ripples in their life and the lives of those around them.

CHAPTER 15

Building Self-Esteem and Self-Acceptance

Affirmation "Me Cards"

Age Range
9–17

Goals:

- Help clients restructure cognitive distortions about themselves and build coping skills.

Materials:

- Self-laminating or magnetic cards (or precut sheets)
- Coloring utensils
- Stickers and other decorative items

Directions:

1. Explain to the client that they will be creating "me cards" with affirmations to help lift their spirits and motivate them during difficult times. Discuss what affirmations are and how they can help improve their well-being. Provide some examples as inspiration, such as:
    - I am fine just the way that I am.
    - It's okay to get angry sometimes.
    - I can make friends by listening.
    - I am lovable and capable.
    - I am beautiful in every way.
    - I am in control of my choices.
    - I can breathe to calm myself.
    - Each day is a new beginning.
2. Ask the client to create their own affirmations, assisting them if needed and providing positive feedback. Have the client write each affirmation on a card and decorate it. Encourage creativity and personal expression in the design of the cards.
3. Explain that the client can read, hold, or carry these affirmation cards with them to boost their mood and reinforce positive thoughts. This is especially helpful before an anxiety-provoking event or experience, such as a family court meeting where the client appears in court. Suggest placing the cards in visible locations, like the client's locker, backpack, or bedroom.
4. Encourage them to share their affirmations with family members for additional support.

Self-Belief Tower

Age Range **7–13**

Goals:

- Help clients develop self-esteem, confidence, and identity through self-reflection and objectivity about their own characteristics.

Materials:

- Plastic cups in blue, red, yellow, and white
- Permanent markers

Directions:

1. Before the session, prepare the cups by writing different characteristics on them. These should be descriptors that the client may identify with and should be color-coded to indicate sad aspects of the self (blue cups), angry aspects (red), and happy aspects (yellow). Leave the white cups blank. Here are some examples of characteristics to include:
   - **Sad (blue):** Crybaby, shy, sensitive, slow, follower, stuck, bored, depressed, stressed out, anxious, nerd, hyper, strange, unhappy, sloppy, messy, dirty
   - **Angry (red):** Smart aleck, bully, grouch, loner, crazy, sneak, pushy, troublemaker, frustrated, aggravated, stubborn, trouble, out of control, aggressive, meanie, nasty, unfriendly
   - **Happy (yellow):** Athletic, artistic, musical, comedian, dreamer, hero, problem solver, entertainer, actor, friendly, leader, champ, dancer, hopeful, helpful, respectful, giving, kind, neat
2. In the session, inform the client that they will be creating a "self-belief tower" of cups that represent different aspects of themselves.
3. Have the client look over all the premade cups and notice the blank ones. Ask them to choose any cups that have characteristics they feel they possess and stack them. Emphasize that they can choose any cups they honestly identify with—the color doesn't matter, nor does the order or number. Encourage them to create their own cup using a blank white one if they feel they have a characteristic that wasn't written down already.
4. When they have completed their tower, have them take a step back and look at the colors, noting which colors are most represented. Let them know which category of trait each color represents and if they have made their own cups, discuss which category (sad, angry, happy) these should belong to.
5. If you find the tower is mostly red or blue, discuss what the client could do to feel like they could add more yellow cups (identify with more happy traits) and take away red or blue cups (create separation from the sad and angry labels).
6. Ask them to create a name for their self-belief tower and take a photo. Let them know you'll repeat this activity in the future to see if anything has changed.

Two Doors to My Self

Age Range **8–17**

Goals:

- Increase objectivity and self-awareness by helping clients express what they perceive as the positive and negative sides of themselves.
- Help integrate split parts of their personality.

Note: This intervention may take more than one session, depending on how intricate the client wants to be with their drawings and self-expression.

Materials:

- Large sheet of paper or poster board
- Coloring utensils
- Scissors

Directions:

1. Explain to the client that they are going to create two doors into themselves. Have them begin by folding the paper in half and turning it so the fold is at the top. On the front of the folded paper, have the client draw a large circle with a line down the middle.
2. Explain that this circle represents their "outside face"—the face that they show to the world on the outside about who they are—and the two parts represent different sides of this self that they show to others. On one side they will create their "outside positive face" and on the other side they will create their "outside negative face."
3. Give them time to create their two faces. Encourage them to draw and write words around the faces to show what they say to the outside world about who they are.
4. Next, have the client lift the top layer open and cut along the center line (through the face) up to the fold. This divides the face into two doors that can be opened and shut independently of each other.
5. Ask the client to open both doors and, on the bottom layer of the paper, draw another big circle with a line down the middle, forming a new face that is hidden beneath the outside face and accessible through the doors.
6. Explain that this is the face that holds their hidden feelings that they *don't* show to the world. It is also divided into two parts: their "inside positive face" and their "inside negative face."
7. Give the client time to construct these two faces. Around the faces, encourage them to draw and write words to represent what they think and feel privately inside their mind.
8. Once they are satisfied with their drawings, discuss their different faces. Encourage the client to explore the doors and to express each side of themselves, inside and out. Help them understand that they are not different parts or a different person every time they are feeling a certain way, but instead are one complex whole with many different feelings. Ask questions such as:
    - Which outside face do you show more often?
    - Can you give a name to the outside positive or negative face?

- Can you talk back to your negative voice inside?
- Which face causes conflict in your life?
- If you could show your inside face to anyone, who would it be?
- Which inside face hides more often from the outside world?

My Ray of Light

Age Range
7–17

Goals:

- Help clients process and transform their traumatic and difficult experiences into sources of personal strength and self-affirmation.

Materials:

- *My Ray of Light* worksheet
- Sheet protector
- Coloring utensils
- Bright or metallic markers or glitter
- Scissors
- Glue
- Photo of the client

Directions:

1. Explain to the client that this activity will help them transform their experiences of adversity and pain into sources of strength and objectivity that can help them build greater self-esteem.
2. Provide the client with the *My Ray of Light* worksheet. Explain that each sunbeam will represent a negative experience or feeling the client has had. You can also make this exercise more specific to the client's circumstances (e.g., their experiences in foster care). Encourage them to take a minute to think about these feelings and experiences and then write them on the sunbeams.
3. Discuss how each challenge they have endured can be seen as a source of strength and resilience. Emphasize that overcoming adversity makes them wiser and stronger.
4. Place the worksheet in a sheet protector and explain that the client will now see how brightly their light shines. Over each negative experience, have them write an affirmation for overcoming adversity. Provide some examples, such as:
    - I am resilient and can overcome any challenge.
    - I am strong and capable.
    - I use my experiences to grow and improve.
    - I am proud of how far I have come.
    - I can achieve my goals despite the obstacles.
    - I matter, and my actions make a difference.
    - I rise above negativity and use it to build my strength.
    - I am a survivor, and my journey makes me unique and powerful.
5. Encourage them to write enough affirmations to fill all their rays of light. They can also decorate their sunbeams with bright colors, metallic markers, and so on.
6. Ask them to place a photo of themselves over the figure in the worksheet and write the statement "From my adversity, I shine bright" above it.

My Ray of Light

Chair of Belonging

Age Range
7–17

Goals:

- Help clients understand that they are just as special as anyone else, that they are not mistakes or victims, and that they deserve to be heard, respected, welcomed, and loved.

Materials:

- Chair figurines
- Decorative items (e.g., feathers, tissue paper, pipe cleaners)
- Large sheet of paper or poster board
- Coloring utensils
- Index cards
- Glue or tape
- Photo of the client (optional)

Directions:

1. Explain to the client that this activity will help them understand that they belong and matter just as much as anyone else. Introduce the concept of "having a seat at the table" and affirm that the client deserves to be heard, respected, welcomed, and cared for, in their family and in the world.
2. Provide the client with all but one of the chair figurines. Ask them to draw a large circle on the paper to symbolize the table and then place chairs around it to represent the members of their current foster or kinship family. Have them write each person's name on an index card and place it next to that individual's chair.
3. Have the client put the remaining chair in the center of the circle. This is their place. Encourage them to decorate the chair to make it their own, symbolizing their unique value and presence.
4. Around their chair, ask the client to write statements that affirm their right to belong (e.g., "I belong here," "I matter just as much as anyone else," "My voice and presence are important"). These can also be written from the perspective of the others at the table (e.g., "You belong here," "We are here for you," "You are not forgotten").
5. Optionally, the client can add a photo of themselves to their special chair to reinforce their place in the scene.
6. Discuss with the client how it feels to see their place among others and to recognize their right to belong. Talk about times when they felt excluded or unwelcome and how they can remind themselves of their worth and belonging. Encourage them to think of ways they can assert their presence and rights in everyday situations.

My Carnival Day

Age Range
7–17

Goals:

- Help clients celebrate and appreciate their unique qualities and interests.

Materials:

- *My Carnival Day* worksheet (copied onto large paper)
- Coloring utensils
- Stickers and other decorative items (optional)

Directions:

1. Explain to the client that this activity will help them celebrate and appreciate their own unique personality and qualities by creating a personalized carnival that happens on a special day just for them.
2. Prompt the client to fill out all the different areas on the *My Carnival Day* worksheet. Encourage them to be as creative and detailed as possible. They can also add drawings, stickers, and other decorations.
    - Ask them to come up with a fun and personal name for their carnival and the specific date on which it is happening.
    - Have them write or draw their favorite food stands and musicians or other entertainment that would be at the carnival.
    - Encourage them to include rides and games they enjoy, such as a dunk tank (decide who gets dunked).
    - Ask them to think about what free giveaways would be meaningful to them and why (e.g., books, toys, video games, art supplies).
    - Have them design a T-shirt that represents them and their carnival, thinking about colors, logos, and phrases.
3. Discuss what each element of their carnival represents and why it's important to them. Talk about the qualities and interests that make them unique and how celebrating these can boost self-esteem and self-awareness.
4. Help the client create positive affirmations about themselves based on their carnival elements (e.g., "I celebrate my unique tastes and interests," "I am proud of who I am," "I deserve to be celebrated").
5. Encourage them to display their carnival poster somewhere visible as a reminder of their unique qualities and the importance of their individuality. Discuss how they can incorporate the spirit of their carnival day into their daily life by taking time to appreciate themselves regularly.

My Carnival Day

Name of Carnival:	Date:
Food Stands:	Entertainment/Music:
Rides:	Games:

Giveaways:

T-Shirt Design:

The Worth Inside Me

Age Range
7–17

Goals:

- Help clients recognize their inner strength and value.

Materials:

- Modeling clay
- Colorful feathers
- Glitter
- Decorative gems
- Cellophane
- Paints (optional)
- Glue

Directions:

1. Explain to the client that the purpose of this activity is to help them recognize their inner worth, strength, and resilience, like a phoenix rising from the ashes. Tell the story about the phoenix—a mythical immortal bird that would set fire to its nest of wood, be consumed by the flames, and rise anew from the ashes, rising stronger and more vibrant than ever before. Relate this symbol of rebirth and resilience to the client's ability to overcome challenges, rise above their old circumstances, and recognize their inner strength.
2. Ask them to sculpt a phoenix out of clay, emphasizing its wings and dynamic pose to represent rising. Encourage them decorate their phoenix with colorful feathers, glitter, and gems. They can use cellophane to create the effect of flames around the phoenix, symbolizing transformation and strength. Offer paints so the client can add vibrant colors to the sculpture.
3. Discuss the process of creating their phoenix and what each element symbolizes to them. Ask them what happened in their own life to destroy their phoenix—what caused it to burn? Talk about their personal experiences of overcoming challenges and how these experiences have contributed to their sense of worth and inner strength.
4. Help the client create positive affirmations related to their worth (e.g., "I am resilient and can rise above any challenge," "My worth is inherent and unchangeable," "I grow stronger from my experiences," "I shine brightly, just like a phoenix").
5. Encourage them to place their phoenix sculpture in a visible location as a daily reminder of their worth and resilience. Discuss how they can use this metaphor in everyday life to remind themselves of their strength and value.

Feel-Good Waterfall

Age Range
6–17

Goals:

- Help clients create a plan to engage in activities that make them feel good, promoting self-care, happiness, and well-being.

Materials:

- *Feel-Good Waterfall Flip Book* template
- Coloring utensils, stickers, and other decorative materials
- Glue or a stapler

Directions:

1. Inform the client that they are going to create a "feel-good plan" consisting of activities and strategies that make them feel happy and healthy.
2. Introduce the metaphor of a waterfall that keeps the feel-good activities flowing and moving along. Explain that just like a waterfall needs a continuous flow of water to keep going, they need to keep engaging in their feel-good activities to stay happy and balanced.
3. Discuss different activities that make them feel good. Break these down into four categories to help them:
    - **Physical activities** (e.g., sports, dancing, going for a walk, playing an instrument)
    - **Creative activities** (e.g., drawing, painting, crafting)
    - **Relaxing activities** (e.g., reading a book, writing, listening to music, taking a bath)
    - **Social activities** (e.g., spending time with friends or family, playing games)
4. Provide the client with the *Feel-Good Waterfall Flip Book* template. Ask them to draw or write their favorite feel-good activities in each box provided.
5. Ask them to cut out each box and glue or staple them on top of one another to form a vertical book that resembles the continuous "flow" of feel-good activities. Encourage them to decorate their flip book to make it colorful and personal.
6. Discuss how each activity makes them feel good and why it's important to take time for self-care. Explain how incorporating at least one of these activities into their daily routine can help keep their happiness flowing and keep their sadness at bay.

The flip book will look like this:

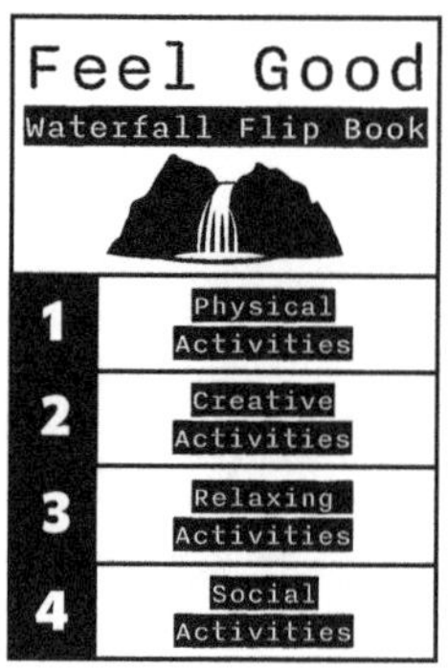

Feel-Good Waterfall Flip Book

Feel Good

Waterfall Flip Book

Glue or staple here

1.
2.
3.

1 Physical Activities

Glue or staple here

1.
2.
3.
4.

2 Creative Activities

Glue or staple here

1.
2.
3.
4.
5.

3 Relaxing Activities

Glue or staple here

1.
2.
3.
4.
5.
6.

4 Social Activities

CHAPTER 16

Raising Resilience

Fall Reaching

Age Range
10–17

Goals:

- Help clients understand and cope with their experiences and emotional states.
- Provide insight, foster resilience, and promote emotional healing.

Materials:

- Large sheets of paper
- Coloring utensils
- Music player

Directions:

1. Explain the concept of "fall reaching" to the client. Discuss how falling can symbolize various challenges and emotional states in their lives, and how reaching out during these times can lead to growth and support. Outline the phases of fall reaching:
    - **The fall:** The feeling of losing control, fear, or being overwhelmed
    - **Reaching out:** Seeking help and support or trying to find stability
    - **Catching on:** Finding something to hold on to, gaining a sense of control or support
    - **Standing up:** Recovery, resilience, and moving forward after a fall
2. Talk to the client about what "the fall" means to them. Have them think about times when they felt like they were falling, losing control, or facing overwhelming challenges. Ask them to draw a picture that represents their fall. This could include images of falling, darkness, chaos, or anything that symbolizes their feelings during challenging times. Prompt them to think about what triggered the fall and how it made them feel.
3. Next, talk about the importance of reaching out for help and support when they feel like they are falling. Discuss different ways they can reach out, such as talking to a trusted adult or friend. Ask them to draw a picture that represents reaching out. This could include images of hands reaching out, people offering support, or other symbols of hope and help. Prompt them to think about who they can reach out to and what kind of support they need.
4. Then ask the client to think about moments when they feel like they have caught on to something that gives them stability or support. Discuss what these moments are like and how the client can recognize them. Ask them to draw a picture that represents catching on. This could include images of holding on to something stable, finding a lifeline, or other symbols of support and security. Prompt them to think about what has helped them feel stable and supported in the past.
5. Finally, talk about the process of standing up after a fall. Discuss the importance of resilience, recovery, and moving forward. Ask them to draw a picture that represents standing up. This could include images of standing tall, overcoming obstacles, or other symbols of strength and resilience. Prompt them to think about what has helped them recover and move forward.
6. Play the song "I'm Still Standing" by Elton John and show them the words as they are sung to instill deeper meaning of resilience for them.

Unbroken Tattoo

Age Range
10–17

Goals:

- Help clients recognize and celebrate their resilience and strength.

Materials:

- Large sheets of paper
- Coloring utensils
- Tattoo stencils or examples (optional)
- Temporary tattoos (optional)

Directions:

1. Explain to the client that they will be creating a tattoo design that symbolizes their resilience, strength, and journey of being "unbroken." Despite their difficult experiences and emotional pain, they have managed to keep moving forward.
2. Talk with the client about what the concept of "unbroken" means to them. Discuss symbols, images, and words that represent their strength and resilience.
3. Encourage them to sketch tattoo ideas that resonate with their personal journey and incorporate the theme of being unbroken. You can offer examples as inspiration, such as:
   - **Symbols:** A phoenix rising, unbreakable chains, a butterfly emerging from a chrysalis, a heart with stitches
   - **Words:** *Resilient*, *survivor*, *strength*, *unbroken*, people's names or initials, dates
   - **Decorative elements:** Flowers, vines, geometric shapes
4. Discuss their design, reflecting on how each element represents their journey and strength. Talk about how this design can serve as a powerful reminder of their resilience.
5. Provide them with some temporary tattoos that symbolize their tattoo to take home.
6. Process with the client:
   - You have been through so much, and yet you keep going. That is true strength.
   - No matter what happened, you are still standing, still growing, and still shining.
   - You are proof that you can face any challenge that arises.
   - FEAR has new meaning: **F**ace **e**verything **a**nd **r**ise!

My Inner Compass

Age Range
10–17

Goals:

- Help clients set and visualize clear goals in various aspects of their lives, making it easier to focus, find balance, overcome hardships, and keep moving in the right direction.
- Remind clients that it is okay to seek help when they are feeling lost.

Materials:

- Large sheet of paper or poster board
- Coloring utensils
- Printout of a compass (optional)
- Stickers and other decorative materials

Directions:

1. Explain to the client that this activity will help them set and visualize goals using the idea of possessing an inner compass that helps them through difficult times by keeping them headed in a positive direction.
2. Have the client draw a large compass with north, south, east, and west labeled (or provide a template of a compass).
3. Introduce the following categories of goals that the client will be setting: personal growth, school/career, relationships, and hobbies/interests. Have the client assign each of the categories to one of the directions on the compass and write down the short-term and long-term goals they want to accomplish in each area. Discuss how each goal contributes to their overall growth and well-being. Here are some examples:
    - **Personal growth:** Learn a new skill, practice self-care, improve their health, read more books
    - **School/career:** Improve their grades, complete a difficult project, learn a new subject, apply for a job or internship
    - **Relationships:** Make new friends, plan a special activity with their family, practice their communication skills, join a club
    - **Hobbies/interests:** Start a new hobby, travel to a new place, participate in a sport, create art
4. Encourage them to decorate the compass to make it personal and meaningful.
5. Use the image of their compass to illustrate how complex and broad their desires are. Discuss how easy it is to get overwhelmed with all that we want to achieve, especially when we are faced with hardships in any of the directions.
6. Explain that of course our goals can change over time, but having a clear idea of what we want to achieve in each direction helps us focus and reduces the potential for setbacks and disappointments. It also helps us become more resilient because when problems arise in one direction, we balance them out by recognizing our successes in the other directions. The compass allows us to stay on a positive course toward self-improvement.

7. Emphasize the importance of asking for help when they feel lost or overwhelmed. Have them write "Ask for help" in the center of the compass as a reminder that it's okay to seek support.
8. Help the client create positive affirmations related to their goals and journey, such as:
   - "I am capable of achieving my goals."
   - "If one direction becomes hard, the other directions can lift me up."
   - "I trust my instincts to guide me."
   - "I can ask for help when I need it."
   - "I am on the path to personal growth and success."
9. Encourage the client to display their compass somewhere visible as a daily reminder of their goals and direction.

Warrior Portal

Age Range **7–17**

Goals:

- Help clients harness their inner strength and resilience.

Materials:

- Poster board or large sheet of paper
- Scissors
- Coloring utensils
- Stickers and other decorative materials

Directions:

1. Explain to the client that this activity will help build strength and resilience through the creation of personal mantras.
2. Talk about the idea of a wounded healer or warrior, someone who has experienced pain and hardship but uses those experiences to help themselves and others.
3. Explain that the client will be creating a "warrior portal" as a way to tap into their inner strength and resilience. Explain that this portal symbolizes entering a space of empowerment and healing.
4. Have the client fold the poster board in half and draw a large circle on it that slightly overlaps the folded edge. Have them cut out this shape—leaving the side with the fold intact—to create a round "door" that can be opened and shut along the fold like a greeting card.
5. Discuss what mantras are: short, powerful statements that can provide motivation and strength. Help the client create a list of personal mantras that resonate with their experiences and aspirations. Examples include:
    - "I am strong and resilient."
    - "I learn from my mistakes."
    - "Failure is an opportunity for positive growth."
    - "My past does not define me."
    - "I can transform my pain into power."
    - "My internal flame cannot be extinguished."
    - "I will walk my path with my chin held high."
    - "I am a warrior of my own life."
6. Ask the client to write their mantras within the portal. Encourage them to decorate the inside and outside of their portal to make it personal and meaningful.
7. Discuss with the client how they can use these mantras in their daily life to build their resilience and self-worth. Reinforce the idea that failures and setbacks are tremendous opportunities for self-reflection and growth. Talk about how some of their negative experiences have made them stronger or wiser.
8. Encourage them to display their warrior portal somewhere visible as a daily reminder of their inner strength and resilience.

Peaks and Valleys

Age Range
8–17

Goals:

- Help clients increase resilience and self-confidence by identifying their strengths and vulnerabilities.

Materials:

- Large sheet of paper or poster board
- Coloring utensils
- Stickers and other decorative materials

Directions:

1. Explain to the client that this activity will help them become stronger and more confident.
2. Ask them to draw a mountain range with multiple peaks and valleys. Explain that the peaks will represent their strengths and achievements while the valleys will symbolize their vulnerabilities and challenges.
3. Have them think about their strengths first. Provide examples, such as honesty, resilience, kindness, determination, or creativity. Encourage them to choose the words that best describe them, or come up with their own, and write one above each peak on their drawing. Discuss moments when they demonstrated these strengths.
4. Then ask them to think about their vulnerabilities or perceived weaknesses. Offer examples like timid, lonely, untrusting, unattractive, or short-tempered. Ask them to write one vulnerability they identify with by each valley in the drawing. Discuss how these vulnerabilities are part of their journey and contribute to their growth.
5. Encourage them to personalize and enhance their mountain drawing. You can ask, "What colors are the peaks and valleys? Are the mountains rocky or smooth, snowcapped or barren?"
6. Discuss how each peak and valley represents different aspects of their life. Reflect on how their strengths have helped them overcome challenges and how acknowledging their vulnerabilities can lead to growth and resilience.
7. Help the client create positive affirmations based on their strengths and vulnerabilities (e.g., "My strengths help me rise to new heights," "I honor my vulnerabilities as part of my journey," "I am proud of my peaks and valleys").
8. Encourage the client to display their mountain drawing somewhere visible as a reminder of their strengths and vulnerabilities.

Future Brag Book

Age Range
7–17

Goals:

- Help clients envision their future and build self-confidence by celebrating their aspirations and potential achievements.

Materials:

- Paper
- Construction paper
- Coloring utensils
- Stickers and other decorative materials
- Photos or printed images (optional)
- Glue or tape
- Stapler

Directions:

1. Explain to the client that the purpose of this activity is to help them envision their future and celebrate their potential achievements through the creation of a "future brag book."
2. Have the client create a book by stapling together at least five pieces of paper, plus two pieces of construction paper as the front and back covers.
3. Encourage them to think about their biggest wishes, fantasies, and desires for each aspect of their life, such as personal achievements, school or career goals, relationships, hobbies, and adventures. For each page in their book, ask them to write or draw what they envision for their future at a different point in time: in five years, in ten years, and so on. Guide them by asking them to complete prompts such as:
   - "______ years from now, I will be called . . ."
   - "I will live . . ."
   - "I will be with . . ."
   - "I will be doing . . ."
4. Encourage them to use the coloring utensils and other decorative materials to personalize each section. They can also include photos or printed images that represent their future achievements. Ask them to decorate the cover, too, and give their future brag book a title.
5. Discuss how visualizing something in detail can help make it come true. Knowing and seeing what they want provides the inspiration to dedicate themselves to achieving it. Affirm that they have the power to shape the future they want through visualization, determination, and hard work. Ask them how each envisioned achievement would make them feel.
6. Reflect on the steps they can take to work toward these goals and dreams. Help them create positive affirmations based on their future brag book, such as:
   - "I am capable of achieving my dreams."
   - "I believe in my potential."
   - "My future is bright and full of possibilities."
7. Encourage the client to keep their future brag book and revisit it regularly as a source of motivation and inspiration.

My Tree of Strength

Age Range
7–17

Goals:

- Help clients identify and celebrate their strengths.

Materials:

- Canvas or poster board
- Precut paper leaves (different colors and sizes)
- Paints and brushes
- Coloring utensils
- Glue or tape

Directions:

1. Explain to the client that this art activity will help them identify and celebrate their strengths. Discuss the metaphor of a "tree of strength," with deep roots that symbolize their foundation and strong branches that represent their growth.
2. Ask them to draw or paint a tree trunk with branches spreading out across the canvas.
3. Provide precut paper leaves in various colors and sizes. Ask them to write one of their strengths on each leaf. Examples might include kindness, determination, creativity, patience, courage, honesty, confidence, gratitude, self-discipline, leadership, curiosity, dependability, generosity, or perseverance.
4. Have them glue the leaves to the branches of the tree. Encourage them to place the leaves where they feel each strength fits best, creating a balanced and full tree. They can add other elements as they wish to personalize and enhance their tree of strength.
5. Discuss with the client how each leaf represents a strength that contributes to their overall resilience and growth. Reflect on specific examples of when they have demonstrated these strengths in their life.
6. Encourage the client to display their tree of strength somewhere visible as a reminder of their strengths and resilience.
7. Process with the client:
    - Even when the limbs of your tree are swaying, you are still able to stay rooted.
    - Your past may have planted you in tough soil, but your seeds of strength push you through.
    - Your branches reach high because you believe in yourself and your future.
    - Each leaf tells a story of victory, blossoming into the unique and powerful person you are.

My Ideal Family

Age Range
8–17

Goals:

- Help clients envision and articulate their ideal family, identifying the qualities and characteristics that would meet all of their needs and provide a nurturing environment for their future.

Materials:

- Poster board or large sheet of paper
- Coloring utensils
- Stickers and other decorative materials
- Wooden peg dolls and clay (for a younger client)
- Photos or printed images (optional)
- Glue or tape

Directions:

1. Explain to the client that the purpose of this activity is to envision their ideal or best possible family situation, focusing on the qualities and characteristics that would meet their needs and provide a nurturing environment.
2. Ask them to think about the qualities and characteristics that are important to them in a family. Discuss what they believe makes a family feel safe, supportive, and loving. Encourage them to reflect on their past experiences and identify or imagine what characteristics were missing from their birth family that led them into foster care (or kinship care, etc.). Stress that this is not about what they don't or didn't have in the past but what they feel they need for the present and future.
3. Provide the client with materials for drawing and collaging (or, for a younger client, some wooden peg dolls and clay to create a model). Ask them to create a visual representation of their ideal family. This could include family members, pets, and the home environment. Have them write down or draw the qualities and characteristics they want in their ideal family. Examples might include love, affection, safety, security, open communication, support, encouragement, fun, laughter, stability, and consistency.
4. Encourage them to use stickers and other decorative materials to personalize and enhance their representation. They can also include photos or printed images.
5. Discuss how creating their ideal family makes them feel. Reflect on how they can use this vision to identify and seek out positive relationships and environments now and in their future.
6. Help the client create positive statements related to their ideal family (e.g., "I deserve a loving and supportive family," "I can create positive relationships in my life," "My ideal family is within reach").
7. Encourage them to display their ideal family representation somewhere visible as a reminder of their vision and goals.

Badge of Courage

Age Range
8–17

Goals:

- Help clients recognize and celebrate their bravery and resilience.

Materials:

- Paper
- Coloring utensils
- Stickers and other decorative materials
- Printouts of blank award ribbons or badges (optional)

Directions:

1. Explain to the client that the purpose of this activity is to help them recognize and celebrate their bravery and resilience by creating and awarding themselves a badge of courage. Discuss the importance of acknowledging their strengths and the courage it takes to navigate the difficult and painful experiences in their life.
2. Encourage them to think about what makes them courageous and resilient and what feelings or situations they have to face that most kids do not.
3. Draw the outline of an award ribbon or badge (or use a premade template). Invite the client to design and decorate their badge of courage. They can include symbols, words, or images that represent their bravery and achievements.
4. Encourage them to write or say out loud a short statement about why they are awarding themselves the badge of courage. Discuss specific examples of bravery, such as overcoming challenges in foster care, staying hopeful, or helping others.
5. Once they are finished, ask them how designing their badge of courage makes them feel. Talk about how they can continue to draw strength from these experiences. Ask them, "If there were one person, other than yourself, that you could receive this award from, who would it be and why?" Whoever they choose, be ready to validate and reassure the client that this person would be proud of them.
6. Assist them in creating positive affirmations related to their badge of courage (e.g., "I am brave and strong," "I have overcome many challenges," "I am proud of my resilience," "I have earned this award").
7. Encourage them to display their badge of courage somewhere visible as a reminder of their strength and bravery.

Foster Care Hero Award

Age Range
6–17

Goals:

- Help clients recognize and celebrate their strengths, achievements, and resilience.

Materials:

- *Foster Care Hero Award* template
- Coloring utensils
- Stickers and other decorative materials

Directions:

1. Before the session, copy the *Foster Care Hero Award* template and fill it out. Also prepare a short statement about the client's unique strengths, achievements, and resilience.
2. In the session, present the award to the client. Explain that you are recognizing and celebrating their strengths, achievements, and resilience by awarding them the Foster Care Hero Award. Discuss the importance of acknowledging their strengths and the courage it takes to navigate life in foster care. Reflect on the client's unique strengths and specific instances where they demonstrated heroism, honesty, bravery, strength, and resilience.
3. Invite the client to personalize their award using the coloring utensils and other decorative materials. Encourage them to add symbols, words, or images that represent their journey.
4. Discuss how receiving this award makes them feel and how they can continue to draw strength from these experiences.
5. Help them congratulate themselves for receiving their award, such as: "Congratulations to me! I am a hero in my own story. It feels good to be seen. I am proud of my achievements and resilience. I have the strength to overcome any challenge."
6. Encourage them to display their Foster Care Hero Award somewhere visible as a reminder of their strengths, achievements, and resilience. Discuss how they can continue to acknowledge and celebrate their heroism in the future.

FOSTER CARE HERO AWARD

Proudly presented to:

____

For their
HONESTY, BRAVERY, and DETERMINATION.
THEIR SUCCESS STORY will be an INSPIRATION
for YEARS TO COME!

From: ____

PHASE 5

Family Trust, Bonding, and Attachment

Many youths in foster care or who have experienced other forms of trauma do not have a basic understanding of trust because it has so often been betrayed. They've been lied to, deceived, avoided, hurt, or subjected to verbal and physical abuse, and they may never have had trust modeled by their families of origin.

Attachment for these children is fragile, like a wilted flower—they need consistent warmth, nurturing, and nourishment every day to grow. This begins with the foster parents or current guardians learning how to fall in love with their child, called "bonding," and how to tend the garden of attachment by planting the seeds of trust.

The family-oriented interventions in the final chapters of this book involve playfulness, acceptance, curiosity, and empathy. They will help clients understand the important role that trust plays in forming strong and sincere attachments. Clients will also learn how the lack of trust contributed to the breakdown of their family of origin.

It is crucial to brief the client's parents or guardians on the nature and intent of these interventions to gain their eager participation. Trust is not won; it is earned. The interventions in this phase offer creative ways for them to earn that trust. They will come to understand the magnitude of their child's experience and the responsibility they hold to not only provide care but to steadfastly supply their child with the essential ingredients of nurturance and dedication.

As Daniel A. Hughes (1997/2004) states, "Trust is the foundation for change" (p. 7). Without trust, the youth cannot feel safe enough to explore their thoughts and feelings, whether with you in the therapy room or at home with their family. Therefore, establishing trust is the primary focus of chapter 14, creating the scaffolding for the final chapter, which supports families in fostering emotional security and healthy attachments. These interventions were inspired by the work of Dr. Hughes, Bryan Post, and Heather Forbes.

Before participating in these interventions, remind the parents or guardians to be aware of seven key nonverbal cues—eye contact, facial expression, tone of voice, gestures, posture, timing, and intensity of response—and how to communicate to their child via these nonverbals. In addition, they should follow their child's lead and attune to these same nonverbal cues in their child, waiting for the child to initiate or disengage. Parents may also use words to reflect back what they see, hear, or feel when observing their child in play: "I see you are smiling and having a wonderful time" or "I hear your laughter" or "I feel so much love—you have so much love in your heart." This creates a synchronized experience with shared attention and reciprocity, as the parent matches the rhythm and affect of their child's experience.

CHAPTER 17

Establishing Trust

Hold On to My Feelings

Age Range
4–17

Goals:

- **Help parents/guardians create a safe and warm holding environment, build trust, and foster secure attachment with the client.**
- **Help the client express and heal their grief from early attachment trauma and separations.**

Note: This intervention is done with the client and their current parents/guardians (e.g., foster parents, adoptive parents) to support secure attachment. It is important to perform this intervention in a comfortable setting, whether that be in your office or a welcoming space at the client's home. Discuss the activity with the parents before the session starts so they understand the method and intention and can join in with an attitude of playfulness, total acceptance, curiosity, and empathy. These positive, nonthreatening attitudes create a model that meets the needs of the client by providing a container for their feelings, producing a therapeutic environment where the client can feel safe, felt, heard, and seen.

Materials:

- Old phone book
- Pillowcase
- Permanent markers
- Notebook and writing utensils

Directions:

1. Introduce the activity to the client by saying something like, "We've noticed you've been holding on to a lot of big feelings and wanted to give you a way to release these feelings by letting you rip up this old phone book. And guess who is going to clean up and hold on to all the feelings? Not you, *we are*."

2. Have one of the parents playfully entice the client to participate by saying, "Wait. I've had some big feelings too." Have them open the phone book, rip out a few pages at a time, and tear the paper into pieces while stating examples of what they are feeling in the form of "I feel ____ because ____" (e.g., "I feel mad because my doctor told me I can't drink soda for breakfast!"). They can also express their frustration, anger, or pain without words via their facial expressions and by throwing the pieces of paper up in the air. Making it seem fun and cathartic is a critical element that allows the client to feel safe to release some of their own pent-up feelings.

3. As the client begins tearing up the phone book to express their own big feelings, keep the following guidelines in mind. These should also be shared with the parents prior to the intervention:
    - It is strongly recommended that the parents encourage the client to use feelings words and "I" statements to help them build emotional intelligence. However, do not force the client if they are nonverbal. Their resistance may be a signal that they are not feeling safe enough or emotionally ready to verbalize at this time.
    - It is recommended to begin the activity with lighthearted feelings and complaints, allowing the client to feel more comfortable with the process before digging into more painful core issues.
    - Prepare the parents to be very aware of their own state of being and to not be reactive or triggered by any feelings their child may share. This intervention is designed to get the big feelings out of the dark and into the light so they can be dealt with and the

client and family can heal. Sometimes a client might say something that is painful or shocking for the parents to hear, such as "I'm mad because I wish I was never adopted!" or "I'm sad because you're not my real parents." Let the client express their feelings without criticism, rejection, anger, or dismissal.

- You and the parents should keep an open, stress-free face, show curiosity (raised eyebrows), and breathe deeply to help calm down and regulate any arousal states the client brings out and stay connected. Encourage the parents to enjoy the client's process by oohing and aahing with amazement as the client rips up the paper. Active and verbal support keeps the parent connected and engaged while increasing levels of oxytocin, the bonding hormone.
- Have the parents bring a small journal or notebook into the intervention. If they feel they are becoming dysregulated and overwhelmed, have them take a moment to write down what it is that is triggering them and ask them to revisit those notes later.

4. If the client is reluctant to participate, some prompting is appropriate. Encourage the parents to ask, "Would you be willing to let Mommy or Daddy speak a feeling you have said before so we can feel it together?" Doing this often entices the client to share or correct a notion, allowing the intervention to progress.
5. Every issue brought up by the client will not be resolved after the first session. Providing the opportunity for this intervention on a regular basis will begin to build more trust and allow the client the freedom to express more pent-up feelings in the future. This is not about "solving" any issues on the spot, but allowing the client a safe space to express them. A good time to stop the activity is after an emotional epiphany, after a particularly positive or emotional exchange, after 45 minutes if the client still seems to be avoiding the deeper issues, or when the client indicates that they're done.
6. Have the client and their parents take a moment and breathe. Encourage them to look at the scattered papers around the room and see them as the client's emotional life. Make statements such as: "Wow! Look at all these feelings! They sure can get messy. Are feelings messy sometimes? Thank you for letting us know about all these. Now, we are going to give them all the love and care that they deserve." (While acknowledging the messiness, be careful not to refer to the paper—symbolizing the client's deepest feelings—as "garbage" or similar.)
7. Have the client take a comfy seat and "supervise" as the parents pick up each feeling (piece or pile of paper), identify it, and place it in a pillowcase while communicating great empathy and care. For example, if the client had expressed, "I'm angry that I can't live with my birth mommy!" their foster mom might say, "I'm sorry, too, that your birth mommy could not be your everyday mommy. This feeling I am going to hold on to and give it lots of love." Encourage the parents to do what they feel is authentic in their hearts at this moment. Some parents kiss each torn piece of paper or hug piles of feelings and do not say much, but convey to the client through facial expressions how much this means to them. Some are brought to tears upon truly understanding the depths of the client's grief and their responsibility to experience these emotions along with their child. The reverse side is witnessing the client's face light up and become amazed by their parents' capacity to be so reflective, open, and honest about the reality of their experiences and the realization that they are truly loved.
8. When all the feelings have been identified and collected, ask the client, "Are there any feelings we have missed?" The client can scan the room and point them out, so all have been acknowledged.

9. Have the parents write a closing response on the pillowcase, either together or individually, such as: "I understand. I respect all of your feelings. I am here to listen and give love. I want to help hold on to your sadness, so you don't have to hold on all by yourself."
10. Have the parents tell the client that they are going to hold on to these feelings and keep them safe until the client tells them to let go of them. This helps the client to feel that their big feelings will be secure and their parents understand and accept them.
11. At a moment when the client is not present or in a private message to the parents, tell them to carry the feelings on their shoulder or arm at home throughout the week to show their child they are holding on to their feelings. When the client sees this, the parents can acknowledge this empathic act with compassion and love. Encourage the parents to do this exercise at home as needed.

Stop, Freeze, Receive

Age Range
4–10

Goals:

- Help the client and their parents/guardians establish a deeper connection, build trust, and nurture feelings of love and safety.
- Help the client feel heard, seen, and respected while building self-regulation, resilience, and attachment.

Materials:

- *Good Parent Messages* handout
- Heart-shaped pillow
- Small trampoline or couch to jump on (optional)

Directions:

1. This intervention is designed for a family session and is particularly effective at the start of the session. Before you begin, ask the parents to reflect on the past week and take mental note of positive things they have noticed as well as what may have been difficult or challenging, yet the client and parents were able to problem-solve together and come back to a place of regulation.
2. Explain that this activity is designed to increase communication and attachment within the family and to help the client learn how to receive and accept positive messages from their parents. Provide the parents with the *Good Parent Messages* handout to use as inspiration and guidance.
3. Have one of the parents hold the heart pillow. Tell that client that at the count of three they are to start jumping in place and keep jumping until the parent says, "Stop!"—at which point they must freeze in place. The parent will then give the heart pillow a big hug and say out loud a message of strength, gratitude, or encouragement for the client.
4. After the verbal message is given, the parent throws the pillow to the client. Instruct the client to take that message in and feel the warmth of the pillow by hugging it and absorbing that sensory message in their heart and soul.
5. Then ask the client to throw the pillow back to one of their parents and begin jumping again, waiting for the next message.
6. Go back and forth for as long as the client wants. This intervention builds trust and instills in the child that they are loved, valued, and safe in their relationship.

Good Parent Messages

Recognizing Strengths	Acknowledging Vulnerabilities
You showed great honesty in facing that.	It is so hard for you when you are not allowed to do that.
You did a great job of controlling your anger when you were mad at me.	You are really hard on yourself when you do something wrong.
It took a lot of courage to bring that up to me.	Nothing seems to be going right for you lately.
You really want to get good at that. I see how important it is for you.	Sometimes you get so upset it seems to ruin your whole day.
Your friend is really important to you.	It seems so hard to just relax and be confident that things will go your way.
You are so brave to tell me how you feel.	It must be hard if you think you're bad.
You have a lot of energy today!	If you think I don't love you, that must be so hard for you.
I am so proud that you told me that you think I don't care. I see how important our relationship is to you.	If you think I don't care, does it affect what you think about yourself?
I appreciate your honesty and deep feelings you expressed to me earlier. I see you and hear you.	I am sorry you do the best you can and it still doesn't feel good enough for you. I see how hard you are on yourself.

Early Life	School Age	Teen
I love you.	I love you.	I love you.
I welcome and cherish you.	I welcome and cherish you.	I welcome and cherish you.
I see you and I hear you.	I see you and I hear you.	I see you and I hear you.
It is not what you do but who you are that I love.	It is not what you do but who you are that I love.	It is not what you do but who you are that I love.
I am proud of you.	I am proud of you.	I am proud of you.
Over and over, I will show you how to trust.	You can trust your inner voice.	I have confidence in you.
I am not leaving.	I am not leaving.	I will not give up on you.
My consistency of meeting your needs will last longer than your chaos.	My consistency of meeting your needs will last longer than your chaos.	My care is more lasting than your rejection.
I will recognize and respond to your needs.	I appreciate that you are different from me.	I appreciate that you are different from me.
Sometimes I will tell you no, and that's because I love you.	My patience is stronger than your anger.	My love is bigger than your hate.

Protect My Heart

Age Range
4–9

Goals:

- Help parents/guardians establish a deeper connection with the client, build trust, and reinforce love and safety.
- Help the client understand that they are truly loved and cared for.

Materials:

- Play-dough or clay in blue and yellow
- Rolling pin
- "I love you" themed book*

Directions:

1. Explain to the client and their parents/guardians that in this activity they are each going to create a replica of their own heart. Give each parent an equal amount of yellow play-dough but give the client a smaller amount of blue play-dough. Encourage them to make their hearts in whatever shape they want.
2. Have the client place their blue heart on the table. If two parents are involved, have them place the client's blue heart between their two yellow hearts (like a sandwich). If just one parent is involved, have them place their heart on top of the client's.
3. Instruct the parents to gently knead, spread, and wrap the yellow hearts around the blue one to cover it. As they do so, encourage the parents to verbalize how they will care for their child's heart, such as "I will keep your heart warm and protect it from harm" and "I will console your heart when it is aching." Prompt the parents as needed by making observations about the client's heart (e.g., "I know your heart is tough and needs so much love and warmth and cuddles and kisses") or posing questions to the parents (e.g., "Can you love their heart for a long, long time, through thick and thin no matter what?").
4. Ask the client if they have any empty feelings or missing pieces of their heart, such as missing family members, a special object they no longer have, old friends, or even lost memories. If they do, have them create another blue heart and ask them to poke holes in it to represent their losses. Ask the parents to use their yellow play-dough to fill in the holes while keeping the shape of the heart. Sometimes the client will want to fill the holes in themselves, but encourage the parents to do it while verbalizing more messages of support and love. Explain to the client that they can let love in and out of their heart and that the love from their parents' hearts is safe and warm.
5. Once the client's play-dough hearts have been enveloped and filled with their parents' love, ask the parents to read an "I love you" themed book to their child.

* There are many books with this theme, such as *I Love You Through and Through* by Bernadette Rossetti-Shustak and illustrated by Caroline Jayne Church.

Wrap Me Up in Love

Age Range
4–17

Goals:

- Help the client's parents/guardians create a safe and warm holding environment, build trust, and foster secure attachment.

Materials:

- Toilet paper (several rolls)
- Wrapping paper, bows, and stickers
- Small chair
- Hand fan
- Snacks

Directions:

1. Inform the client and their parents/guardians that they are going to wrap each other up in toilet paper one at a time. Most kids think this is hilarious and want to be wrapped up first.
2. Set a small chair in the center of the room and have the client sit in it.
3. Instruct the parents to start wrapping toilet paper at the client's feet and work their way up the entire body, excluding the face (unless the child demands it!). As they do so, have them verbalize that they are wrapping the client in a web or cocoon of warmth, happiness, love, security, and so on. Encourage them to be creative and express their love and care for their child.
4. Ask the client how it feels to be wrapped up in love. Let them respond in full and sit in the warmth of the wrap. This creates a womb-like experience of feeling safe and secure, fostering unconditional love between the client and their parents.
5. Encourage the parents to decorate the wrap by adding wrapping paper, stickers, and bows. Have them demonstrate further care by fanning the client and checking in to see how they feel and what they need (e.g., juice, a snack, a love sticker).
6. Once the decoration is complete, have the parents say they are going to count to three and on three the client can stand up and break free from the toilet paper.
7. You can repeat the process with the child wrapping their parents if they wish to do so.
8. During the intervention parents can verbally express to the client the following:
   - No matter what happens, my love will always be wrapped around you.
   - You are safe in my love. Nothing can take that away.
   - This wrapping is a hug that never disappears, even when you can't see it.
   - You belong here, always. My love surrounds you like this wrap.
   - This love is your shield and will hold you up even when things feel hard.
   - You can always come to me, no matter what. My love will always catch you.
   - Even when we are apart, this love stays with you, gently wrapping around your heart.

Tower of Trust

Age Range
6–10

Goals:

- Help the client and their parents/guardians identify and define what builds trust and what breaks trust within their family.

Materials:

- Wooden tumbling tower blocks in four colors (nine of each color)
- *Tower of Trust Cards* handout cut into cards
- Index cards
- Writing utensils

Directions:

1. Explain to the client and their parents/guardians that they are going to use wooden tumbling tower blocks to build a "tower of trust." Discuss how some actions cause trust to be broken, like how removing a block from a tower can make it less stable. But trust can be rebuilt over time, which is like adding new blocks to the tower that make it even taller than before.
2. Ask them to create a tower with the blocks in a random order of colors, with three blocks on the bottom in one direction, the next three stacked on top in the opposite direction, and so on until there is a twelve-story tower.
3. Explain the meaning of each color block (substituting different colors if needed based on your selection): blue is building trust, red is breaking down trust, green is repairing trust, and yellow is sprouting new trust. Define and give examples of these categories if needed.
4. Lay the game cards face down in a pile. Explain that the family will read each card together, decide which category the example on the card belongs in, and follow the corresponding instructions:
    - **Building trust (blue block):** If the card suggests an action that builds trust, the family must pull out a blue block and add it to the top of the tower.
    - **Breaking down trust (red block):** If the card suggests an action that breaks trust, the family must remove a red block from the tower.
    - **Repairing trust (green block):** If the card suggests an action that repairs trust, the family must pull out a green block to fill any gap in the tower. If there are no gaps, place the green block on top of the tower.
    - **Sprouting trust (yellow block):** If the card suggests an action that sprouts new trust, the family must pull out a yellow block to fill any gap in the tower. If there are no gaps, place the yellow block on top of the tower.
5. This activity also serves as an assessment tool. Pay attention to the stories and examples shared by the family members as they reflect on past relationships and trust experiences. This can provide valuable insights into their dynamics and individual perceptions of trust. Provide blank index cards for the client to create their own variables of trust to add to the deck, to personalize this intervention.

Tower of Trust Cards

Offering genuine apologies and acknowledging mistakes	Taking steps to make up for wrongdoings	Discussing issues openly and honestly to resolve misunderstandings
Demonstrating consistent behavior over time to rebuild confidence	Praising and encouraging positive growth in others	Building memories by creating positive experiences together
Engaging in activities that promote teamwork and cooperation	Encouraging open and honest discussions about feelings and expectations	Establishing and respecting healthy boundaries within the relationship
Working together toward common goals and celebrating achievements	Disregarding or belittling someone's feelings, needs, or opinions	Being unreliable or unpredictable in behavior and actions
Keeping promises and consistently following through on commitments	Paying attention and showing interest when someone is speaking	Offering help and support without being asked
Being truthful and open in all interactions	Being dependable and showing up when needed	Showing consideration and respect for each other's feelings and opinions
Being dishonest and withholding important information	Failing to follow through on commitments	Sharing someone's secrets or personal information without permission

Musical Hats

Age Range
5–17

Goals:

- Help the family establish rapport, trust, and empathy.
- Normalize emotional responses, encourage sharing about themselves, and build self-esteem.

Materials:

- Variety of hats
- Name tag stickers
- Music player

Directions:

1. Introduce to the family an assortment of hats and ask, "If you could be a hat, which one would you be?" Have them each pick one hat. Take a few moments and ask each person what was special about the hat they chose and what it says about them. Have each person write their name on a name tag sticker and stick it to the front of their hat.
2. Have the family sit in a circle. Explain that this game is called "Musical Hats" and tell them the rules: While the music is playing, they will pass the hats clockwise around the circle. When you stop the music, they must all freeze, read the name on the hat in their hands, put it on their head, and wait their turn for you to ask them a question.
3. Moving clockwise, ask each participant a question about the person whose hat they are wearing. If they don't know the answer, have them take a guess. After each answer, the person then tells them if they were correct or incorrect and gives them the right answer. Here are some suggestions of questions to ask the family members:
   - What is their favorite color?
   - What is their favorite activity?
   - What is their favorite meal?
   - What is their favorite song?
   - What do you think they are happy about?
   - What do you think they are sad about?
   - What do you think they wish for?
   - What do you have in common with this person?
   - What makes you different from this person?
   - What do you want this person to know about you?
   - What do you think is important to this person?

Secure Nest Sculpture

Age Range
4–10

Goals:

- Increase trust, attachment, love, and resilience within the family while reducing the sense of abandonment, loss, and unimportance in the client.

Materials:

- Twigs from nature (two to five inches long)
- Modeling clay
- Shredded paper
- Aluminum foil
- Paper cutouts of leaves

Directions:

1. Explain to the client and their parents/guardians that they are going to make a sculpture that visually represents their family's secure nest. Just as birds do, they will take great care in constructing the nest, ensuring the family will be safe and warm even on cold and stormy days.
2. First, ask the family members to each craft a small bird out of the clay to represent themselves. They can use whatever colors they choose and use twigs to add a beak and legs if they wish.
3. Then have them craft the foundation for the nest by creating a bowl shape that is big enough to fit all the bird figurines inside. Encourage them to decorate the nest with foil, twigs, and shredded paper, making a it safe and comfortable.
4. Next, have them write on paper leaves what trust means to them and their family and lay these on the bottom of the nest to make it comfortable, like a blanket of leaves.
5. Finally, have them each place their bird in the nest.
6. Encourage dialogue and sharing during the creation of the nest. Ask questions such as:
   - Why did you choose to put those twigs there?
   - Where will each family member sleep?
   - Will it be warm enough?
   - How do you make sure no one falls out?
   - How high in the tree will it go?
7. Discuss how it feels to have created this nest together. Invite them to take it home to their real "nest" as a reminder of their security, trust, and connection.

My Trust Mandala

Age Range: **8–17**

Goals:

- Increase the client's sense of belonging, self-esteem, and confidence within their family and develop healthy attachments and trust.

Materials:

- Paper
- Coloring utensils
- Assortment of stencils

Directions:

1. Explain to the family that the parents/guardians are going to support the client while they create a trust symbol, called a mandala, that will remind them of how they are building trust within the family.
2. Have the client draw or trace a large circle on the paper and divide it into three sections. They can divide it like a bull's-eye, like a pie chart, or another way that is meaningful to them.
3. Ask the client to choose three symbols of trust to combine in their mandala. They can draw, use stencils, and write inside the circle to represent how they define and feel about trust within their family. Provide examples of trust symbols as inspiration, such as:
   - **Handshake:** Trust is a commitment to uphold a promise and mutual respect.
   - **Lock and key:** Trust grants access; a lock provides security and protection.
   - **Heart to heart:** Trust, love, and care are at the heart of any strong bond.
   - **Bridge:** Trust creates connection and the ability to overcome obstacles.
   - **Anchor:** This represents a steady trusting foundation in turbulent times.
   - **Chain:** Each link contributes to the chain's overall strength, forming an unbreakable bond.
   - **Compass:** Trust takes guidance, direction, and reliability.
   - **Eagle:** Trust involves belief in someone's abilities and their vision for the future.
   - **Sun:** Trust in the warmth, light, and reliability of caring people.
   - **Scales of justice:** Trust is essential for balance, fairness, and equity.
   - **Tree:** Trust grows over time and provides support and shelter.
   - **Dove:** Trust there is peace, serenity, and harmony within.
   - **Shield:** Trust protects and defends the value of relationships.
   - **Phoenix:** Trust, once broken, can be rebuilt stronger than before.
4. Encourage the client to share with their parents why the symbols are important to them and how they are feeling by asking questions such as:
   - What does this trust symbol mean to you?
   - Why did you choose that symbol?
   - What can your parents do to strengthen this symbol of trust?
5. Encourage the family to take the trust mandala home as a reminder of their trust, care, and commitment to each other.

CHAPTER 18

Strengthening Bonds

Make a Connection

Age Range: **4–17**

Goals:

- Help the client and their parents/guardians strengthen their bonds, communication skills, emotional regulation, and empathy.
- Reduce feelings of anxiety and displacement by fostering a sense of connection and understanding.

Materials:

- None needed

Directions:

1. Explain to the client and their parent/guardian that this activity is designed to help them understand how their brains can work together to make connections, improve communication, and build empathy.
2. Explain that "Make a Connection" is a game where they will each think of a word and try to make a connection between their words. Go over the instructions:
    a. Have the client and parent sit facing each other.
    b. Ask both participants to silently think of any object.
    c. Have them count to three together and say their words out loud at the same time.
    d. If they identify a relationship between their two words (e.g., "book" and "shelf"), they have made a connection. They can high-five each other when successful.
    e. If they do not identify any relationship between their words, they will keep playing with new words until they make a connection.
3. After each round, discuss why they think the words were or were not connected. Encourage them to talk about how they felt when they made a connection and how they felt when they didn't.
4. After they are successful making object connections, choose new categories (e.g., animals, food, school items) to narrow down the words and make it easier to find connections. You can also explore the following variations:
    - **Story Connection:** After saying the words, the client and parent will create a short story that includes both words. This fosters creative thinking and collaboration.
    - **Emotion Connection:** Ask them to think of words that describe feelings and then discuss how the words they choose connect to each other's emotional experiences.
5. Encourage them to use this exercise as a tool whenever they feel disconnected or misunderstood.

"I Message" Egg Hunt

Age Range: **4–16**

Goals:

- Develop trust, attachment, and love while reducing reactivity, dysregulation, and anxiety within the family.
- Provide a safe and warm holding environment for the family members to convey loving messages to one another, build trust, and secure the attachment.

Materials:

- Twelve plastic Easter eggs
- Small pieces of paper
- Writing utensils

Directions:

1. Inform the client and their parents/guardians that they are going to play a fun hide-and-seek game designed to strengthen their family bond through honest and positive messaging.
2. Have the parents write "I messages" on paper, fold them up, and put each message inside a plastic egg. The messages must be positive and loving. For example:
    - I appreciate you when you help me with the groceries.
    - I love your smile.
    - I care about your feelings.
    - I notice what a great friend you are.
    - I see how hard you are working at school.
3. The client can also write their own positive "I messages" for the parents if they wish. Assist if necessary.
4. When the messages are ready, ask the client to close their eyes while the parents hide the eggs around the room.
5. Have the client go on a scavenger hunt for the eggs. Give them some direction by yelling out "hot" when they get close to an egg and "cold" when they stray far away.
6. Once an egg is found, have the client open it up and hand it to the parent to read it to them face to face. If the client has written their own messages to their parents, have the client read those messages to the parents.

Family Handprint

Age Range:
4–12

Goals:

- Increase a sense of importance, belonging, security, and attachment between the client and their family while decreasing their sense of alienation and abandonment.

Materials:

- Poster board
- Finger paints
- Paper plates
- Bowl with water
- Towel
- Coloring utensils
- Stickers, glitter, and other decorative items

Directions:

1. Explain to the family that they are going to create a family collage out of each person's handprint. The client will be the leader, director, and curator of the handprints.
2. Set up a workspace with the poster board and finger paints. Pour different colors of paints onto paper plates. Have a bowl of water and a towel ready for cleaning hands between prints.
3. Ask the client to make decisions about the collage and to guide the other family members through the process:
   - How many handprints will each person make—one hand or both?
   - What are the color choices for each family member?
   - How will the handprints be placed on the poster board (e.g., in a circle, overlapping, scattered)?
4. Encourage each family member to write their name and a positive word or phrase that represents them near their handprint. They can also add stickers, glitter, drawings, or other decorations that represent the family's interests or shared memories.
5. Once the collage is complete, gather the family and ask the following questions:
   - What are your thoughts about this family collage?
   - Who in your family collage do you want to learn more about?
   - How does it feel to be connected to each other in this way?
6. Ask the client to reflect on their experience with these questions:
   - What is something special about this family that is different from other families you have lived with?
   - What do you most need to stay connected and trusting with your family today?
   - What are some positive feelings or thoughts you have about this activity and your family?
7. Encourage the family to find a special place in their home to display the family handprint collage as a reminder of their connection, unity, and sense of togetherness.

Musical Bags

Age Range: **8–17**

Goals:

- Reduce feelings of fear, worry, and anxiety in the child client by providing a fun, safe environment where the family members can learn more about each other and increase trust and attachment.

Materials:

- Paper lunch bags
- Markers
- Slips of paper

Directions:

1. Inform the client and their parents/guardians that they will be playing a fun game to help them get to know each other better.
2. Give each person several lunch bags. On each bag, have them write a question or prompt for the others to answer. Assist them in formulating their questions as they relate to their needs and feelings. For instance, the client may create bags that say:
    - What do Mommy and Daddy love about me?
    - When I am scared/sad/mad, Mommy or Daddy can . . .
    - I'm happy when Mommy or Daddy . . .
    - I'm unhappy when Mommy or Daddy . . .
    - What do I love about Mommy and Daddy?

    The parents may create bags that say:

    - I am proud of [*client's name*] because . . .
    - [*Name*] gets scared/sad/mad when I . . .
    - [*Name*] is happy when I . . .
    - What I love about [*name*] is . . .
    - My feelings get hurt when [*name*] does . . .
3. Have the parents and client write their answers to the questions on slips of paper and put them in the corresponding bags.
4. For each bag, have the person who wrote the question read it aloud along with the answers. They and the others can then respond, either by agreeing with the answer or correcting the answer as to what their needs are and what they want the other family members to know.

Family Memory of Feelings

Age Range: **5–12**

Goals:

- **Help the client externalize and identify memories while reducing feelings of grief, loss, and alienation.**
- **Foster open communication, understanding, bonding, and attachment among the family members.**

Note: This intervention works well with new clients. It is an effective, unthreatening way to build rapport and develop an understanding of the family dynamics and the client's life and personality.

Materials:

- **Memory card game, either standard or a custom family photo game (see variation below)**

Directions:

1. Before the session, if you will be using the family photo variation, ask the client's parents/guardians for about twelve photos showing the client with their other family members and each family member individually. You will need two copies of each photo, printed out at the same size to create a set of custom memory cards.
2. In the session, explain to the client and their parents/guardians that they will be playing a memory game as a way to share about their family memories. Shuffle the cards and place them face down in a grid.
3. Have the client play the memory game by turning over the pictures two at a time until they find a match. (If the two pictures they turn over do not match, the client should turn them face down again and try again.)
4. Once they have a match, ask them to verbalize a memory that relates to the picture. Prompt them if necessary by asking questions. If you are using a standard memory game, you might ask questions like:
    - Picture of a cake: What has been your favorite birthday?
    - Picture of a bird: If you could fly, where would you fly to?
    - Picture of a cat: How are you like a cat?
    - Picture of a dog: Who in your family is like a dog?

    If you are using family photos, ask questions like:

    - How old are you in this picture?
    - What are you doing?
    - Who is with you?
    - What do you remember most about that day?
    - Who is this a picture of?
    - What was it like the first time you met this person?
    - What does this person do to make you laugh or smile?
    - What does this person like to do? Eat? Watch?
5. Continue until all the cards have been matched and the memories explored.

Gotcha! You're Doing Good!

Age Range: **8–17**

Goals:

- Promote open and clear communication, bonding, and understanding between family members while decreasing the client's sense of alienation, isolation, and repression.
- Help parents/guardians attune to the client's needs while allowing the client to feel empowered within the family dynamic.

Note: This intervention is very effective to use with birth parents (as well as with foster parents or the client's current guardians). Clients usually fear the negative impulses, behaviors, or outbursts of their birth parent that led to the separation, and having the birth parent participate in this exercise empowers the client, who becomes eager to encourage more good behaviors. It also helps the birth parent attune to the needs of their child by providing the communication and positive attachment the client desperately craves.

Materials:

- Index cards (24 multicolored)
- Coloring utensils
- Jar
- Adhesive label or paper and tape

Directions:

1. Explain to the client and their parents/guardians that this intervention is designed to help the client communicate to the parents the things they do that the client enjoys or respects. The client will do this by creating "Gotcha! You're Doing Good!" cards for their parents. They will give one of these cards to their parents when they catch them doing something that they like and want their parents to do more often.
2. Have the client write on one side of each index card, "Gotcha! You're Doing Good!" Make a dozen to start. Have them label the jar "The Good Jar." They can also decorate and personalize the jar and cards (leaving the other side of the cards blank to be filled in later).
3. Explain to the client there are two ways to give their parents a reward:
   - Give their parent the card and tell them out loud what they did well.
   - Write on the back of the card what the parent did well and then hand them the card.
4. Instruct the parents that when they receive a card, they must acknowledge the gift with a "thank you" and, after reading or hearing the message, place it in the Good Jar. At the end of each week if the parents have received six or more cards, the client and parents can decide on an outing or activity to celebrate the parents' good behavior and the client's good communication.

My Family Wishing Stone

Age Range: **4–17**

Goals:

- Help the family establish a deeper connection and solidify boundaries while decreasing feelings of isolation and anxiety.

Materials:

- Modeling clay
- Rolling pin
- River rocks
- Plastic knife

Directions:

1. Explain to the family that they are going to create a family wishing stone together by each making a handprint in a piece of clay and then connecting their hands into one stone.
2. Give each family member an equal amount of clay. Have them roll and shape their clay into a piece that is about half an inch thick. Then they can press their hand into the clay to create an imprint.
3. Bring the hands of clay together in the center of the table and add one more piece of clay, also a half inch thick, to connect them all together at the center. Each family member can knead and connect their clay to the center clay.
4. Invite the family members to place river rocks around the molded hands for decoration. To complete the family stone, use the knife to carve their last name (e.g., "The Jones Family" or "The Díaz-Petersons") on the centerpiece. They can add decorative rocks around the name as well.
5. Ask each family member to say a wish for their family, something either for the present or for the future. They can also say wishes for each individual family member if they choose to. Allow whatever the family members feel they need to say to acknowledge their connection, bond, and love as a family. Some examples include:
    - Our handprints symbolize that every member of our family is uniquely valued.
    - Each handprint in our family stone represents a pledge to care for one another.
    - Our family is built on connection. Each handprint is a sign that we are all in this together.
    - Just like these handprints leave an imprint, our family leaves an imprint in our hearts and souls.
6. Encourage the family to take their stone home as a reminder of this connection.

Forget-Me-Not Bags

Age Range: **8–17**

Goals:

- Help the parent/guardian prepare the client for a temporary separation to continue to foster bonding and attachment; reduce the client's fear, worry, and anxiety; and increase their sense of belonging and being loved.

Materials:

- Two small fabric or paper bags
- Twenty precut paper hearts
- Stickers (hearts, happy faces, etc.)
- Feathers or pom-poms
- Coloring utensils

Directions:

1. Inform the client and their parent/guardian that they will be creating "forget-me-not" bags to help them know that they are thinking of each other while they are temporarily separated (this may be due to the parent taking a trip for work or some other reason).
2. Give the client and parent one bag each. On the bag, have them write the other's name (the name of the person they will miss while they are separated).
3. Next, have each person write messages for the other on paper hearts and place them in the bag. Invite them to also use the feathers and pom-poms as a sensory reminder of the tenderness they feel and want to give to each other. If necessary, help them formulate what they will write to let each other know that they are thinking about them while they are apart. This might include what they love about each other, what they will miss about each other, and reminders of their connection.

   For instance, the client's forget-me-nots may say:

   - We are not apart—we are forever in each other's hearts.
   - I want you to know . . .
   - Please remember . . .
   - I feel . . .
   - I need . . .

   The parent's forget-me-nots may say:

   - You have the strength to get through this.
   - I'm thinking of you.
   - I'm holding you in my heart.
   - I'll be home soon.
   - Keep going—you're doing great!
4. When they have finished writing their forget-me-nots, have them exchange bags and read out loud the messages that were written to them.

5. Instruct the parent to pack their forget-me-not bag in their suitcase, show the client that it's there, safe and sound, and promise to read their heart notes every day while they are away. Tell the client to keep their forget-me-not bag close to them while their parent is away and read the heart notes whenever they need to.
6. Complete the activity by saying, "Though miles may lie between us, we are never far apart, for family doesn't count miles—it's measured by the heart. You will forget me not." Have this written on two paper hearts and place one in each of their bags.

References

For your convenience, purchasers can download and print the worksheets from this book at **pesipubs.com/atrisktoolbox**

Balint, M. (1968). *The basic fault: Therapeutic aspects of regression.* Tavistock Publications.

Boston Center for Contemplative Practice. (2019, April 16). *Imagine ideal parents by Dr. Daniel P. Brown* [Video]. YouTube. https://www.youtube.com/watch?v=z2au4jtL0O4&t=81s

Dana, D. (2020). *Polyvagal exercises for safety and connection: 50 client-centered practices.* W. W. Norton.

Hartman, A. (1995). Diagrammatic assessment of family relationships. *Families in Society, 76*(2), 111–122.

Hobday, A., & Ollier, K. (1998). *Creative therapy: Activities with children and adolescents.* Wiley.

Hughes, D. A. (2004). *Facilitating developmental attachment: The road to emotional recovery and behavioral change in foster and adopted children.* Jason Aronson. (Original work published 1997)

Kabat-Zinn, J. (2023). *Wherever you go, there you are: Mindfulness meditation in everyday life* (30th anniversary ed.). Hachette Go. (Original work published 1994)

Kaiser Greenland, S. (2016). *Mindful games: Sharing mindfulness and meditation with children, teens, and families.* Shambhala.

Kedmy, E. (2023). *The mandala way: A creative journey into healing and self-empowerment.* Watkins.

Kübler-Ross, E. (1969). *On death and dying.* Macmillan.

Kübler-Ross, E., & Kessler, D. (2005). *On grief and grieving: Finding the meaning of grief through the five stages of loss.* Scribner.

Levine, P. A. (2010). *In an unspoken voice: How the body releases trauma and restores goodness.* North Atlantic Books.

Levine, P. A., & Kline, M. (2007). *Trauma through a child's eyes: Awakening the ordinary miracle of healing.* North Atlantic Books.

Oaklander, V. (1978). *Windows to our children: A Gestalt approach to children and adolescents.* Gestalt Journal Press.

Parnell, L. (2008). *Tapping in: A step-by-step guide to activating your healing resources through bilateral stimulation.* Sounds True.

Rosenberg, L., & Guy, D. (1998). *Breath by breath: The liberating practice of insight meditation.* Shambhala.

Rosenberg, M. B. (2015). *Nonviolent communication: A language of life.* PuddleDancer Press.

Siegel, D. J. (2010). *Mindsight: The new science of personal transformation.* Bantam Books.

van der Kolk, B. A. (2014). *The body keeps the score: Brain, mind, and body in the healing of trauma.* Penguin.

van Gulden, H., & Vick, C. (2005). *Learning the dance of attachment: An adoptive/foster parent's guide to nurturing healthy development.* Authors.

West, C. (2021). *We all have parts.* (S. Gong, Illus.). PESI Publishing.

Williams, M., Teasdale, J., Segal, Z., & Kabat-Zinn, J. (2007). *The mindful way through depression: Freeing yourself from chronic unhappiness.* The Guilford Press.

Zweig, C., & Abrams, J. (Eds.). (1991). *Meeting the shadow: The hidden power of the dark side of human nature.* Jeremy P. Tarcher.

About the Author

Jeanette Yoffe, MA, MFT, has specialized for the past 20 years in the treatment of children, teens, and adults with histories of abuse, neglect, adoption, or multiple foster care placements. She is the founder of Celia Center, Inc., a non-profit organization supporting all members of the foster care and adoption constellation as well as professionals working in the field. She is also the clinical director of Yoffe Therapy, Inc., a mental health center in Los Angeles that provides services to families, children, teens, and adults connected by foster care and adoption.